- How the core process of followe
  leadership works and how to impl
  proven self-leadership strategies

- How organizations and managers can make
  the challenging transition to self-leadership

- How to use teams to empower followers
  and how to take the entire team concept to
  the next level

- How a total culture of self-leadership can
  create a company of heroes

- What can be learned from the examples of
  such real-life SuperLeaders as Jack Welch,
  CEO of General Electric; Ricardo Semler,
  CEO of Semler Industries; and Dennis
  Bakke, CEO of AES Corporation

An invaluable resource for all managers and
supervisors, *Company of Heroes* is a blueprint
for all those who want to build the new, more
dynamic organizations of the future *now*.

HENRY P. SIMS, JR., is Professor of Man-
agement and Organization at the Maryland
Business School, and **CHARLES C. MANZ**
is Professor of Management at Arizona State
University. They are the coauthors of *Super-
Leadership* and *Business Without Bosses*.

Company of Heroes

Other Books by Charles C. Manz and Henry P. Sims, Jr.

by Charles C. Manz and Henry P. Sims, Jr.

Business Without Bosses: How Self-Managing Teams Are Building High-Performing Companies
Wiley, 1993; paperback, 1995

SuperLeadership: Leading Others to Lead Themselves
Prentice Hall, 1989; Berkley, paperback, 1990

by Charles C. Manz

Mastering Self-Leadership
Prentice Hall Press, 1992

The Art of Self-Leadership
Prentice Hall Press, 1983

by Henry P. Sims, Jr.

The New Leadership Paradigm
Henry P. Sims, Jr., and Peter Lorenzi
Sage, 1992

The Thinking Organization
Henry P. Sims, Jr., and Dennis Gioia
Jossey Bass, 1986

COMPANY OF HEROES
Unleashing the Power of Self-Leadership

Henry P. Sims, Jr.

Charles C. Manz

JOHN WILEY & SONS, INC.
New York • Chichester • Brisbane • Toronto • Singapore

About the Authors

Henry P. Sims, Jr., and Charles C. Manz are international scholars and consultants on the topics of leadership and self-managing teams. Dr. Sims is Professor of Management and Organization at the Maryland Business School. Dr. Manz was a Marvin Bower Fellow at the Harvard Business School and is currently Professor of Management at Arizona State University.

Their theoretical and practical work on leadership and teams has been published in over 150 articles and 7 books. Their award-winning book on leadership, *SuperLeadership*, was published in 1989 to wide critical acclaim. Their book on the topic of self-managing teams is entitled *Business Without Bosses* (Wiley, 1993).

Drs. Sims and Manz conduct a wide range of training and consulting activities. Their stock in trade is a three-hour interactive workshop on leadership. Both are frequent keynote and after-dinner speakers, and they conduct workshops on the design specifics of self-managing teams. On occasion, they conduct five-day executive development programs that extend beyond SuperLeadership and teamwork. Their workshops are always highly interactive and include significant participant involvement, cases and exercises, and videotaped cases.

Drs. Sims and Manz have served as consultants and executive development leaders with many organizations, including General Motors, Ford Motor Company, Marriott Corporation, Motorola Corporation, American Express, Procter & Gamble, Allied Signal, 3M, Dial, Unisys, Prudential, The Mayo Clinic, the Epilepsy Foundation, Defense Logistic Agency, Academy for Educational Development, and U.S. Agency for International Development.

*To
Laurie and Karen*

Contents

CONTENTS

PART IV: CREATING
A COMPANY OF HEROES

Preface

Would you like to be part of a company of heroes? There is a way you can make this happen. A company of heroes can be created by unleashing the power of self-leadership. That's what this book is all about: how a remarkable kind of leadership, SuperLeadership, can develop and enhance heroic self-leadership in others.

Over the past decade, organizations have struggled to find a form of leadership that can release the creativity and initiative of each employee. In today's competitive world, we need followers who are heroes. Together, leaders can create a company of heroes. SuperLeaders can make this happen, and you can be a Super-Leader—a leader who leads others to lead themselves.

This book is about leading others to be heroic self-leaders.

Throughout history, society has been preoccupied with heroes—great military leaders, outstanding athletes, powerful political leaders, visionary social reformers. Ghandi, Martin Luther King, Jr., George Washington, Alexander the Great, Joan of Arc, Winston Churchill, and many other names are emblazoned on our consciousness. In the business world, Henry Ford, Lee Iacocca, Alfred Sloan, and Jack Welch come to mind. The heroic role these people have played inspires a sense of hope for the future, a hope that great leaders will help us through the many challenges ahead. In many societies we have learned to base our visions and dreams for ourselves and the world on the actions and abilities of such heroic people.

Today the popular press fawns on a myth of heroic leadership. We are dominated by images of dashing leaders striking dramatic poses and taking swift action. Yet, is this a true portrait of what we need to lead today's complex contemporary organizations? Have we become addicted to a vision of heroic leadership?

Historically, a great leader was seen as one who does something to a follower. At first, this leader was viewed as a "strong man" type that was associated with masculinity and dominance and the exercise of influence based on fear. We think of John Wayne knocking heads or perhaps a ruthless and intimidating political leader. Later, leaders were viewed as "transactors," who provided goals and rewards in exchange for compliance from followers.

Are we addicted to a myth of heroic leadership?

In today's media, the most prominent view of leadership is the heroic leader—sometimes called the visionary leader, the transformational leader, or the charismatic leader. This type of leader is attributed with a magical charisma and wisdom that attracts followers to a greater-than-life vision.

None of these leadership types, however, brings the follower to the fore. All emphasize the leader at the expense of the follower. The popular obsession with the leader can indeed be inspiring but also limiting. When leaders are placed on a heroic pedestal, followers become dependent and insignificant. In our rapidly changing, highly complex, and competitive world we need the full contributions of everyone, not just a handful of prominent heroic leaders. We need to go back to basics—to bring the follower back into the equation.

There are many ways to exercise leadership, and each type has advantages and disadvantages. In this book, we especially address the advantages of shifting the spotlight away from leaders so that followers can become heroes themselves. Collectively, these followers can become a company of heroes.

THE NEEDED SHIFT IN LEADERSHIP

We are suffering a profound leadership crisis that is threatening the existence of historically successful organizations. In large part, this crisis has occurred because we have stopped thinking about the real effect of leadership on the follower. Instead, we let a romantic myth govern our beliefs about leadership.

The popular press fawns on a myth of heroic leadership.

Today, leadership is especially important because of several recent trends challenging contemporary organizations. First, world competition has pressured companies to utilize their human resources more fully. Second, the workforce itself has changed a great deal in the last few decades; the baby boomers, for example, have carried into their organization roles their elevated expectations and needs for greater meaning in their work lives.

As a consequence, organizations have increasingly experimented with innovative work designs. Widespread introduction of modern management techniques such as quality circles, self-managed work teams, Japanese business practices, and flatter organization structures have led to the inherent dilemma of how to lead employees who are increasingly encouraged and required to become self-managed. The result is a major knowledge gap about appropriate leader behavior under conditions of increasing employee participation. Indeed, it's time for a true paradigm shift in our thinking about leadership.

SUPERLEADERSHIP

The SuperLeadership approach focuses on the follower instead of some aggrandized version of heroic leadership. The leader becomes "super" by creating followers who are extraordinary self-leaders. The strength of one becomes the strength of many when the power of self-leadership is unleashed.

The SuperLeader is a giant step beyond this myth of heroic leadership. The SuperLeader has the capacity to create followers who are self-leaders—a company of self-leading heroes. Previous views of leadership always focus on the leader, and the talent of followers is often wasted. In this book, we propose a different view of leadership. We call this view SuperLeadership—leading others to lead themselves.

True leadership comes from within. In the end, achievement flows from follower self-leadership.

SuperLeadership is a new paradigm that will help us to release the talent, energy, enthusiasm, and expertise of everyone in the organization—not just the people at the top. The most effective leader will be the one who transforms ordinary followers into a company of heroes by leading them to lead themselves.

SO WHAT'S NEW HERE?

We previously wrote about leadership in *SuperLeadership* and *Business Without Bosses*. So what's new? *Company of Heroes* adds these features:

- We take a much more "how-to" approach than we did in *SuperLeadership*, which presented overall philosophical concepts. This book emphasizes pragmatic action and implementation—that is, executing SuperLeadership.
- SuperLeadership is compared with other historical viewpoints of leadership, especially visionary or heroic leadership. We flesh out each of these historical models of leadership and we show how SuperLeadership is indeed different from them and much more in tune with the needs of today.

- We devote special attention to the core process of follower self-leadership. Proven self-leadership strategies are examined in detail.
- We emphasize how organizations and managers can successfully make the challenging transition to SuperLeadership.
- We emphasize the use of teams as a means to empower followers.
- We emphasize how a total culture of self-leadership can create a company of heroes.
- We provide many vivid real-life examples of SuperLeadership in action. For example, with teams, we emphasize white-collar or knowledge-worker teams.
- We feature distinct profiles and stories of prominent business leaders such as Jack Welch of GE, Ricardo Semler of Brazil, and Dennis Bakke of AES.

Most of all, this book concentrates on specific steps that executives can implement *now* to improve their organizations. Some specific steps for becoming a SuperLeader that we will cover include becoming a self-leader and serving as a self-leadership model for others; facilitating the transition of followers to self-leadership through the use of goals, rewards, and other leadership strategies; promoting empowered self-led teamwork; and facilitating a self-leadership culture. Through SuperLeadership, followers become important leaders in their own right, and the organization can become a highly effective force for success and progress that unleashes the full talents of everyone.

WHY READ THIS BOOK?

The current vogue is to conceptualize contemporary leadership as vision. For example, most current leadership books seem to be saying that effective executives are visionary leaders, and ineffective leaders are merely managers. We don't quarrel with the necessity of vision from the top leader of an organization or with the notion that effective leadership is something beyond just being a good manager. Nevertheless, the emphasis on vision may be old wine in new bottles; it's still an inordinate focus on the leader and omits the follower from the equation.

An obsession with vision omits the follower from the equation.

Instead, we focus on how leaders can generate excellent performance by getting followers to lead themselves. Look at the cover story of a recent issue of *Fortune* magazine: "Who Needs a Boss?" Other articles present the idea of a "postheroic" leader or a "brave new leader." We were involved in this issue as early as 1980 and were prominently featured in a personal interview in *U.S. News and World Report* in which these ideas were developed. The *Fortune* story clearly shows that the time for this form of leadership has arrived. How can today's executives create extraordinary self-leaders throughout their organizations? How can we create an organization filled with heroes? The answer is to put the spotlight on the follower. There is no other leadership approach that views the follower so prominently. This focus on the follower is *the* central element of SuperLeadership. SuperLeaders empower their followers. SuperLeaders lead others to lead themselves.

The SuperLeader develops many pillars of strength throughout the organization.

By unleashing the powerful self-leadership capacity that resides within each person, the SuperLeader creates extraordinarily effective organizations character-ized by many pillars of strength. Together, these powerful self-leaders equal a company of heroes.

HENRY P. SIMS, JR.
CHARLES C. MANZ

August 1995

Acknowledgments

This book is a result of an extended company of heroes. We especially express our appreciation to our colleagues who helped us with the preparation of the various stories presented throughout the book: Christopher P. Neck, Gregory Stewart, Barry Bateman, Frank Shipper, Alan B. Cheney, Stephen Carroll, Kenneth G. Brown, John S. Tabor, Amy L. Kristof, Joe S. Anderson, Waskito Tjiptosasmito, Janice A. Klein, Pamela J. Derfus, Peter Lorenzi, Craig Pearce, Gregory E. Prussia, and Kenneth A. Smith. Indeed, without their efforts, this book would be much less interesting and informative. Many of these authors were the experts or key links that were critical to the process of developing the inside information for each of the stories.

We are also very grateful to the many others who helped make the writing and printing of this book a reality. We thank all the helpful people at Wiley, especially John Mahaney, our acquisitions editor, who helped create the vision for the book. We also thank our current editor, Janet Coleman, for her support in the later writing stages.

Our respective universities, the University of Maryland–College Park and Arizona State University (especially the Business Colleges at each), have supported our research and writing over the years. We especially thank Larry Ponley, Ed Locke, and Luis Gomez-Mejia.

There are many other colleagues we need to recognize: Michael Beyerlein, Tom Cummings, Linda Trevino, Richard Hackman, Dennis Gioia, Robert House, Ed Lawler, Ted Levitt, Fred Luthans, Barry Macy, Tom Peters, Richard Cherry, Jonathan Cox, and Phil Podsakoff. All of these people have significantly affected our thinking and writing over the years.

We owe special thanks to the many innovative companies and their managers and employees who have inspired us and given us hope that companies of heroes are not only possible to create but in fact are emerging all around us. We have captured some of their stories in our writing.

Finally, as always, we are grateful for our supportive families. The energy we have been able to spend on writing this and our other books and articles has been greatly facilitated by their patience, encouragement, and understanding.

H.P.S.
C.C.M.

Company of Heroes

Part I

Beyond Heroic Leadership

UNLEASHING THE POWER OF SELF-LEADERSHIP

There is an old Norse word, *Laed*, meaning "to determine the course of a ship." We can easily see how our modern word *lead* comes from this ancient expression. And, we can even visualize the modern version of a leader as the person who guides the course of a ship. (Think of the image of George Washington crossing the Delaware.) In business, we usually consider a CEO to be a leader, who guides the course of the organization.

In today's changing world, how should this guidance take place? Is the contemporary CEO the modern version of the ship captain who drives the galley slaves through threat of the whip. Or is the captain the first among equals, guiding the course of the ship by creating a team of caring and empowered shipmates? Can the captain create a crew of self-leaders?

We continue to read about leadership every day. Most of us would regard the designation as "leader" to be an honor—in a very real sense, a kind of hero. Few would refuse it. But where does that leave the follower? If we honor the leader, does it mean the follower is devoid of honor? We think not. In fact, the essence of this book is to honor followers by emphasizing the notion of self-leadership. Followers who are capable self-leaders are heroes. And when we have a company of capable self-leaders, we have a company of heroes.

To be a leader is a kind of hero, but where does that leave the follower? Can't the follower be a hero too?

Finding leaders who can produce heroic self-leaders as followers is the challenge. The question of how to lead best produces many divergent views. One view is the myth of the modern heroic leader. But heroic leaders tend to rob followers of their chance to be leaders and thus be heroes themselves.

In this book, we address the past, the present, and the future of leadership. We revisit many of the primary leadership themes of history. Our discussion serves as our manifesto on leadership that stretches from the past into the future. It ranges from leadership through intimidation and exploitation, to leadership through exchange, to leadership through inspiration, and finally to leadership through empowerment. Most of all, we express our belief that as we move into the twenty-first century, successful organizations will be those loaded with leaders—self-leaders. These organizations will be companies of heroes.

THAT CHANGING WORLD

We all know that the world is changing at an unprecedented rate, and everything is in constant flux, from the economy to markets. The workplace is beset by changes of all sorts from all sides. The workforce itself is best characterized by diversity and change—a complex mix of baby boomers and baby busters from a variety of ethnic and sociocultural backgrounds. As we approach the new century, the organizations that survive and flourish will be the ones that fully tap into the capabilities of the entire workforce. No longer can one individual, or a small group of individuals, be expected to have all the answers and make all the decisions in an effective way that meets the needs of everyone else. Instead of *one* hero, we need *companies* of heroes.

Now is the time for a new breed of leader. A recent article in *Fortune* called for a "postheroic" leader who places less emphasis on control and more on empowerment.[1] We call this new breed the *SuperLeader*: one who leads others to lead themselves. This is a lot harder than it sounds. Perhaps the biggest obstacle is mental. We've been chained to the concept of a boss for decades and have become obsessed with the notion of leaders as heroic figures.

But these views of leadership are ineffective because they place the leader—whether boss or hero—at center stage. In contrast, the *true* postheroic leader places followers at center stage and brings out their inner leadership capabilities. He or she leads others to become self-leaders. The transition to becoming an empowering SuperLeader is very challenging. As a *Fortune* article points out, "Ninety-five percent of American Managers today say the right thing. Five percent actually do it."[2]

Instead of *one* hero, we need a *company* of heroes.

Consider the interesting case of former president Jimmy Carter. As president, he had all the authority of the office and the potential to be a heroic leader, yet he lost his bid for reelection. But it's Carter's postpresidency leadership that is the object of our curiosity. As former president, Carter has no direct, formal authority; he leads without the power of office or authority. Yet his life is remarkable because his leadership empowers others. Through his actions, he creates heroic self-leaders.

JIMMY CARTER: PRESIDENT EMERITUS AND EMPOWERING SUPERLEADER

There have been many critics of the Jimmy Carter presidency. Certainly the most cutting judgment of all was the rejection of his presidential leadership by the American electorate in his bid for reelection. Yet, in contrast, some would argue that Jimmy Carter has been the most effective and respected former president of all time. He has been characterized as an uncommon mixture of real accomplishment and public failure. What is there about the leadership of Jimmy Carter's post-presidency that seems so remarkable?

As we examine the record, we see elements of leadership remarkably similar to our concepts of SuperLeadership—that is, leading others to lead themselves. Clearly, Carter has been an empowering leader as president emeritus. Following are some examples of how he has used his reputation and prestige to influence others in extraordinarily positive, constructive ways.

First has been his role as a conciliator and conflict resolver. The most prominent examples of this role are his efforts to resolve the nuclear stalemate with North Korea, a Sudan cease-fire, the bloodless occupation of Haiti, and the cease-fire in Bosnia. He has created the Carter Center at Emory University, where people can come together to resolve conflict. Carter seems to have a special capacity to influence quarreling parties to stop and reflect on the parameters of the conflict, and then make decisions that lead to constructive and positive ends. And he does all of this without direct power. He merely has the capacity to bring people together to make decisions that are in their own best interests. He has been described as a diplomat without portfolio.

Carter remains passionate about democratic political processes and grass-roots political empowerment, expressed mainly through his influence in ensuring honest elections in developing countries. He has been a high-profile election monitor in Nicaragua and Panama.

Perhaps the best example of his empowering leadership role is his public and passionate support of the Habitat for Humanity project, a non-profit organization that brings people together to construct a type of "up from your own bootstraps" private housing for the poor and homeless. Through housing, the organization facilitates stability and dignity by helping people to help themselves. The image of Carter wielding hammer and saw is a model that many have come to emulate.

Carter seems to be most effective when he leads *without* authority.

Carter is a model of how to bring success out of defeat. The failed reelection campaign, along with the failure of his personal business while it was in a blind trust, was a psychological low point in his life. After losing the presidency, he was described as "an all-but-shattered man."* But Carter is an unfailing opportunity thinker rather than an obstacle thinker. "When I have a setback and a disappointment," he said, "I look for the future. How can I build upon this and even sometimes use it for advantage?"† He also tries to convey this unflagging optimism to others.

One way to view the difference between Carter the president versus Carter the president emeritus is to think first of President Carter leading with authority and then later as leading without authority. By "leading with authority," we mean leadership based on the legitimate power that derives from office. Certainly, the U.S. presidency is one of the most powerful leadership roles in the world. As president, Carter led with authority, but he was extensively criticized as an ineffective micromanager. The power of *former* presidents, however, is remarkable for the absence of legitimate power. Former presidents must rely on their reputation, prestige, expertise, and networking to exercise influence. Interestingly, Carter's effectiveness seems to be strengthened when he attempts to lead without authority.

After his years of quiet toil in the political wilderness, many have come to "consider Carter as one of the greatest ex-presidents America's ever had" and "one of our national assets."‡ Some might think of him as a

---

*Wayne King, "Carter Redux," *New York Times Magazine*, December 10, 1989.
†"Biography—Jimmy Carter: To the White House and Beyond," program aired on the Arts and Entertainment cable television channel, April 1995.
‡Ibid.

"postheroic" leader, who leads through example, energy, initiative, a sense of values, and initiative. We see Carter as a SuperLeader who leads others to lead themselves.

Most of us have been conditioned to expect someone to be in charge, to direct us. We've been chained to this concept of a boss. Today, the socially desirable image of a boss is one who is inspiring and has a vision that we can rally around. And certainly an inspiring leader is preferable to a tyrant who rants and raves and intimidates followers. Nevertheless, even the inspiring heroic boss hogs the spotlight, and is expected to be the primary source of wisdom and direction. The follower still gets ignored. To achieve the potential of a high-performance empowered organization, we need to leave our boss baggage behind. We need a radically new understanding of what it is to be an effective leader. We need an empowering SuperLeader.

A SuperLeader brings out the effective self-leadership potential of others and leads others to lead themselves. The SuperLeader has the strength of ten (or more) because that strength is based on the experience, knowledge, and capability of many.

With more traditional leadership approaches, the leader is a boss or the hero at center stage. The leader does the thinking, provides the guidance for where the organization will go, and serves as the primary pillar of strength. If that pillar is removed, the organization is likely to collapse. In fact, a common military strategy over the centuries has been to eliminate the opponent's leader in battle in order to throw the enemy into disarray. Without this dominant figure, followers become disoriented. They don't know what to do next.

A SuperLeader leads others to lead themselves.

In contrast, under the guidance of a SuperLeader, each individual follower becomes a pillar of strength. An organization with multiple pillars of strength—that is, many competent self-leaders—will not collapse when the leader is absent or gone. The most effective leader, the SuperLeader, helps create followers who are quite capable of carrying on very well through self-leadership. The SuperLeader leads others to lead themselves so that the organization can thrive without constant external direction.

The SuperLeader transcends the myth of heroic leadership. The spotlight is placed on the followers. The SuperLeader doesn't try to be the hero but instead creates followers who are heroes for themselves and for each other. That's what this book is all about: creating a company of heroes through SuperLeadership.

BEYOND BOSS-REX

It's not surprising that many organizations still organize their work around the traditional boss concept. After all, according to conventional wisdom, someone has to be in charge. And besides, without bosses, human nature will eventually lead to a lack of effort and total chaos—so the logic goes. Consequently, we end up with organizations that are overly dependent on the thinking, wishes, and style of one particular individual who is recognized as the boss. Add to that the tradition that has been passed down for years: if employees are not performing the way the boss wants, then it's time to coerce and intimidate. Threats and punishment become central tools of the boss–centered organization.

Let us call this kind of leader *Boss-Rex*. Just like the ancient dinosaur king tyrannosaurus rex, Boss-Rex attracts a great deal of attention. Not many people like Boss-Rex, and they make many derogatory comments about this boss. Nevertheless, Boss-Rex is provided a great deal of deference and at least superficial respect from subordinates. In a perverse sense, Boss-Rex often becomes the dark hero of the work environment. Bureaucracy and hierarchy allow this kind of leader to thrive. Control is a major objective, and the Boss-Rex leader is able to gain a great deal of control—that is, compliance—through intimidation and threat.

Boss-Rex influences others through intimidation and threat.

Boss-Rex is an efficient breeder; many smaller versions spring up in a hierarchical organization. Generation after generation can quickly spawn, and before long, an organization can be overrun with Boss-Rexes, who check up on other less powerful Boss-Rexes, who check up on others, and so forth. As new people enter the organization, they quickly learn who holds the power and influence. Thus, the Boss-Rex can quickly take on a monstrous but mighty image. If imitation is the greatest form of flattery, then Boss-Rex receives a great deal of flattery in traditional hierarchical organizations.

This cycle can go on for years and even decades, or at least until more efficient competitors emerge who have shed these wasteful layers and achieved higher efficiency and innovation. Today, more voices than ever are crying out for the extinction of Boss-Rex. A recent cover story in *Business Week* on the horizontal organization (as opposed to the hierarchical organization) began with this statement: "Wanted: Bureaucracy basher, willing to challenge convention, assume big risks, and rewrite the accepted rules of industrial order."[3]

DOES THE HORIZONTAL ORGANIZATION SIGNAL THE DEATH OF HIERARCHY?

As we approach the new century, the hierarchical organization may be facing a very bleak future.* Is it terminal, destined to become extinct? The concept of the horizontal corporation suggests this possibility. Many of the leading companies in the world—AT&T, Motorola, GE, Du Pont, Texas Instruments, IDS, WL Gore—are making or have already made sweeping changes that are moving them closer to a flattened decentralized organization. The traditional hierarchical and bureaucratic organization is being challenged as never before.

Model companies used in the past organized themselves into neat, tightly managed functional boxes; today they are practicing the three big Ds: downsizing, delayering, and decentralizing. Hierarchy and functional boundaries are being torn down while multidisciplinary work units that manage themselves are being used as key organizational building blocks. GE's Jack Welch calls for a "boundaryless organization." The approach requires nontraditional strategies: reducing supervision, introducing employee empowerment, and emphasizing work teams over traditional structures.

Downsizing, delayering, and decentralizing are creating horizontal organizations. Self-leadership is the power that drives these new organizational forms.

Organizations moving to horizontal designs institute the following key practices:

- Flatten the organization, removing unnecessary layers of management and supervision.

---

*Source: John A. Byrne, "The Horizontal Corporation," *Business Week,* December 20, 1993, pp. 76–81. See also Charles C. Manz and Henry P. Sims, Jr., *Business Without Bosses* (New York: John Wiley, 1993).

- Organize around key work processes (such as product development) rather than traditional functions.

- Place employees in work teams with the responsibility and authority largely to manage themselves.

- Reward employees on the basis of relevant work skills they possess and team performance.

- Base primary emphasis in measuring organizational performance on customer satisfaction with the organization's products or services.

- Create plenty of occasions for employees to have regular contact with customers and suppliers.

- Provide employees with significant information (even sensitive information) and training to help them make effective decisions and perform their work well.

At first glance, the road to the horizontal organization might seem to be cold and inhumane; in fact, transitions to the horizontal organization have often been associated with slash-and-burn downsizing and reengineering, with employees bearing the brunt of past management mistakes. Yet, in an apparent paradox, the horizontal organization is precisely the kind of environment in which self-leadership thrives. Moreover, getting to self-leadership does not require a slash-and-burn approach, just a different kind of leadership. The initiative that comes from self-leadership drives horizontal designs.

Wanted: SuperLeaders to build horizontal companies of heroes.

New organizational designs, such as the horizontal organization, require a reallocation of the locus of power. Self-leadership is the power that drives the horizontal organization.

Fortunately, we hear similar cries for change from many sources, and we find striking examples of companies and leaders that have already chosen this path of change. For example, Ricardo Semler has evicted the Boss-Rex concept from his Brazilian company, Semco, and replaced it with a highly empowered workforce. His company has enjoyed tremendous bottom-line gains.

THE UNCONVENTIONAL LEADERSHIP OF RICARDO SEMLER

Top-down directive management has been widely accepted in thousands of companies.* Recently, however, this long-accepted norm has been challenged in many organizations, among them, the Brazilian equipment producer, Semco. Its unorthodox CEO, Ricardo Semler, believes there is a danger in concentrating too much decision making in the hands of elite leaders. Semler views himself as a catalyst rather than a wielder of power and central decision maker. His leadership turns ordinary workers into empowered self-leaders who become their own managers. He bets the future of the company on the decisions and performance of its employees.

Semler's leadership turns workers into self-leaders. He bets the future on creating a company of heroes.

This is not the way it has always been at Semco. At first, Semler tried to follow the example of his father, the company founder, when he took over as CEO, and he acted as a hard-driving disciplinarian. But he found that this style spawned workers who didn't care, subsequently producing unsatisfactory organizational performance. Moreover, he was working 18-hour days and experiencing a great deal of stress. After advice from his doctor to slow down, Semler began to make changes.

Before we can lead others, we must learn to lead ourselves.

He realized before he reorganized Semco that he had to reorganize himself. This is notably consistent with our SuperLeadership view: Before you can lead others, learn to lead yourself. Semler began to delegate, cut back on his own micromanaging, and empowered his workforce. He proceeded to remove nine layers of management and redesigned the company to have a core of upper management en-

---

*Sources: Ricardo Semler, *Maverick: The Success Story Behind the World's Most Unusual Workplace* (New York: Warner Books, 1993); Frank O'Donnell, "When Workers Are Bosses," *Washington Post,* September 14, 1993, p. B–2.

11

circled by middle management and workers. Some of the more notable specifics of Semler's approach include these elements:

- Workers set their own hours.
- Some workers set their own salaries.
- There are no receptionists.
- There are no office walls.
- Managers are evaluated by their employees.
- Employees vote on all major decisions.
- Employees share 22 percent of all company profits.
- The CEO has essentially delegated his authority to make decisions.

Since these changes have been put into place, Semco's sales have increased 600 percent. Perhaps even more important, a remarkably high trust level between management and workers bodes well for future success. In the words of one Semco worker, "The company became a paradise to work in. Nobody wants to leave."[†]

Despite these dramatic trends, the resilience of the Boss–Rex leader should not be underestimated. It has been said that power is intoxicating. Even if fewer and fewer are willing to revere a modern Boss-Rex, this type of leader is often quite satisfied to relish the feeling of power. If we are truly to create companies of heroes, the Boss-Rexes of this world will have to be dealt with. Boss-Rex is always ready to arise at any time. We believe that many managers secretly long for the good old days when being a Boss-Rex was okay. We note with interest the popularity of business titles like *Management Secrets of Attila the Hun* and *Confessions of an S.O.B.*

"Wanted: Bureaucracy basher, willing to challenge convention and assume big risks."

Perhaps there is a little Boss-Rex inside of each of us wanting to come down hard on those followers we view as lazy, incompetent, or problem employees. But

---

[†]O'Donnell, "When Workers Are Bosses," p. B–2.

we must remember that when a Boss-Rex is on the loose, a defensive, hostile organization is likely to be the outcome.

BEYOND THE VISIONARY HERO

Boss-Rex is not the most powerful and dangerous leader in all the land; another is potentially even more dangerous. Like Boss-Rex, this leader is dominating and commanding, but in an often subtle and attractive way. We call this leader the *Visionary Hero.*

The Visionary Hero can create a captivating vision that inspires a sense of purpose for followers. Sometimes the vision is backed by strong personal charisma. Others follow out of a sense of emotional commitment, not just compliance, as they do for Boss-Rex. Followers go above and beyond the call of duty. Sometimes the vision can lead to a wonderful new social reform or excellent organization performance. Alas, sometimes it can lead down a path to destruction.

Vision can lead to wonderful reform—or it can lead down a path to destruction.

The all-star roster of Visionary Heroes includes names of some of the most revered leaders in history: Ghandi, Martin Luther King, Jr., and JFK. The list also includes some of the most infamous: Hitler, Jim Jones, and David Koresh. (Clearly these individuals are not "heroes" but perhaps "antiheroes.") Visionary Heroes are most important in times of crisis and major change, when communicating an inspiring purpose-filled vision may mean the difference between organizational collapse or survival and success. The survivors of Chrysler's near-bankruptcy would likely confirm the importance of the visionary role Lee Iacocca played.

Visionary Heroes occupy center stage and dominate the spotlight, just as Boss-Rex does, but unlike Boss-Rex, they are widely liked and admired. Like Boss-Rex, they are expected to do all the thinking and have all the answers—and that is where the weakness lies. When either type of leader becomes the central pillar of strength for the organization, followers are kept weak, dependent, and vulnerable.

The Visionary Hero creates vulnerability by becoming a single pillar of strength. The SuperLeader creates many pillars of strength.

A PREVIEW: LEADING OTHERS TO LEAD THEMSELVES

In the next few chapters, we develop in some detail the historical themes of leadership that have emerged over time. In particular, you will recognize the prominent historical roles of Boss-Rex and the Visionary Hero. We discuss the advantages and disadvantages of each, and present prominent examples of different types of leaders.

Then in contrast to Boss-Rex and the Visionary Hero, we propose a distinct type of leadership that focuses on developing the self-leadership capabilities of followers. We want followers who can become effective self-leaders by developing and using a set of practical skills for increased personal effectiveness. Self-leadership is the critical part of our thesis and is the focus of Part II of this book. The specifics of putting self-leadership into practice are set out in detail in Parts III and IV.

Self-leadership is both a philosophy and a set of practical skills that people can apply to themselves.

Yes, Boss-Rex should command some fear and caution, but we also preach caution with the Visionary Hero. As empowerment and teamwork move more fully to the forefront, we need to go beyond this myth of heroic visionary leadership as the ideal. Our organizations need a postheroic leader, one who can fully unleash the power of follower self-leadership. It's time to move the spotlight from the heroic leader to the heroic follower. It's time to create a company of heroes.

STRONGMEN, TRANSACTORS, VISIONARY HEROES, AND SUPERLEADERS

Fundamentally, leadership means influence—the ability to influence others. We sometimes associate the words *charismatic*, or even *heroic*, with leadership. Typically, the spotlight is on the leader, with the follower a forgotten part of the leadership equation—usually taken for granted.

Leadership is important to all of us. Each of us wants to be an effective leader when we are called upon to lead, and we want effective leaders to lead us. But the notion of leadership is elusive, ambiguous, even romantic. Maybe we can't really describe good leadership, but we know it when we see it. We do know, however, that leadership is often embodied in what the leader chooses to say. Consider the following story. Think about the aircraft carrier captain as a decision maker who chooses what his own words should be.

LEADERSHIP AS A DECISION: CHOOSING WHAT TO SAY

Here's a true story that will help you understand that leaders have a choice over what they say.* We'll use an old storyteller device: tell the

---

*Source: We first heard this story from Dr. Denise Rosseau.

story but then stop and ask you to finish it. We'll ask you to create an ending by speculating on various words that a leader might choose to influence followers.

The Aircraft Carrier Captain

It's nighttime. The huge aircraft carrier is headed into the wind. Operations are in full swing; about every 75 seconds, a plane is launched. Recovery of planes is also taking place. This is a night operations training exercise that will receive a performance score by observers.

About 1 A.M. the carrier group admiral retires and goes to bed. Shortly after, the carrier captain leaves the bridge and also retires. This captain is new; he has been in command for only three weeks. He realizes his command will be watched very closely during this important exercise.

Operations continue; you can feel the special tension during night operations. The carrier continues to launch and recover the planes with a quiet professionalism.

Down below, in the bowels of the ship, a young seaman—an apprentice mechanic—finishes his shift. He returns his tools to the cabinet, checking each item off the checklist. Earlier he had been working on the flight deck.

The sailor feels his stomach tighten: a wrench is missing. He searches his kit and his pockets carefully. He inspects the area meticulously but still can't find it. He knows he's in trouble if the chief petty officer finds out. Briefly, he considers hitting the sack; no one will ever know.

Now, you may be asking why all this fuss about a wrench, but the sailor knows the potential damage a wrench can cause if it's sucked into an aircraft engine during a launch. It can cause a crash.

Reluctantly he goes to his chief petty officer and reports the missing wrench. The report quickly goes up the chain of command. Within minutes, the air boss orders launch operations to be suspended while a walkdown of the huge deck is undertaken. (In a walkdown, a line of officers and enlisted men walk shoulder to shoulder across the deck, from one end to the other, searching every square inch for debris.)

Because of the delay, the score for the exercise is ruined.

Early the next morning, the young seaman who lost the wrench is escorted by a marine to the captain's office. Needless to say, the captain is disturbed that the first exercise under his command will not be considered a success. The young seaman comes

16

to attention before the captain. The captain hesitates, takes a breath, and then says . . .

Well, what does the captain say?

This is a leadership incident, and we will allow you to speculate about the real ending for a moment or two. What do *you* think the captain would say?

For most of us, leadership implies action and command. We intuitively see a leader as taking charge by barking brisk instruction and command. There is frequently an overtone of power, threat, and intimidation with this type of leader. We call this leader the Strongman. For most of us, our stereotypical view of a military leader fits this image. For example, if the captain were a Strongman leader, he might choose to say:

> *"You screwed up! I'm going to make an example out of you. You'll stand trial for this. I'm going to throw your butt in the brig!"*

But perhaps this image is somewhat out of alignment with more contemporary viewpoints of leadership. We expect modern leaders, even in the military professions, to be more professional. Sometimes this type of leadership is dependent on an exchange relationship between the leader and the follower. That is, the follower contributes knowledge or labor, and the leader and/or organization provides rewards and security. For example, if our aircraft carrier captain were a Transactor, he might choose to say:

> *"You're paid to do your job, and I expect you to do it right!"*

But this type of exchange is seen as too mundane and unexciting for most contemporary leadership theorists. They would say that the Transactor depends too much on extrinsic rewards and fails to capture the potential excitement and enthusiasm that can energize each follower. The leadership enthusiasts of today would want the captain to be "charismatic" or "transforming"—to provide a clear and inspiring vision to followers. For example, if the aircraft carrier captain were a Visionary Hero, he might choose to say:

> *"We must remember our mission! We're here to protect our country. It takes each one of us doing our own job if we are going to fulfill our mission!"*

But even this contemporary view of leadership is not without criticism. Some would say that the Visionary Hero tends to develop dependent followers, despite all of their enthusiasm. Followers of the Visionary Hero find difficulty in taking independent action on their own. They become overly attached to the charisma of the leader or captured by the top-down vision. The leader, in fact, may even have the power to lead them astray.

We believe that leadership in today's fast-changing environment should be empowering to followers. Followers are not there to carry out the wishes of the leader but to develop a capacity to think and act on their own. For example, even lowly apprentice seamen in a modern navy must exercise judgment, and sometimes this judgment directly influences the lives of others. At times, the seaman must act as a self-leader. Perhaps the captain of this sailor might act as a SuperLeader—one who leads others to lead themselves. A SuperLeader creates and develops followers who are skilled and capable of empowered self-leadership. After all, true leadership comes from within each follower.

The apprentice seaman is no exception. If the aircraft carrier captain were a SuperLeader, he might choose to say:

"Son, I want to congratulate you for reporting that missing wrench. I know it would have been easy to ignore it, but you faced up to it and did your duty. You did the right thing. I know that you're the kind of person we can count on to make this ship the best in the navy."

In fact, this captain indeed was a SuperLeader, and by the next day, this highly symbolic act of leadership was known all over the ship. This crew was 100 percent behind their new captain, and he had a very successful tour of duty.

We can achieve excellence if leaders are dedicated to tapping the vast potential within each of us. This is the task of the SuperLeader: to unleash the powerful self-leadership capability within each follower. Typically, we have a misplaced focus when we talk about leadership. We suggest that we not focus on leaders as heroes but on leaders as hero-makers. Is the spotlight on the leader—or on the follower?

Our personal viewpoint is that a revolution is taking place in American organizations, and we have only begun to discover the power and impact of this change. The fire of competition is building new kinds of organizations. We still have problems and challenges, but we are optimistic about the fundamental capability of modern organizations. The cutting edge of this change has taken place in manufacturing organizations, but we are now starting to see similar results in the service sector and perhaps even in the government sector. There is hope that people will have an opportunity to work in SuperLeader types of organizations and thus have an opportunity to achieve their full potential as empowered self-leaders.

Opinions on successful leadership have changed significantly over time. Here, we present a simplified historical perspective on different approaches to leadership, noting that four different types of leader can be distinguished: the Strongman, the Transactor, the Visionary Hero, and the SuperLeader. These different approaches to leadership practice have emerged over time, but each of them is still widely practiced today.

Types of Leaders

	Strongman	Transactor	Visionary Hero	SuperLeader
Focus	Commands	Rewards	Visions	Self-leaders
Type of power	Position/ authority	Reward	Relational/ inspirational	Shared
Source of wisdom and direction	Leader	Leader	Leader	Mostly followers (self-leaders, then leaders)
Subordinate response	Fear-based compliance	Calculative compliance	Emotional commitment based on leader's vision	Commitment based on psychological ownership

STRONGMAN

The *Strongman* view of leadership is perhaps the earliest leadership form emphasized in our culture and the most representative of the notion of leader as boss. Previously, we coined the term *Boss-Rex* to indicate that this type of leader should be extinct, like dinosaurs. We use the masculine pronoun purposely because when this leadership approach was most prevalent, it was almost a completely male-dominated process. Today the Strongman view of leadership is still widely found in many organizations, although not as highly regarded.

This view of leadership creates an image of a John Wayne–type figure who is not afraid to knock some heads to get followers to do what he wants. The expertise for knowing what should be done rests almost entirely in the leader. It is he who sizes up the situation and, based on some seemingly superior strength, skill, and courage, delivers firm commands to the workers. If the job is not performed as directed, some significant form of punishment will be delivered to the guilty party. The focus is on the leader, whose power stems primarily from his position in the organization. He is the boss, the primary source of wisdom and direction. Subordinates comply out of fear.

The strongman view creates an image of a John Wayne type, ready to knock some heads.

The Strongman leader is alive and well today. Many world political leaders, football coaches, and high-level executives in large corporations fit this model. As one example, a Strongman apparently managed to work his way up the corporate hierarchy at Kellogg Co. At the top, the conflict between this Strongman and the more genteel culture of Kellogg became apparent. Eventually this venerable Battle Creek cereal maker terminated its president in an unusual action. Accounts described this person as "abrasive and often unwilling to listen . . . , very abrupt . . . , more inclined to manage without being questioned." He was known for deriding unimpressive presentations as a CE (career-ending) performance. CEO Frank Lorenzo would also likely be identified as a prototypical Strongman by most employees who experienced his leadership at Eastern Airlines. Even President Bill Clinton apparently has a streak of Strongman within him.

BILL CLINTON: WHAT'S MY LEADERSHIP STYLE TODAY?

What kind of leader is President Bill Clinton? At different times, at different places, Clinton has behaved in a way consistent with all of the leader types we describe.

Clinton as Strongman: Anger

According to Bob Woodward, President Bill Clinton has a well-known propensity to anger—an emotion that is a typical characteristic found in a Strongman leader.* Writing in his book *The Agenda*, Woodward reports on an incident in Macon, Georgia, on September 1, 1992. During a campaign speech, residents of the town were roped off from the event, separated from candidate Clinton.

Clinton saw this decision as a mistake and was furious at his staff for allowing it to happen. He angrily attempted to identify the unlucky aide who had made this unfortunate decision. According to Woodward, Clinton said, "I want him dead, dead. I want him horsewhipped."

Apparently his rage continued for three days, although his sug-

---

*Bob Woodward, *The Agenda: Inside the Clinton White House* (New York: Simon and Schuster, 1994), pp. 55–56.

gested punishment of the hapless staff member diminished in intensity. After "horsewhipped," Clinton demanded, "I want him fired," but finally mellowed to say, "Damn it, I hope he gets a real talking to."

Clinton as Transactor: The Horsetrader

Clinton has been known to engage in the politics of exchange, an age-old tradition in political life. For example, in the days leading up to the 1993 Senate vote on his economic package, he engaged in a flurry of personal negotiation to secure the votes of reluctant senators.

One particular target was Senator Dennis DeConcini, Democrat from Arizona, who was reluctant to support the president's position.[†] "I need your vote," exclaimed Clinton. "What can we do?"

In the end, the economic plan was altered by lowering slightly the number of people whose social security would be taxed—a change that appealed to DeConcini's constituency of retired persons in Arizona. This example is only one of many stories that point out President Clinton's willingness to influence by the tactics of the Transactor.

Clinton as Visionary Hero: The Inaugural Speech

Bill Clinton's inaugural speech clearly shows elements of the Visionary Hero—for example:

"Profound and powerful forces are shaking . . . our world, and the urgent question . . . is whether we can make change our friend and not our enemy."

"A spring reborn in the world's oldest democracy, that brings forth the vision and courage to reinvent America."

"Our greatest strength is the power of our ideas, which are still new in many lands."

"Though we march to the music of our time, our mission is timeless."

"To renew America, we must be bold."

"I challenge a new generation of . . . Americans to a season of service—to act on your own idealism."[‡]

To use a well-worn catchphrase, Bill Clinton certainly knows how to "talk the talk." Whether he can also "walk the walk" we will leave to the historians to decide.

[†] Ibid., p. 283.
[‡] *Washington Post*, January 21, 1993, p. A20.

Clinton as SuperLeader: Helping People to Help Themselves

By early 1995, welfare reform had reached the front burner as a national policy issue, with both Republicans and Democrats apparently intent on transforming a system that everyone agreed had fostered widespread social dependency. In his State of the Union address in early 1995, President Clinton sounded like a SuperLeader as he spoke about this issue:

> *Our administration gave two dozen states the right to slash through federal rules and regulations to reform their own welfare systems and to try to promote work and responsibility over welfare and dependency. . . . Our goal must be to liberate people and lift them up from dependence to independence, from welfare to work . . . to responsible parenting. . . . We should promote responsibility."§*

Bill Clinton: Layer upon Layer

President Clinton is indeed a complex leader. At times, he can clearly be a Visionary. Certainly in his relations with Congress, his pragmatic horsetrading is very Transactor-like. Also, the incident Woodward reported, along with other incidents, suggests that Clinton has a clear streak of Strongman in his leadership repertoire. His effort to reinvent government is a step in the direction of empowerment.

Will the real Bill Clinton please step forth?

TRANSACTOR

The second view of leadership is that of a *Transactor*. As time passed in our culture, the dominance of the Strongman view of leadership diminished, and a different view of influence, using the power of rewards, began to emerge. The emphasis increasingly was placed on a rational exchange—exchange of rewards for work performed. Even Frederick Taylor, the father of scientific management, emphasized the importance of providing incentives to get workers to do work.

The transactor depends on exchange: "Here's what I expect from you. Here's what I'll do for you."

---

§*New York Times*, January 25, 1995, p. A30.

With the Transactor type of leader, the focus is on goals and rewards as the driving motivator. The leader's power stems from an ability to provide rewards to followers. In exchange, the followers do the work. The source of wisdom and direction still rests with the leader. Subordinates will tend to take a calculative view of their work: "I will do what the boss asks as long as the rewards keep coming."

Perhaps one of the most prototypical Transactor organizations in the world today is Pepsico, and it has been very successful with this approach. Some have described the company with phrases like "boot camp," "60-hour weeks," "back-breaking standards that are methodically raised." Those who can't compete are washed out. Those who do compete successfully are rewarded, and very handsomely: first-class air travel, fully loaded company cars, stock options, bonuses that can hit 90 percent of salary. Those who are comfortable and successful in this culture receive the spoils; those who are not comfortable and do not succeed tend to leave early in their careers.

VISIONARY HERO

The next type of leader, *Visionary Hero*, probably represents the current most popular view. Here the focus is on the leader's ability to create highly motivating and absorbing visions. The leader represents a kind of heroic figure who is somehow able to create an almost larger-than-life vision for the workforce to follow. If organizations can find those leaders who are able to capture what's important and wrap it up into some kind of purposeful vision, then the rest of the workforce will have the clarifying beacon that will light the way to the promised land.

With the Visionary Hero, the focus is on the leader's vision, and the leader's power is based on the followers' desire to relate to the vision and to the leader personally. Once again, the leader represents the source of wisdom and direction. Followers, at least in theory, are expected to commit to the vision and the leader.

"Charisma can be the undoing of leaders."
—Peter Drucker

The notion of the visionary leader has received a great deal of attention over the last decade. Great visionary leaders throughout history have left an inspiring legacy for us all. People such as Ghandi, Martin Luther King, Joan of Arc, and John F. Kennedy are thought of as attractive models to emulate. In many ways the visionary approach is held up as the ideal leadership approach for leaders to strive toward. Nevertheless, visionary leadership is not perfect. Peter Drucker, for example, believes that charisma can become the undoing of leaders. He believes that they can become inflexible, convinced of their own infallibility, and slow to change. Drucker suggests that the most effective leaders are those who are not afraid of developing strength in their subordinates and associates—which brings us to SuperLeadership.

SUPERLEADER

The final view of leadership is the *SuperLeader:* the one who creates a company of heroes. We do not use the word *Super* to create an image of a larger-than-life figure who has all the answers or is able to bend the will of others to his or her own. On the contrary, this leader focuses largely on followers. Leaders becomes "super"—that is, possessing the strength and wisdom of many persons—by helping to unleash the abilities of the "followers" (self-leaders) who surround them.

The focus of SuperLeadership is on followers who become self-leaders. Power is more balanced between leaders and followers. The leader's task becomes that of helping followers to develop the necessary capabilities, and especially self-leadership skills, to be able to contribute more fully to the organization. Thus, leaders and followers (who are becoming strong self-leaders) together represent the source of wisdom and direction. Followers (self-leaders), in turn, experience commitment and ownership of their work.

SuperLeadership is a perspective that reaches beyond concepts of heroic leadership—as a solid answer to today's primary leadership challenges. In the past, the idea of a leader implied that the spotlight was on the leader, who was the source of dynamism, energy, and vision. An alternate viewpoint, more suited to today's environment, is to place the spotlight on the follower.

Recently the notion of "postheroic" leadership has emerged in the popular management literature. For the most part, the specifics of this kind of leadership remain undefined. We believe that this label represents a desire to find something beyond the Visionary Hero. In truth, the so-called postheroic leader sounds suspiciously like the SuperLeader.

**SuperLeadership reaches beyond heroic leadership.
SuperLeaders create heroic followers.**

For the SuperLeader, the essence of the challenge is to lead followers to discover the potentialities that lie within themselves. Instead of becoming a hero, a SuperLeader creates heroic followers by unleashing the power of self-leadership.

How can a SuperLeader lead others to become positive effective self-leaders? How can a SuperLeader lead others to lead themselves?

We will present an array of practical strategies to accomplish these ends later in this book. As you will see, some of the elements included in the other leadership views are part of SuperLeadership (e.g., the use of rewards), but the focus of the leadership process and the basis of power and the relationship of the SuperLeader with followers are very different.

The following chapters in this part of the book examine each of the leadership approaches briefly introduced in this chapter. All of these approaches have a place under specific conditions, so it is important to understand thoroughly the typical leader behaviors that accompany each and the likely impact that each will have on followers. Nevertheless, let us be clear that we are indeed advocates of Super-Leadership. We believe that SuperLeadership has the power to deal with the special challenges of the twenty-first century. There are a variety of ways to exert significant leadership influence over followers, but only SuperLeadership offers the ingredients for creating a company of heroes.

THE STRONGMAN

The whole earth shook as he approached with long, powerful strides. Everything in his path scurried out of the way as he entered the area. He rolled his head back and let out a mighty roar. All those present shook with fear. He barked out commands, and everyone sprang into action. All thinking seemed to cease; only frantic activity remained. A faint smile came to the mighty creature's face as he studied the commotion he had created. He settled heavily on his throne as he considered the next directives he would bark to his subjects. Absolutely no one challenged his right to dominate, for he was the supreme ruler of all the land. He was the Boss-Rex.

The traditional Boss-Rex leader is a strongman who operates from a traditional top-down, overt-control orientation. The Strongman leads through commands and relies on position power (boss status) as the basis for influence. Intimidation and domination are the order of the day for this type of leader.

For decades, no one challenged his right to dominate. He was the ruler—the Boss-Rex.

Consider the following account, which summarizes a true story of a Strongman leader in action and how his leadership pattern may eventually have been his undoing.

OFF WITH HIS HEAD: FORMER BOSS-REX'S LEADERSHIP COSTS HIS JOB

Richard Snyder had built an impressive publishing empire at Simon & Schuster.* He had led the company from a struggling $40 million operation in 1979 to over $2 billion in revenues in 1993. Life was good at the top as he guided the firm to tremendous financial growth and success as the CEO. By most measures, he was a rip-roaring success.

The only limitation on his decision discretion was his duty to report to Martin Davis, CEO of the parent company, Paramount. According to reports, he found his relationship with Davis a painful source of frustration and discomfort. Then when Viacom Inc. acquired Paramount, Davis had been removed. Snyder said that he wanted his new relationship to work, and his first meetings with Viacom management were described as quite cordial. He claimed to have been euphoric when Viacom entered the scene. But a few months later, Snyder found himself fired by Viacom president Frank Biondi, Jr., who cited a "difference in style." Snyder reportedly couldn't understand what went wrong. He just didn't get it.

There is not total agreement on what went wrong, but accounts of Snyder's leadership and personal demeanor provide some strong clues. Snyder's leadership was generally described as reigning by intimidation and fear. When *Newsweek* interviewed people associated with Snyder, they found that he was "loathed as a boss." He was specifically described as managing "by fear and intimidation," "erratic," "demanding," and "imperious."[1]

Reportedly Snyder was such a dominant figure that many myths were created about his horrendous deeds. There were stories about "power lunches," spotless soles of his shoes because of his being driven everywhere, and forcing his driver to change his name to sound more dignified. Many stories involved elevators. Supposedly Snyder was prone to fire employees whom he had contact with while riding the elevator. Many employees got the message and declined to enter an elevator when Snyder was on board. Snyder liked it that way.

According to reports, Viacom realized that the amount of conflict that Snyder's style was creating couldn't continue. Ironically, Frank Biondi,

---

*Source: Meg Cox and Johnnie L. Roberts, "How the Despotic Boss of Simon & Schuster Found Himself Jobless," *Wall Street Journal*, July 6, 1994, pp. A7, A9.
†Michael Meyer and Nancy Hass, "Simon Says 'Out!'" *Newsweek*, June 27, 1994, pp. 42–44.

who fired Snyder, has been described as a low-key, soft-spoken man who rarely fires anyone. Nevertheless, it was apparently clear that Snyder's Strongman leadership style did not fit the Viacom culture. In the end, Richard Snyder's Boss-Rex approach that had reportedly instilled terror and fear in many a subordinate apparently led to his demise.

A Boss-Rex tends to suppress creativity and initiative, and that seemed to have happened at Simon & Schuster with a Boss-Rex. According to *Newsweek*, Snyder "demanded too much control. People were afraid to express their opinions, to be creative. There was no room for dissent."[‡]

Leadership thinking and practice has undergone significant evolution. Inspiring and empowering others, not intimidation and control, form the mantle of modern leaders. Dinosaurs failed to make the evolutionary changes they needed to survive. Boss-Rex types are still around, but more and more they are likely to find themselves subject to the same fate as Richard Snyder.

STRONGMAN BEHAVIORS

The Strongman especially relies on a set of leader behaviors that clearly establish followers as compliant subordinates: command and direction, assigned goals, intimidation, and reprimand.

Command and Direction

The Strongman views leadership as a process of commanding others to gain their compliance to his or her wishes. Strong direction serves as a primary control device to ensure that subordinates become an extension of this leader's will. Much like a military leader in the middle of a raging battle, the Strongman barks out orders to manipulate troops into position. Followers largely become instruments of the Strongman's thoughts about what should be done. The leader thinks and directs, and others do what they are told.

George Patton shouting at troops as he directs them into battle comes to mind, as does Leona Helmsley berating employees to ensure that they carry out her every whim. Regardless of the specific leader, the behavior falls into a similar pattern: a self-proclaimed king or queen who dominates with a commanding presence, bent on directing followers as though pawns on a life-sized chess board. *Commander, director,* and *Boss-Rex* are all labels that suit the Strongman well.

[‡]Ibid., p. 44.

> ### Sometimes the Strongman seems to be a self-proclaimed king or queen bent on dominating followers as though pawns on a life-sized chess board.

Assigned Goals

The Strongman frequently relies on goals as a management tool, but these are usually assigned or required goals. Indeed, much research has confirmed the ability of goals to channel effort and stimulate higher performance. The Strongman leader is not particularly concerned with the subordinates' view of the goals—only that the goals are achieved. The Strongman establishes the goals alone and then assigns them to followers. After all, the Strongman does not expect—in fact, does not want—followers to think; the only concern is that they obey. Goals become just one more device for commanding and directing.

In addition to helping to establish direction, the goals serve as useful benchmarks for measuring subordinate performance. Indeed, goals are very useful to the Strongman in identifying poor subordinate performance and occasions to intimidate and punish. Goals are used to set the standard by which the Strongman evaluates and deals with subordinates. Followers who do measure up to the standards are safe—for the moment. Those who do not measure up are dealt with harshly.

Intimidation

"He rolled his head back and let out a mighty roar." This sentence from the opening paragraph of this chapter captures a central characteristic of the Strongman leader: intimidation as a primary foundation for exerting influence. Much like the classic image of a disciplinarian teacher who continuously keeps students on the edge of their seats by establishing a sense of fear in the classroom, the Strongman uses intimidation. Fearful subordinates tend to be compliant ones, at least as long as the feared boss is around. They know if they do not do what they are told, they will have serious problems from the tyrant of their work area.

> ### The essence of Boss-Rex is intimidation.

The key is to establish a tense atmosphere that never quite lets employees relax for fear of what the Strongman may do to them if they do not meet his or her expectations. The essence of Boss-Rex is fashioned from acts of intimidation, and the Strongman uses this powerful device to establish control by publicly berating a subordinate, knocking over a piece of furniture, coldly staring down an employee while describing his or her incompetence in private, or something else.

Reprimand

The ultimate tool for creating the compliant atmosphere that the Strongman seeks is to enforce domination through reprimand. The more old-fashioned term for reprimand, of course, is punishment. If subordinates choose not to do what they are told or perhaps make a mistake as they try, the Strongman makes the proverbial trip to the woodshed—a verbal attack, perhaps, or something more concrete, such as a distasteful job assignment, a cut in pay, or a demotion.

Based on the principles of behavior modification, punishment involves delivering a negative consequence for undesired behavior. The intent is to eliminate or reduce an undesired targeted behavior, or at least its frequency of use. The obvious shortcoming of this approach is that it focuses on what *not* to do rather than what *should* be done. It also dwells on past failure rather than future improvement. Add to this the tendency for Strongman leaders to use reprimand to dominate people, even when they really haven't done anything wrong, and you have an especially troubling situation.

Effective leaders use reprimand only as a last-resort strategy that is reserved for seriously negative follower behavior that is obviously unethical or harms others in some way. The Strongman leader, in contrast, relies on punishment as a primary influence tool, tossing out reprimands much like a baseball pitcher throws curveballs to strike out batters.

FOLLOWERS OF THE STRONGMAN

The practice of Strongman leadership tends to promote the development of a certain type of follower. They are compliant. Rather than expending effort on creativity, innovation, or value-added thinking, they are much more concerned with guessing what the leader wants. "If I could only read the boss's mind, then I could do what she wants and I'd be safe" is the kind of thinking that dominates subordinate thinking. Unfortunately, this is true whether what the boss is thinking is correct or not. Maintaining the status quo by satisfying the boss, not continuous improvement, is the main concern. The Strongman leader's followers are characterized by the classic term *yes-men* or more recently *yes-persons*.

Followers of Strongman leaders are the classic yes-persons.

Here is a summary of the Strongman behaviors and the type of follower this person spawns:

Typical Leader Behaviors

Command and direction

Assigned goals

Intimidation

Reprimand

Type of Followers

Yes-persons

Consider the following story about a Strongman in action in an organization that stimulates prolific breeding of this kind of leader. Although this case is fictitious, it reflects our observations of many Strongman leaders over our years of consulting and research in countless organizations.

A BOSS-REX BREEDING GROUND

Everyone seemed polite and cordial during the first week on the job. Training and orientation focused on useful information regarding the company's operating systems and some overall guidelines for functioning as a new entry-level manager. John Miller was able to apply some of the information over the next few months, and other information he simply filed away. In retrospect, he could not remember anything that would indicate any official policy that managers were expected to direct and control their subordinates firmly and deal with mistakes harshly.

That is part of the reason it came as such a shock, about a year into the job, when he heard what one of his fellow trainees, Pete Jones, said as they stood before the company bulletin board. An announcement was posted indicating that Paula Worth had just been promoted to a divisional manager position. "Yep," said Pete. "She's plenty tough enough for that position. She really knows how to kick butt to get the work out. I hope I can develop into a strong enough leader to advance like she has." With that he turned and shouted at one of his employees who appeared to be struggling with setting up a display a few yards away: "Hey! What the hell are you doing?" He cursed under his breath as he stomped off in the direction of the employee.

John carefully studied him as he left to make sure that this was the same very friendly and polite person he had gone through training with. "Pete would never have talked like this a year ago," John thought to himself.

In fact, John had been noticing a disturbing pattern throughout the organization for some time. He began to see what appeared to be an overriding management philosophy in the company. Time and time again he observed managers at all levels strongly berating their subordinates to gain their compliance. And he noticed that the people who were promoted tended to be the toughest managers, who intimidated, directed, and reprimanded their employees until they were molded into compliant subordinates.

In one particularly striking personal episode, he had been chewed out by his boss, the division manager, for his proposed department operating plan for the next year. Then, when all the department managers and the division manager met with the group vice president to review all of the departments' plans, he observed this same division manager become the target of a public and spiteful attack. The vice president let him know in no uncertain terms, and for all to see, his dissatisfaction with the way the division manager had directed the planning process. Finally, the chain of events climaxed in another meeting when the president of the company berated all of *his* managers, with special attention directed at the same vice president who had given the devil to John's division manager.

Clearly, this organization had a chain of intimidation that extended from the top to the bottom. Leadership was learned by observing the Strongman behaviors of those who had survived and ascended the corporate ladder.

Ultimately John decided he did not view his own leadership as consistent with the authoritarian approach that he knew he would have to adopt to advance in his career, and he left the organization. A few years later, he was interested to read that the company had been acquired after it had experienced serious financial difficulties. Reports in the press suggested that it had not sufficiently adapted to the dramatic change and competitive pressure of its environment. The reports indicated that this was surprising since the company had always prided itself in hiring the most aggressive managers in the industry.

THE
TRANSACTOR

Conversation in the anteroom of the Helsinki hotel was animated, perhaps fueled by the generous bar that had been open for 45 minutes. Dozens of men and women clustered in small groups, eagerly awaiting the main event. Finally the large double doors to the ballroom opened, and the sound of inspiring music was heard. Following their leader, entrepreneur Pekka Puduisu, the group eagerly moved into the larger room.

Their eyes focused on the large central table, lighted by candles and decorated by a magnificent floral centerpiece—and stacks of cash arranged around the edges of the table. There were dozens of stacks, one for each person in the room. Each stack was a different height, although all were substantial, and some seemed quite high. The stacks were orderly piles of Finnish currency (roughly equivalent to piles of twenty-dollar bills), and on top of each was a card on which a name and amount had been imprinted.

Then Pekka delivered a short speech, thanking all of the company supervisors for their contributions in the past year and ending with a short inspirational word about the possibilities of the coming year. With a laugh, he suggested that each supervisor find his or her own pile. For the next few minutes, chaos reigned as the crowd milled around the table. Many were clearly delighted when they found their own stack. A few seemed disappointed, but the overall good cheer of the crowd was apparent.

Later I talked to Pekka over dinner. "I do this each year to honor and reward the company supervisors," he said. "It's a special way to let them know how important they are to the company. We wouldn't be anywhere without them. We make a special ceremony to deliver this annual profit-sharing bonus, and it creates motivation for the year ahead. I think paying the bonus in after-tax cash has a special impact."[1]

Perhaps the most common type of leadership practiced today is what we call the Transactor approach. The Transactor leader focuses on the power of rewards for getting followers to perform. Clearly Pekka uses a Transactor approach when he pays his annual bonus to company supervisors.

Phrases like "What's in it for me?" (from followers) and "I'll make it worth your while" (from leaders) especially characterize the Transactor approach. Consider the following dialogue between Mary and Bill illustrating classic Transactor behavior.

THE (NOT SO) SUBTLE EXCHANGE

"Bill, I would like you to coordinate the new project for implementing the Z process into our operations. I realize that it will add to your normal responsibilities, but I really need you to do this for me."

"I understand that you want someone to take the central role on that project, Mary, but you know I really am loaded down with other pressing tasks right now."

"I realize that, Bill, but believe me, if you do a good job on this, I will make it worth your while. In fact, I've been seriously considering your request that I nominate you for that new incentive program in our division. That program could have a major impact on your career, you know."

"Yes, I agree. I guess if the Z process goes well, it could help us both out."

"That's true, Bill, and I especially hope we can have the Z process in place by the first of the year. I know you're busy, but I'm quite confident that if you do this for me, I can help you get that bonus. And I could enter a formal commendation letter in your file that would look awfully good for the upcoming promotion decisions. I'd also like to publicly recognize your contribution to my department year-end summary presentation at the annual division meeting."

"You have a way with words, Mary. Well, boss, I think I'm going to do whatever it takes to make the project a big success, and soon."

"That's what I like to hear, Bill. You meet the January 1 target, and the payoffs will more than cover your sacrifice."

TRANSACTOR BEHAVIORS

Four categories of leader behavior are especially prominent in the Transactor approach: interactive goal setting, contingent personal reward, contingent material reward, and contingent reprimand.

> ## Phrases like "What's in it for me?" and "I'll make it worth your while" characterize the Transactor approach.

Interactive Goal Setting

Goals tend to be important to the Transactor leader. By identifying specific performance goals (such as, "Fully implement the new Z process into operations by January 1"), followers have definite targets to guide their performance efforts. Research has in fact indicated that goals can affect performance positively, especially if they are specific and challenging but realistic and achievable.

> ## Quantitative measures are the baseline by which leader-follower transactions are conducted.

Although research is not entirely definitive on this point, usually it is recommended that leader and follower together set goals. In essence, the goal sets the stage for the Transactor exchange. To set up the transaction, the Transactor leader tends to involve followers in setting goals, although clearly the goals are designed to satisfy the leader's wishes. Goals serve as a management tool for channeling follower effort, and they establish a framework for allocating rewards. Of course, goals are an integral part of a system of management that depends on quantitative measurements to drive the process. Consider the case of the Whiz Kids at Ford Motor Company, who were instrumental in establishing professional management at Ford after World War II. Statistics and measures were their bible, and these measures became the framework for a culture of Transactor leadership at Ford.

WHIZ KIDS: THE FORD TRANSACTORS

Peter Lorenzi

Henry Ford, Sr., had shown a Strongman style in building and running the Ford Motor Company during the first half of the twentieth century. By the end of World War II, the company was in financial turmoil, about to go bankrupt. The company's rescuers in the postwar era were a small group of brash, gifted young men, all veterans of the U.S. Army, who came to be known as "Whiz Kids." These high-profile executives initiated a significant change in the cultural pattern of leadership at Ford.

The Transactor era at Ford began with Ernest Breech and Tex Thornton, achieved its heyday under Robert McNamara, and culminated in the late 1980s. Along the way, Lee Iacocca—out of sync with his style of visionary, heroic leadership—found his career cut short at Ford.

After years of declining market share and profits, the Whiz Kids changed the way Ford operated. Their approach to running the organization was based on close, numerical control of all the operations of the production and sales process. The Transactor's belief in the power of "running the numbers" superseded other beliefs and considerations. As author John Byrne has noted, "Eventually they would unwittingly become ministers of a management theology that dominated American business and social culture. The numbers-only mentality they begat would lead to an emphasis on cost control rather than quality, on finance instead of manufacturing, and on paper rather than people."*

At Ford, managing by the numbers became the bedrock upon which Transactor leadership would thrive.

The numbers became an obsession at Ford. They were the basis for setting goals, evaluating results, doling out rewards, and making or breaking careers. Under Henry Ford, the company had been run in a top-down authoritarian, yet haphazard, fashion. What the Whiz Kids showed was that an auto company, much like the war effort, could be run with a common theme: statistics, careful controls, and so-called professional management. In essence, numbers became the medium of exchange, and the baseline upon which a dominant Transactor leadership culture was established.

According to Byrne, "Their belief in the numbers gave us systems that promoted efficiency at the expense of responsiveness. A postwar generation became slaves to numbers, taught to squeeze out costs in every part and every product while building looming hierarchies of white-collar staffs that centralized authority and decision making. For the efficiencies of cutting costs and gaining control, we sacrificed all notions of product quality and customer satisfaction, and we obliterated individual initiative." Following the war, the American economy experienced rapid

---

*John A. Byrne, *The Whiz Kids* (Garden City, N.Y.: Doubleday, 1993). All quotations are from this book.

expansion, providing people throughout the world the products they had done without or lost during the war. Byrne says, "For a time, however, their ideas worked brilliantly. American business needed discipline, order, control." Clearly, in the postwar period, Ford needed order.

The record of prominence of the Whiz Kids was impressive. Six became Ford vice presidents; two became Ford presidents; and one became dean of the Stanford Business School. Three left Ford to become presidents or CEOs of major American corporations. Two took companies public: one took a firm from $3 million in sales to $100 million in less than four years in the early 1950s.

Of all the Whiz Kids, Robert McNamara, who served as Ford president, became the most famous of the group. Later McNamara attempted to bring the numbers philosophy to the management of the Vietnam war—an approach that history has reviewed with widespread criticism.

The Whiz Kids developed a top-down system of numbers-oriented management that concentrated on rewards as the main motivational driver.

The Whiz Kids also left a legacy to American management. The systems they created were based on the belief that not only did management know best but management could manage anything if only they had the right numbers.

The Ford experience was a precursor of a later debate about the so-called dichotomy between management and leadership. Ford would become a particular example of a leadership culture known as "management." Leadership was based on mastery of the numbers, on the close monitoring of work results, and a belief in the power of financial controls to motivate people and to manage operations. Later, in the 1980s, Ford would react to this culture in an attempt to rediscover innovation, creativity, and quality through a special emphasis on developing human resources.

Contingent Personal Reward

Goals are important, but the use of contingent rewards is the defining characteristic of the Transactor leader. The term *contingent* means based on performing the action desired by the leader. That is, the Transactors offer rewards in exchange for the performance of followers of what the leader wishes. For example, the reward might be given in exchange for achievement of a goal. In a sense, rewards become leader payments in completing a transaction with followers. (A cynic might even describe the reward as a type of bribe.) Regardless, rewards serve as the basis for stimulating follower motivation for achieving the leader's ends.

One prominent category of this type of leader activity is contingent personal rewards, which focus on less tangible incentives such as praise and recognition— the "pat on the back" approach. Considerable evidence has suggested the power of these less formal and less costly rewards for influencing employee performance when they are tied directly to specific desired behaviors. That means praise and recognition should not be used randomly but rather should be provided *only* when targeted desired behaviors are performed.

The exchange of leader material reward in return for follower compliance is the essence of Transactor leadership.

Most people enjoy appreciation and praise, especially if this is done publicly so that wider recognition is enjoyed in front of peers. Generally, we are in favor of contingent rewards as an effective leader behavior. Over time, followers learn that personal rewards can be received in exchange for behavior and performance that complies with what the leader wants done. A transactional process is set into motion that enables the leader to exercise a great deal of influence.

Contingent Material Reward

Material rewards too can provide the basis for exchange between leaders and followers. Again, *contingent* means based on performance. Pay raises, bonuses, promotion opportunities, and so forth can serve this purpose. Frequently, these material rewards can have an even more powerful impact than personal rewards. Pay and promotion might be thought of as the big Ps in the traditional Transactor's tool kit. Money and career advancement are primary symbols of the American dream.

It is important that these material rewards be made contingent on desired performance. The skilled Transactor leader is very aware of this and holds out concrete incentives as the primary carrot for gaining subordinate compliance. "If you want more money and if you want to get ahead in your career, then do what I ask you to do," is the essence of the Transactor leader's message to followers. Consequently, the primary incentives for work performance are clearly distinguished from the job at hand. Whether an employee enjoys or believes in the work is not the issue. Rather, if employees want the incentives, they must perform the work as the Transactor directs.

If the price is right, followers normally comply with the Transactor leader's wishes.

An important part of the exchange process within larger organizations traditionally has been the material reward loosely known as job security—that is, an employee provided services in exchange for an understanding that a job would be available for life. But this element of the exchange equation seems to have disappeared as downsizing has spread.

LOYALTY LOST

Not too long ago, job security used to be part of the exchange formula between employer and employee. The organization (especially if it were a large organization) provided job security—sometimes a job for life. In exchange, the employee provided loyalty. In fact, loyalty seemed to work both ways: the company was loyal to the employee and the employee was loyal to the company. For decades, the loyalty ethic powered business organizations.

But times change, and both job security and loyalty seem to be vestiges of a past era. Companies continue to downsize and unload employees. Those who remain keep their head down and hope the guilt of survival will not be too difficult.

In retrospect, it's clear that this reciprocal loyalty was a form of paternalism. Employees cling to the belief and hope that top management will do the right thing for the company, and they fervently hope that they personally will continue to survive.

For leaders who have always depended on the exchange relationship, the basis for their power is now under severe threat. They no longer can depend on the reciprocal relationship between the employee and the organization. Now that mutual loyalty has become lost, a new form of leadership power is needed. We suggest that new leaders will enhance their own power by creating empowered followers who are capable of high achievement through effective self-leadership. The time for Transactor leadership is past; the time for self-leadership is now.

Because of the tangible value attached to material rewards, they especially create the psychology of a transaction. Transactor leaders purchase work effort from subordinates with whatever material incentives they have to offer. If the price is right, followers will normally comply with the leader's wishes. This enables Transactor leaders to exercise definite influence, but it can also create the conditions for suboptimal subordinate employees because the process does not engage the psychological ownership of the follower. Effort or desire to achieve might stop once the conditions for the transaction have been fulfilled.

Contingent Reprimand

Goals, and especially rewards, are the most significant tools of the Transactor leader. Nevertheless, similar to the Strongman leader, the Transactor also relies on reprimand. The central process that maintains the leader-follower relationship is exchange. If the follower does and achieves what the leader wants (e.g., meets the established goals), personal or material rewards are provided. If the goals are not reached, reprimand is the consequence.

Reprimand discourages risk taking and innovation; maintaining the status quo becomes the aim.

This is not to say that the Transactor tends to be a highly punitive leader. The Transactor is not typically drawn to punishment as an emotionally driven central part of the leadership experience. Rather, punishments are simply a logical part of a rationally based exchange relationship. If the follower delivers positive results, the leader offers positive consequences (rewards) in exchange. If the follower delivers negative results, then negative consequences (punishments) are provided in exchange. In fact, we recognize that reprimand is sometimes necessary and should be a part of a leader's behavioral repertoire. Following are some guidelines that will help a leader reprimand in a more effective manner:

- *Praise in public, punish in private.* Public praise can inspire everyone. Public punishment can be embarrassing and dysfunctional.
- *Reprimand following the behavior.* Delayed reprimand is often misunderstood and misinterpreted. To be effective, the reprimand must reaffirm the connection between the undesirable behavior and the reprimand.
- *Focus on the undesirable behavior, not the person.* It's the behavior that needs to be corrected. Behavior can be changed more easily than the person.
- *Make sure the desired behavior is made clear.* In itself, reprimand tells what *not* to do. Make sure the person also knows *what* to do.
- *Balance reprimand with positive approaches.* Keep on the lookout for good things that happen that can be reinforced. Don't always focus on the negative.

- *Make reprimands contingent on undesired behavior.* The connection between undesirable behavior and the reprimand must be made absolutely clear if future behavior is to be improved.

Unfortunately, whether punishments are delivered with an emotional commitment (as the Strongman tends to do) or delivered out of a more detached rationale, the impact on followers can be very much the same. Risk taking and innovation tend to be discouraged. Compliance (doing the minimum of what is asked) rather than commitment (a willingness to go above and beyond the call of duty) is fostered. Maintaining the status quo (whether it is desirable or not) and satisfying the boss, rather than continuous improvement, becomes the aim. In contrast, the most effective leaders have a special capacity to encourage followers to control their own behavior rather than depending on the reprimand as a significant influence factor.

FOLLOWERS OF THE TRANSACTOR

The Transactor leader tends to have followers who are very sensitive to rewards. In fact, Transactor leadership can establish the breeding ground for skilled calculators—followers who become so tuned into the transactional relationship they have with their boss that they begin to weigh any contribution they might make against the rewards they could receive in exchange. "What's in it for me?" is the battle cry of calculators created by Transactors. Consequently, getting something in return, rather than a commitment to continuous improvement, becomes the dominant concern of employees.

Followers of Transactor leaders are calculators who ask, "What's in it for me?"

Of course, employees should receive recognition and compensation for what they do. But the pure Transactor-type leader tends to create an undue focus on rewards. Ideally, personal and material rewards should contribute to employee motivation, but more as added support for a strong inner drive to outstanding performance and continuous improvement over time. Pride in work and commitment to peers (the rest of the team) will tend to produce a longer-term increase in performance. An overly strong focus on rewards tends to produce compliance (a willingness to do the minimum of what is asked, and little more) in order to receive rewards in return.

The following list sets out the primary leadership strategies used by the Transactor and identifies the kind of followers the Transactor tends to create:

Typical Leader Behaviors

Interactive goal setting

Contingent personal reward

Contingent material reward

Contingent reprimand

Type of Followers

"Calculators"

In summary, Transactor leaders rely on goals that set up contingent rewards and reprimands to establish a relationship based on exchange with subordinate employees. As a consequence, they tend to produce calculating, compliant followers—not enough to compete effectively in the long run, especially with organizations that create a company of heroes.

THE VISIONARY HERO

We often think of the Visionary Hero in images that conjure up a leader on a rearing white horse, calling, "Follow me!" Visionary Heroes are inspiring. One of them, Theodore Roosevelt, said, "Far better it is to dare mighty things, to win glorious triumphs, than to . . . live in the gray twilight that knows not victory nor defeat."[1] Almost four decades later, Franklin Roosevelt declared, "This generation of Americans has a rendezvous with destiny."[2]

Traditional approaches to leadership, such as Strongman and Transactor, tend to produce follower compliance—the minimum of what the leader asks. Yet both approaches to leadership can be appropriate under certain conditions. Some situations require only that a routine task be completed, and rewarding people in exchange for performance is enough. Sometimes, such as during a dangerous emergency (e.g., a battle during war), strong, directive leadership designed to save lives may prove most beneficial.

The Visionary Hero creates follower excitement and emotional involvement.

Strongman and Transactor leadership, however, do not fit well with the objective of creating long-term commitment so that people are willing to go above and beyond the call of duty. Here we concentrate on the Visionary Hero as a popularly prescribed leadership for establishing commitment to a common purpose. This approach is very important during a major organizational change or crisis, although it poses problems for achieving long-term employee empowerment. The main advantage of a Visionary Hero is the sense of mission and direction that he or she provides as an overall guiding light for the organization.

WE AREN'T JUST TALKING SMALL POTATOES: VISIONARY LEADERSHIP IN BIOTECHNOLOGY

Craig Pearce

Small Potatoes Inc. (SPI) is an entrepreneurial biotechnology company, based in Madison, Wisconsin, that produces small potatoes—potatoes about the size of a pea—with a patented production technology, in state-of-the-art bioreactors. These pea-sized potatoes—"micro-tubers" to industry insiders—are then used as seed potatoes. In an interview, Peter Joyce, the founder and president of SPI, explains: "Micro-tubers offer several advantages over conventional seed potato production methods: they can be produced year round; they are grown in a pathogen free environment; they cost less in terms of shipping and handling; they can be produced in any climate; and they can be easily transformed through gene-splicing."

Joyce's Formative Experiences

Peter Joyce is a Visionary Hero. He founded SPI in 1988 on a shoestring budget and a vision stemming from a fledgling idea that he and his major professor, Brent McCown, were working on in the laboratories of the University of Wisconsin at Madison while Joyce was pursuing his master's degree in horticulture. "We knew we were on to something . . . and I wanted to see the vision realized. That's why I started SPI. . . . I saw the great potential of the technology to reshape the entire potato industry."

"I just decided I had to get the ball rolling."

Joyce got his first leadership experience while a Peace Corps volunteer in Guatemala. There, he said, "I was thrust into a leadership position. . . . I helped the locals with many improvement projects in agricultural production and building infrastructure." One of his most memorable experiences was when building a road through the countryside and a landowner wanted the project stopped. "Most people didn't want to continue working on the project because the landowner threatened their lives. Nobody (with the exception of one person) wanted to work on the project because they were afraid . . . so I just decided that I had to get the ball rolling. I started tearing down (with the help of one other person) the fence that protected a landowner's property so that we could finish the road. . . .

I guess this gave everyone the courage they needed. We finished the road soon after that . . . and that's when I realized how important it is to be persistent and to be committed to your vision."

Small Potatoes Today

Today Joyce is still tearing down new frontiers—except now he is focused on developing new and better potato production techniques. Small Potatoes is recognized as a world leader in the micro-tuber field; it sells seed potatoes throughout North America and has begun discussions with several European organizations. Its production techniques are about 150 times more efficient than its closest competitor. When asked about his vision for Small Potatoes, Joyce replied, "I see us one day dominating the world market for seed potatoes. We can do it because we are able to provide a low-cost, high-quality product and we're committed to constantly improving."

Joyce's vision for the future includes addressing part of the world hunger crisis: "Our technology will be particularly important for developing countries that cannot produce their own seed stock due to environmental factors . . . and when they get this technology it will produce some jobs on the one hand, but more importantly it will help lower the cost of staple food products." Moreover, Joyce claims that through gene splicing and transformation of potatoes, they will be able to scale-up new varieties of potatoes that are resistant to disease and insect damage, thereby eliminating the need for environmentally damaging insecticides and pesticides.

We can help to solve the world hunger crisis.

Small Potatoes has had a steady record of growth since its formation. It won the highly competitive Phase I and Phase II Small Business Innovative Research grants from the U.S. Department of Agriculture and successfully funded a first-round equity financing that has permitted it to increase research and development. In the future, Joyce plans to take the company to the point of an initial public offering or to sell the company to one of the currently established leaders in the potato industry.

Joyce's Leadership

Joyce believes in leading by example and in giving his employees room to make their own mistakes, though he admits that it is sometimes difficult to watch someone make mistakes that could be avoided. For instance, one front that Small Potatoes is pursuing is the development of an automated planting machine specifically designed for its micro-tubers. He offered some advice to the project leader that was not followed, and they lost a couple of weeks on the project, but "I like to take a long-run view with my employees. If I solve all of their problems for them now, they won't be as valuable to us in the future."

In sum, Joyce says, "Leadership is all about having a vision of where you are going, and motivating your people to follow that vision." It appears that Peter Joyce discovered a way to stimulate dramatic change by using the best parts of a visionary approach, while at times blending in a good dose of SuperLeadership.

VISIONARY HERO BEHAVIOR

Visionary Hero specific behaviors are communication of the leader's vision, emphasis of the leader's values, exhortation, and inspirational persuasion.

Communication of the Leader's Vision

As the label implies, the central activity of the Visionary Hero leader is to create and communicate a vision that followers can pursue. Currently a popular view is the notion that good leaders influence others through the power of a purposeful vision. History has repeatedly distinguished outstanding visionary leaders who have held out a captivating visionary banner at a crucial time that pointed the way to a better world. Ghandi, Martin Luther King, and many others exemplify this inspiring form of leadership. Unfortunately, Adolph Hitler, Jim Jones, and David Koresh stand out as well.

A leader can influence followers by communicating a meaningful vision.

The main point is that a leader can achieve significant influence over followers by effectively communicating a meaningful vision that is seen as both timely and important to them. Using language and imagery that followers will respond to is crucial. The vision may be created by the leader, but the most influential Visionary Heroes will communicate the vision so that it is readily adopted by followers. Connecting the vision to historical points of pride (honored ancestors or notable past achievements) or issues of current emotional concern are examples of how the leader can achieve this end.

The Visionary Hero leader uses a captivating vision as the central influence tool for gaining the commitment of followers and communicates the vision in a form that others can rally around.

Emphasis of the Leader's Values

Vision is a central influence mechanism for the visionary hero. So is communication of key leader values, largely achieved through the vision itself but accomplished in a variety of ways. The key is for the leader to be absolutely clear about the values that are central to the performance that is expected. Values can provide basic guides for employee decisions and behaviors. For example, if the leader communicates the value that "the customer is always right," certain behaviors are implied that are consistent with that value. "Ethical behavior is more important than profits" implies another set of behaviors. And "we beat the competition at all costs" will tend to bring out yet another set of behaviors.

The values that are communicated can generate intense energy and attraction in followers. Followers can commit to values that they believe are worthy and provide a sense of purpose. The values need not be ethical and consistent with the common good; for example, Hitler espoused corrupt and evil values. Rather, the values need only appeal to the followers as meaningful and important to them. When difficult situations arise, followers can rely on the values to help them stay true to the overall vision of the organization. At the heart of visions that leaders create are usually a set of central values. By making these values readily apparent, the Visionary Hero leader can establish an internal control mechanism in followers than ensures that they act as the leader desires.

The Visionary Hero does not rely on threat and intimidation or reward to influence followers. Rather, he or she instills adherence to a set of values that control followers from within. The Visionary Hero especially arouses emotions within followers.

Exhortation

While vision and values provide the primary content of visionary hero leadership, exhortation exemplifies the process involved. The leader exhorts followers to behave and perform in ways that the leader prescribes. Whereas the Strongman leader starts threatening and intimidating and the Transactor digs into a big reward sack, the Visionary Hero exhorts: "You can do it. You can succeed in reaching our important purpose. Never give up! We will be victorious in the end."

The Visionary Hero leader exhorts followers ever onward to victory in the cause.

Speech is often an important vehicle through which a leader communicates a vision. We are reminded of Martin Luther King's "I Have a Dream" speech and the exhortation of Coach Knute Rockne at Notre Dame ("Win one for the Gipper!"). Rhetoric has always been associated with charismatic leadership.

Inspirational Persuasion

Inspirational persuasion is a closely related leader behavior to exhortation. The leader combines words that create images, energy, and emotion to persuade followers to adhere to the values and pursue (the vision) the leader has communicated. Many inspirational speeches throughout history exemplify this important part of Visionary Hero leadership. Consider John Kennedy's "Ask not what your country can do for you. Ask what you can do for your country" and Mao Tsetung's "So many deeds cry out to be done. . . . Seize the day. Seize the hour."

"If you can't energize others, you can't be a leader."
—Jack Welch, CEO of General Electric[3]

The idea is to use the power of words to move others to commit, of their own will, to what the leader wants. If an emotional speech or an energizing pep talk can persuade followers to accomplish what the leader wishes, then threat, intimidation, contingent rewards, or any other form of external control is less necessary. Once persuasion succeeds, followers are programmed from within.

VISIONARY HERO FOLLOWERS

The influential Visionary Hero leader tends to create enthusiastic followers. They not only comply with what the leader wants but are willing to go above and beyond the call of duty to serve the leader and his or her cause.

The followers of the Visionary Hero sometimes might be described as enthusiastic sheep. It is true that followers are often inspired and enthusiastic. But their inspiration, enthusiasm, and commitment tend to be largely dependent on the leader. If the leader leaves, they often lose their resolve, and the organization is vulnerable to collapse. After all, it was the leader's values and vision, communicated with inspirational persuasion and exhortation, that provided the influence to begin with. Without the leader, the inner drive and commitment of followers tend to drain away.

Followers of the visionary hero might be described as enthusiastic sheep.

SUMMARY

Following is a summary of Visionary Hero behaviors and the type of followers this leadership type inspires:

Typical Leader Behaviors

Communication of leader's vision

Emphasis of leader's values

Exhortation

Inspirational persuasion

Type of Followers

Enthusiastic sheep

Visionary Hero leaders can be important in times of crisis or a major organizational change. They can often rally the troops in a hurry, without having to resort to threat and intimidation. But remember that the Visionary Hero is *the* hero of a work system. We must be wary of the values of a powerful Visionary Hero leader.

Most of all, we must guard against follower overdependency on this leader. A leader who takes central stage as the primary organizational hero often robs followers of the opportunity to become heroes themselves. If we want a company of heroes, we cannot rely on a Visionary Hero approach over the long haul. Rather, a different kind of leader is needed to bring out the heroic potential of others—the SuperLeader.

THE
SUPERLEADER

General Dwight Eisenhower understood the essence of SuperLeadership. He wrote, "The more you develop people now, the greater will be your confidence in them when you . . . thrust bigger and bigger jobs upon them."[1]

In the previous three chapters we briefly described three alternative approaches to leadership: the Strongman, the Transactor, and the Visionary Hero. Each of these perspectives reflects a top-down theme of leadership suggesting that leaders influence others to do what the leader wants done—a theme consistent with the central myth that has guided leadership practice for many years. That is, leaders are expected to direct and control others based on their superior wisdom and knowledge. Followers are expected to follow. Nevertheless, at times, each of these patterns is an appropriate approach to leadership.

In this chapter, we introduce the primary leader behaviors that are consistent with creating a company of heroes. We call this SuperLeadership: leading others to lead themselves. SuperLeaders work to develop followers who are effective self-leaders.

A SuperLeader unleashes the power of follower self–leadership.

SUPERLEADER BEHAVIOR

The SuperLeader is best understood in terms of some main categories of defining behavior: mastering and modeling self-leadership, facilitating the transition of followers to self-leadership, fostering teamwork, and facilitating a self–leadership culture.

Mastering and Modeling Self-Leadership

At the heart of SuperLeadership is a process we call self-leadership—a set of skills for effectively influencing our own behavior and thinking. The next part of the book examines a variety of strategies for establishing greater self-discipline, more natural enjoyment and motivation in our work activities, and more constructive thinking patterns and habits. Each of these types of self-leadership behavior is important for establishing a balanced, constructive personal system of self-influence. For each of us, self-leadership is the key to achieve our own aspirations of high performance. And most of all, if we hope to lead others to be self-leaders, we must first lead ourselves.

To lead others, first lead yourself.

Leading ourselves enables us to better understand and facilitate what we hope to bring out in others: personal responsibility, initiative, self-motivation, continuous personal improvement, and overall effectiveness. Perhaps even more important, by mastering our own self-leadership, we are in an ideal position to demonstrate and exemplify, or model, the process for others. People pay significant attention to the actions of visible figures of influence. As leaders, we need to talk the talk and walk it as well. By mastering and modeling self-leadership, we trigger one of the most powerful and constructive forms of leadership influence. In fact, a leader's own self-leadership serves as a primary catalyst for the transition of followers from dependence to independence and personal development.

Facilitating the Transition of Followers to Self-Leadership

The most dramatic results of SuperLeadership are realized through the transition of followers to self-leaders. In traditional leadership systems, followers learn to look to the leader for guidance and direction. They may have different primary motivations for doing so (fear, monetary incentives, an inspiring vision, and so forth), but the result tends to be dependence on the leader and an inability to decide and act independently. Employee empowerment and teamwork call for a different kind of follower stance—one in which employees possess the capability and confidence to make decisions, to innovate, and to act on their own.

Some of the ways leaders can help followers with this transition are very obvious: delegate tasks, allow some honest mistakes to be made in the spirit of progress, and provide training and learning opportunities in key competence areas. In addition, key leader behaviors can be employed directly to help the process along. In particular, goals, feedback, and rewards are crucial. Goals that identify specific challenging but achievable performance and personal development targets for followers can provide constructive direction during the transition. They become even more powerful the more they are defined, and consequently "owned," by followers themselves. Feedback regarding follower progress and rewards for accomplishments provide crucial information and motivation as well. Over time followers should develop the ability to be a primary source of their own feedback and rewards in order to become fully empowered.

Each of these issues will be discussed in more detail later in this book. The important point for now is that a large part of the SuperLeader role is to help employees make the transition from traditional followers to independent self-leaders, as well as interdependent team members.

Fostering Teamwork

In our previous book, *Business Without Bosses,* we described in detail how several organizations have implemented empowered work teams and the challenges they encountered and the lessons they learned along the way. Teamwork has become a major tool for organizational competitiveness and effectiveness. In fact, for the most part, teamwork has become the defining method by which self-leadership is implemented. SuperLeadership fully recognizes the power of worker teams and includes facilitating teamwork as a primary leader activity. A leader who stimulates and helps teams to develop and thrive sets in motion a powerful mechanism for high performance. Not only can teams serve as a source of support and socially based motivation, they also enable constructive coordination and integration of effort.

SuperLeaders guide empowered teams to become high-performing units.

At a fundamental level, the SuperLeader views follower capability, knowledge, and experience as primary sources of overall effectiveness. Teams can provide a mechanism for not only tapping into this tremendous resource but also for enabling a constructive combination of individual talent and effort. In the end, the SuperLeader's own effectiveness is best measured by the capability and performance of those whom he or she leads. Consequently, guiding and enabling teams to become high-performing units is a major SuperLeader priority.

Facilitating a Self-Leadership Culture

Each of the categories of SuperLeader behavior we have discussed so far is very important in its own right. A primary mechanism for holding all these activities together is the development of a sustaining culture that supports employee self-leadership. The culture provides a set of generally agreed upon values, beliefs, and norms that make it clear that initiative, taking responsibility, and in general exercising self-leadership is not only okay but is expected.

Self-leadership feeds upon itself when everyone is doing it.

If the SuperLeader successfully applies the other leader behaviors—practicing and modeling self-leadership, guiding the empowerment transition of employees, facilitating teamwork—then a culture supportive of self-leadership should largely unfold as a natural consequence. Nevertheless, facilitating a self-leadership culture is an important category of leader activity, and the SuperLeader directs special attention to helping it along. For example, status symbols may be systematically removed, language may be altered to focus on team effort as opposed to individual competition ("we" versus "I" or "he or she"), special recognition may be given for initiative as opposed to compliant performance, and restrictive rules and policies may be eliminated.

SUPERLEADER FOLLOWERS

SuperLeaders tend to develop followers who are both independent and interdependent self-leaders at the same time: that is, followers who become very capable of standing on their own two feet as well as effectively contributing to a team. They make mistakes but they learn from them and are not afraid to take reasonable risks. A spirit of continuous improvement tends to permeate the workforce. Followers have a sense of ownership and pride in their work. Eventually they rise above the traditional concept of follower. They become effective, empowered, confident, self-leaders—heroes in their own right.

The following list summarizes SuperLeader behavior and characterizes those who follow this leader:

Typical Leader Behaviors

Mastering and modeling self-leadership

Facilitating the transition of followers to self-leadership

Fostering self-leadership teamwork

Facilitating a self-leadership culture

Type of Followers

Self-leaders

LEADERSHIP TYPES: A COMPARISON

Finally, we contrast SuperLeadership with the previously described three approaches—Strongman, Transactor, and Visionary Hero—to delineate more clearly how SuperLeadership is a substantial paradigm shift from previous leadership perspectives. Also, we focus on the question of why a new leadership perspective, like SuperLeadership, is needed to meet the challenges of employee empowerment and teamwork.

The following model suggests the external conditions under which each of the four types of leadership is likely to fit best. This framework is based on two primary situational features: the type of follower involvement that is needed (compliance versus commitment) and the degree of urgency in the situation (low or high).

	URGENCY	
	Low	High
Commitment	SuperLeader	Visionary Hero
Compliance	Transactor	Strongman

FOLLOWER INVOLVEMENT

The first important condition is the nature of urgency of the situation—that is, the time frame in which a decision must be made, a problem solved, or an action taken. At one extreme, the urgency is high, say, an emergency or a crisis. The gravity of the situation clearly demands action soon. The second important condition is the degree of follower involvement that is desired. For example, do we want the follower merely to comply with the wishes of the leader, or do we want the follower to be enkindled with some psychological ownership? Do we want the follower to be committed?

If follower compliance is adequate (employees simply doing the minimum of what is asked and little more), then the Transactor or the Strongman approach will suffice. If the situation is also urgent (a state of crisis exists, such as an urgent product recall), then the Strongman approach fits better than the more gradual Transactor approach.

On the other hand, if follower commitment is needed (a willingness to go beyond the minimum of what is asked, to go above and beyond the call of duty), then either the Visionary Hero or the SuperLeader approach will be more effective. Both of these approaches have the capacity to inspire the follower. And if the situation is urgent (e.g., the organization is on the brink of bankruptcy) then the Visionary Hero approach fits better, at least in the short run. If a long-term view is taken, where the intent is to develop and nurture empowered team-oriented followers, then the SuperLeader is the best alternative.

SuperLeadership reflects a long-term view with an intent to develop empowered and committed team-oriented followers.

This model suggests that SuperLeadership is simply one choice among several different leadership alternatives. That is, on a situation-by-situation basis, a leader might choose which of the types of leadership best fits the situation, and go with that approach. This may or may not be SuperLeadership. This conclusion, however, is oversimplified and requires further consideration. Regardless of the situational factors, there are some definite trade-offs and consequences resulting from each type of leadership. Sometimes it may be better to choose an approach that may not fit as well in the short run in order to avoid long-term problems and enjoy long-term benefits. SuperLeadership is clearly a philosophy that is intended for the long haul.

The following list helps clarify this issue by introducing a major contrasting feature between the leadership types. A comparison is made between the primary source of wisdom and knowledge that drives each form of leadership, an extremely important issue given the exploding growth of information and technology that requires organizations to operate from state-of-the-art knowledge to remain competitive.

Primary Source of Wisdom and Knowledge

From the Leader	*From the Follower*
Strongman	SuperLeader
Transactor	
Visionary Hero	

THE SUPERLEADER: LEADERSHIP FOR TODAY AND TOMORROW

Years ago, it might have been adequate to rely on the wisdom and knowledge of one individual in a position of status and power. Today, successful organizations realize the need for knowledge, creativity, and experience from all their human resources if they are to survive, let alone prosper. This is a primary driver behind the recent spread of team-based organizations across nearly every major industry. The myth of heroic leadership does not fit with today's complex and rapidly changing world. Of the four types of leadership, only SuperLeadership relies on followers as the primary source of wisdom and knowledge. Only SuperLeadership can release the power of self-leadership.

Individuals who do their jobs day in day out are the world-class experts in their own specific work. They are the day-to-day heroes. SuperLeadership recognizes this capability, and is the only leadership view that is deliberately designed to tap this tremendous source of competitiveness and progress.

SuperLeaders rely on followers as the primary source of wisdom and knowledge.

Another related and very important issue is the impact of leadership on the growth of followers. Traditional leadership frequently creates weak and dependent followers who are not capable of standing on their own. Particularly troubling is a self-fulfilling cycle that is frequently set in motion. How many times have we all heard executives say they would like to use empowering leadership but their followers are simply not capable or willing to handle the increased responsibility? They do not realize that their own leadership may be the cause of follower incapacity. Leadership that works well in the short term may be interfering with the opportunity of followers for growth toward independence and interdependence (e.g., in empowered teams) as well as the confidence to handle the increased responsibility of empowerment. Whether a leader relies on commands, rewards, or a leader-created vision, the result tends to be follower dependence.

SuperLeadership is the approach best geared to achieve follower independence. By definition, it involves leading others to lead themselves, to stand on their own two feet. Other leadership practices are designed to influence followers to do what the word implies: follow the leader. When employees learn to be traditional followers, they will always look to the leader, the central organizational pillar, for wisdom and direction. And if that pillar fails, is removed, or simply leaves, the organization, like a house of cards, may well collapse.

Here, in summary, are the consequences of the four leadership types:

Strongman	Leads to *dependent* followers
Transactor	Leads to *dependent* followers
Visionary Hero	Leads to *dependent* followers
SuperLeader	Leads to *independent* followers

When SuperLeadership is effectively implemented, the organization is able to go beyond the myth of heroic leadership. Instead of being supported by only one (or very few) central pillars of strength, the organization is supported by countless sturdy pillars. SuperLeadership can help an organization ascend above the myth of heroic leadership to the solid ground of a company of heroes.

SuperLeadership goes beyond the myth of heroic leadership. Thus, the organization is supported by countless pillars of strength.

Even when dramatically changing times call for visionary leadership, SuperLeadership is often needed just as much. Perhaps there is no other case where this was more true than in the leadership challenge faced by Mikhail Gorbachev of the former Soviet Union. Indeed, there is a great deal we can learn from this man. He made a fascinating contribution to history and perhaps to the evolution toward a new, more complex kind of leadership that is demanded by the challenges of the late 1990s and beyond.

GORBACHEV: VISIONARY HERO, SUPERLEADER, OR NONLEADER?

Highly visible leaders such as Mikhail Gorbachev, who stimulate great expectations and hope, are particularly vulnerable to criticism based on a number of commonly held leadership myths—that is, leaders are expected to have the answers, light the way, know all, and see all. In short, they are expected to be superhuman. The reality, of course, is that leaders turn out to be human, just like everyone else. But even more important, if the spotlight focuses on the leader too long or too much, a condition of follower dependence and weakness is fostered, and the system is largely limited to the knowledge and abilities of one fallible human being who happens to be called a leader. When the leader leaves, the system is likely to collapse. At the same time, we need to recognize the unique demands of leadership during times of major change, when the leader may need to occupy an active, central role.

Our concern about taking this line of thinking too far is that we end up continuing to feed the myths of leaders as stand-out heroes who are different from all the rest. Day-to-day leadership under contemporary conditions calls for something else. Even times of change require more than a strong, inspiring, pioneering central leader. In writing about Gorbachev, authors Bolman and Deal sum it up especially well:

> Gorbachev often clung to the belief that he needed to control events to move them in the right direction. In so doing, he overlooked what his constituents really needed from him. They needed a leader who allied with and supported the forces for decentralization and autonomy that were emerging across the Soviet Union. They also needed a vision of a radically restructured Soviet Union that honored the aspirations of its multiple peoples to control their own destinies while building viable relations with each other and the rest of the world.*

Visionary Hero leadership is appropriate for times of stress or crisis. But what about the long haul? What comes after the visionary leader?

---

*L. G. Bolman and T. E. Deal, "Leadership Lessons from Mikhail Gorbachev," *Human Resource Development Quarterly* 3 (1992): 3–23.

Despite his many apparent contributions, Gorbachev has been criticized for not introducing enough change, for not going far enough. We must subject ourselves to the same challenge regarding our views of leadership. As we move toward the twenty-first century, new views of leadership are needed to tap the potential of all. Espousing the exercise of dramatic leadership that guides people into new, uncharted territory and creates great waves of change can be a dangerous trap. Adolph Hitler, Jim Jones, and many others have already taught us this. In the end, leadership energy needs to come from and be in the people themselves.

In some important ways Gorbachev did serve as a Visionary Hero, leading a major shift toward a new form of government for his people. But was he also a SuperLeader—a leader of others to lead themselves? The most obvious response is that he probably was more instrumental in moving the ultimate communist power toward the democratic principles of self-governance than any other. In this sense, he demonstrated dramatic SuperLeadership. And in a relative sense, he accepted the role and necessity of stepping out of the spotlight and moving on with his life, in stark contrast to many major leaders when they step down from power.[†] In a television interview conducted about the time he was leaving power, Gorbachev indicated that he believed he had done all he could, and he sincerely wanted the democratic movement to succeed, though he would not be the central leadership figure.

We are still left with questions about how well his people will fare in the wake of his leadership. Was he effective in helping others to be able to lead themselves? Was he an effective SuperLeader? Chaos, turmoil, and hunger are rampant in the former Soviet Union. There is an old saying that captures much of the SuperLeadership philosophy: "Give a man a fish and he will be fed for a day; teach a man how to fish, and he will be fed for a lifetime." So far, it seems clear that Gorbachev's leadership has not given his people a fish for today. The question that remains is, Did he help them to learn enough to be able to fish for themselves in the years to come?

[†]Jeffrey Sonnenfeld, *The Hero's Farewell: What Happens When CEOs Retire* (New York: Oxford University Press, 1988).

Part II

Heroic Self-Leadership

THE FIRST STEP IN SUPER-LEADERSHIP

Becoming a Self-Leader

Almost all theories and viewpoints of leadership concentrate on the way the leader is or on something the leader does. The forgotten person in the leadership equation is the follower. In this chapter, we reverse that perspective, putting the spotlight on the follower.

Most of the time, we think of followers almost as we think of robots. The follower is the target of the leader's attempt at influence, and, like a robot, the follower is presumed to carry out what the leader wishes. But followers are not really like robots at all. In a company of heroes, we don't want followers who are robots; we want followers who are self-led heroes. Followers are living, thinking, and behaving human beings. Each is an individual—a unique person. Most important, each follower has a mind of his or her own. Therefore, each follower will respond to a leader in a unique way.

The follower is the forgotten person in the leadership equation.

As we shift our focus from the leader to the follower, we ask the important question: What do we expect from followers within a system of SuperLeadership?

EMPOWERED FOLLOWERSHIP: WHAT IS IT? HOW DO YOU GET IT?

George Diaz sat back in his chair with a frown and threw up his hands in a gesture of frustration as he turned to his friend and consultant, Dr. Ricardo Marquez-Sanchez. He had just returned from his first meeting with his staff.

"The main thing I wanted from the meeting today was some input regarding the capital expenditure budget. When we got to that part of the meeting, the controller presented the draft plan that had been developed under the direction of the previous CEO. I had reviewed the plan, of course, but I think it needed some serious reevaluation. I told them the plan was only a start and that I wanted a thorough reevaluation—that it was not engraved in stone."

George had recently been appointed CEO of State Enterprise, a publicly owned enterprise (owned by the government but operated as an ostensibly private firm). The previous CEO was a well-known national executive who held a degree from the London School of Economics and had had a rapid career ascent mainly through the finance area, until he had been named CEO. He was widely regarded as brilliant but tough and demanding. His subordinates knew that the main thing he wanted from them was to carry out his wishes efficiently. These were the same subordinates George had faced in his first staff meeting. During his seven-year tenure as CEO, he was credited with rationalizing the management of the organization, mainly through his emphasis on modern systems.

Strong-minded leaders, no matter how brilliant and capable, are likely to have a legacy of passive, dependent followers.

Overall, the performance of the enterprise had been dismal when the previous CEO took control, with a ten-year record of losses and cost overruns that had been covered by government appropriations. Now the enterprise was generally on a break-even basis, with only a modest amount of government appropriations required in the previous year. This improvement was mainly accomplished through severe cost control and tightening of operations. Yet the performance of the enterprise was still regarded as mediocre and not competitive. The organization was seen as stodgy and conservative and was a leader in virtually nothing. Creativity and innovation were nonexistent.

The minister of public enterprises knew that the previous CEO had made progress, but in his confidential conversations with George, he indicated a need for change. "We are desperate," he had said to George as they discussed his appointment. "The only way the enterprise remains in business is because of government protection, which must change soon. The enterprise must be made competitive. Our goal is to privatize the company within two years. I have every confidence that you can provide the leadership to prepare the organization for privatization."

George had hired Ricardo as a confidential consultant to advise him during his first six months at the helm. Now he was discussing the experience of his first staff meeting.

"I asked them, 'What are your ideas? How should this budget be changed?'" he continued. "You've never seen such shocked, blank looks in all your life. Most of them looked down at the table. I didn't get a single answer.

"Furthermore, I've met with each major department head individually, and I get the same kind of response. I asked each of them to fill me in on the plans of their department for the coming year, and in every case, I get that same blank look. Not one of them has presented a reasonable plan."

If people have never been asked to perform on their own, it will take some time and effort to develop their self-leadership.

"I think I'm in trouble," he said ruefully. "I need widespread participation and initiative if we are to increase our innovation and competitiveness. I don't know if I have a single subordinate who has the capability to assume responsibility on his or her own. Do you have any suggestions?"

George Diaz has a challenging problem. His subordinates need to develop their skills of empowered followership. In considering this case, try to develop answers to the following questions:

What is empowered "followership"? Try to develop your answer in terms of specific skills and thought patterns. Another way to ask the question is, "What are the specific skills and responsibilities of a subordinate under a system of participative management?"

How is empowered followership different from our traditional definition of followership?

THE IDEAL FOLLOWER

In many of our executive development workshops, we ask, "How would you define your ideal follower?" Not surprisingly, we receive a variety of answers. At one extreme is this: "My ideal follower is one who will carry out my orders in the way I want them carried out!" Obviously this person sees the essence of followership as compliance—that is, complying to the wishes of the leader. (Perhaps this leader might have preferred to have a slave rather than a follower.)

Another might define an ideal follower as "a person who carries out the vision of the organization." This person sees followership as an instrument to implement a top-down vision of the organization. Again, the essence of this viewpoint of followership is compliance, albeit enthusiastic compliance. Instead of compliance to command, the leader wants compliance to a vision that is expounded by a self-centered leader. The role of the follower is to carry out the mission of the leader—another form of follower compliance, although this leader would hope to inspire some enthusiasm and excitement in the follower.

Actually the real definition of ideal followership depends on one's definition of leadership; that is, the behavior that we want from a follower depends on our viewpoint of what the leader should be. For example, a Strongman leader is likely to desire a yes-person who is much like a compliant robot. A Transactor wants a follower who will respond to rewards. A Visionary Hero is likely to desire an "enthusiastic sheep" as an ideal follower. Clearly, the natures of leadership and followership are tightly linked together.

The real definition of an ideal follower depends on one's definition of leadership.

In a system of SuperLeadership, the ideal follower is defined as one who leads one's self. SuperLeaders wants self-leaders. In this chapter, we introduce this notion of self-leadership. Later, in the next few chapters, we further clarify and specify details of the various components of self-leadership. Our ideal follower is definitely no robot! We expect our ideal follower—the self-leader—to be a person who is an expert at initiative and self-responsibility, can stand on his or her own, who draws on the inner self as the main source of influence for behavior. In this part of the book, we attempt to articulate an expanded and more comprehensive viewpoint of how followers can exert self-influence to achieve high performance.[1] In essence, a SuperLeader redefines our ideas of followership. The SuperLeader expects a radical new follower role, characterized by a high degree of self-influence.

SELF-LEADERSHIP

We use the term *self-leadership* to describe the influence that followers exert over themselves to shape and control their own behavior. Self-leadership is one of several terms that denote self-influence; others are *self-regulation, self-management, self-direction,* and *self-control.* These labels are all appropriate, but we prefer *self-leadership* because it indicates an expanded view of self-control that includes both behavioral and cognitive perspectives of how individuals influence themselves.

Most of all, the notion of self-leadership suggests purposeful leadership of self toward personal standards of behavior and performance. That is, effective self-leaders deliberately and consciously attempt to influence their own thinking and behavior through a wide variety of self-influence strategies. They begin by asking the fundamental question: "How can I help myself to perform better? What can I do to achieve high performance?"

Self-leadership suggests purposeful attempts to influence one's own thinking and behavior.

The concept of self-leadership implies that followers look first within themselves for sources of motivation and control. Self-leadership means independence—a certain capability to perform well, sometimes even in the face of an external environment that does not encourage excellence. The self-leader says, "First, I depend on myself to do it."

We do not deny that organizations provide external control systems that exert considerable influence over the way people behave. The reward or compensation system is one example. Nevertheless, these control systems do not access individual initiative directly. Rather, these systems are filtered through a self-influence system. In fact, self-influence is the ultimate system. In the end, all control comes from within.

This viewpoint suggests that individuals can strive toward excellent performance even in the absence of a supportive organizational control system. From a hypothetical standpoint, this system of self-regulation could occur indefinitely.

WHAT'S THE INCENTIVE?

"What's the incentive?" complained Dick, as he had lunch with Rashida. They were both newly appointed supervisors of the Motor Vehicle Administration. "We're all paid the same. Our boss doesn't give any sign that she recognizes a good supervisor from a bad supervisor. If we go by past history, we both will have to serve more than ten years as a supervisor before we might get promoted to manager. I just don't see any reason why I should try to perform at a high level!"

"You're right about one thing," replied Rashida. "The agency doesn't really do much to encourage you to do your job well. But despite that, if you look around, you can find many people who really try to do a good job. It's clear that they care, and they want to make a real contribution. They *do* want to serve the public."

**In the end, high performance really comes
from within.**

"Why do suppose that is?" wondered Dick. "What's in it for them to do a good job?"

"Well," answered Rashida, "some people learn somewhere that if you do a job, it's worth doing well. They seem to have some inner self that tells them they should try to perform well, and that they're not here to goof off. Look at Calvin, for example. He's been here ten years, but he's always looking for a way to do his job better, and he always has this conviction that we should serve the citizens better. If we could understand what Calvin has, put it in a bottle, and dispense it to everyone, then we would have a much better group working here."

"Perhaps you're right," mused Dick.

"You know," said Rashida, "in the end, it's you yourself that sustains and encourages yourself toward good performance. The organization can help—or the organization can get in the way. But in the end, a substantial part really comes from within."

The converse is also true. Given the most supportive and encouraging organizational control system, an employee might fail to respond. This would be an example of an ineffective or impotent self-influence system, at least from the perspective of what the organization wants. Not everyone has developed the skills and behaviors of effective self-leadership.

The SuperLeader strives to develop self-leadership capabilities in each follower. We also recognize that organizational systems are critical for enhancing self-leadership, but for the moment, we focus on the concept of self-leadership itself. What is self-leadership? What are the various kinds of self-leadership? How does one exercise self-leadership? We are temporarily suspending our interest in the issue of how the external leader and the external organizational environment can influence followers to develop the concepts, behaviors, and thought patterns that characterize self-leadership. How do we lead ourselves?

SELF-LEADERSHIP AS A HIGH PERFORMANCE PATTERN

Individuals can achieve more if they understand the nature of their own high-performance pattern.[2] When we gain insight about ourself, especially if we understand how we achieve success, then we can attain more sustainable results. Further, when we understand our own high-performance pattern, we are in a better position to help other people to understand *their* own high performance pattern. Development of our own and others' high-performance pattern is an important part of becoming a hero in a company of heroes.

High performance can be defined as producing results much better than originally expected. A high-performance pattern is a typical sequence of behavior and thoughts that one engages in when carrying out an activity associated with high achievement.[3] Most of the time, high performance means that a person has been exceptionally effective at his or her own self-leadership.

Further, each individual comes to an organization with a different and unique set of self-leadership skills. Some have a well-established pattern of high performance. Others do not but can learn. Indeed, we firmly believe that individual self-leadership skills can be learned, and this is a critical element in building a company of heroes.

A pattern of high performance represents one's self-leadership capabilities.

In the chapters that follow, we develop detailed ideas of how self-leadership can be woven into a fabric of high performance. Yet in the end, the application of self-leadership is uniquely individual; one prescription does not work for all. Each of us must find our own way of adapting the more generic principles of self-leadership to our own situation. When we do this, we can apply this self-leadership pattern over and over again in the pursuit of high performance.

WHY IS SELF-LEADERSHIP IMPORTANT?

Organization structures and processes are changing—and changing radically. The horizontal organization is but one example of the drastic changes in today's organizational environment. Consider the conventions regarding span of control. In older days, one might have heard the following prescription intoned: "The optimum number of subordinates reporting to a manager or supervisor is seven." Today such a prescription would seem ridiculous for several reasons. First, the dogmatic tone of the prescription is contrary to a more contemporary situation-based managerial philosophy. Second, this prescription generally results in tall organizational structures—the converse of today's trend to flatter, more horizontal structures. Finally, the prescription presumes a control mentality on the part of the manager—that is, a view that a major function of a manager is to control the behavior of subordinates.

Self-leadership gives followers confidence in themselves.

Today, spans of control might be 15, or, perhaps even 25 subordinates reporting to a single manager. We have even encountered a manager who had 125 subordinates! We do not recommend a span of control this large, but with larger numbers of subordinates, managers are not able to exert detailed external control over subordinates. Instead, today's leader must vest more control in the hands of followers. To carry out this notion in an effective manner, followers must clearly be self-leaders.

Moreover, self-leadership gives followers confidence in themselves. As they become more and more skilled at self-leadership, they initiate, risk, innovate, persist, and sustain themselves more. They become more flexible and responsive. They become more heroic in facing specific challenges. We call this notion *self-efficacy*, or the belief in one's self that one has the experience, talent, and capability to carry out the tasks required for high performance. Self-leaders have strong self-efficacy. In fact, a recent study suggests that self-leadership positively affects performance because it increases self-efficacy. Strong self-efficacy leads to innovation and high performance.

THE EFFECT OF SELF-LEADERSHIP AND SELF-EFFICACY ON PERFORMANCE

Joe S. Anderson and Gregory E. Prussia

A recent study of aspiring entrepreneurs found that self-leadership strengthens performance; however, its effect on performance results from an initial positive boost in a person's self-perceptions of ability (self-efficacy). Researchers at a major southwestern university surveyed over 150 respondents to find out how often they used self-leadership behaviors, cognitions, and perceptions.* They also surveyed the respondents' levels of task-specific self-efficacy—in other words, how strongly they believed in their own performance ability. Later the researchers evaluated respondents' actual performance on three different dimensions.

A statistical model was developed to evaluate these relationships. Self-leadership skills were represented in the model by survey questions that probed three dimensions: behavior-focused strategies, natural reward strategies, and constructive thought strategies. The subjects' confidence in successful completion of the tasks—task-specific self-efficacy—was represented by two different measures. Finally, performance was measured on three different types of tasks: a writing assignment, an oral presentation, and the results of an exam given to the respondents.

Self-leadership works because it enhances the person's own sense of self-efficacy.

The results of the study indicated that self-leadership skills directly and positively influence confidence in the ability to succeed on tasks (their self-efficacy). In turn, this perceived self-efficacy was found to have a direct, positive effect on performance. Interestingly, the study found that the influence of self-leadership skills on performance was channeled through individual perceptions of self-efficacy. In other words, it appears that self-leadership practices help people develop a higher level of per-

---

*G. Prussia, J. Anderson, and C. Manz, "Self-Leadership and Performance Outcomes: The Mediating Influence of Self-Efficacy," paper presented at the Decision Sciences Annual Conference, Honolulu, Hawaii, 1994.

sonal confidence in their own abilities, and, this increase in confidence brings about improved performance.

Self-efficacy is important because of its capacity to influence performance:

- It influences the *choice* of behaviors. People tend to avoid tasks they believe they will not perform well. They select tasks in which they have confidence.
- It influences *persistence* and *effort expended*. People with high self-efficacy will persevere even in the face of extreme difficulty.
- It influences *thought patterns*. People with low self-efficacy tend to dwell on their weaknesses and expect failure. People with high self-efficacy tend to focus on their ability to succeed in completing the task.

No matter what kind of management and organizational influences surround us, ultimately these forces are potent only to the extent that they affect our self-influence process. Consequently, a person who has an underdeveloped self-leadership capability will be both a poor self-leader and a poor follower. Leading a person with poor self-leadership skills requires a manager to look over an employee's shoulder continuously and provide very close direction and control—a frustrating process.

Individual self-leadership is all the more critical now that organizations are becoming more horizontal and aggressively pursuing employee involvement and empowered teamwork. Technical skills for producing a product or delivering a service are no longer enough. Even adding social skills to help employees communicate better, conduct their own meetings, resolve conflicts, and so forth does not adequately address skill needs. Today's employees need self-leadership skills so they can more fully master their own behavior and minds for high performance. The process of instilling a strong skill base for the practice of self-leadership by everyone in the organization is at the heart of creating an empowered company of heroes.

TYPES OF SELF-LEADERSHIP STRATEGIES

Overall, self-leadership is a comprehensive self-influence perspective concerned with approaching both distasteful and naturally motivating tasks. Self-leadership lies at the heart of the empowerment process. All of us lead ourselves to some degree. We have personal standards and evaluate and react to our behaviors. Sometimes we feel good about ourselves, and sometimes we get down on ourselves. All these things may largely take place outside our conscious awareness, but they are extremely important because they are the substance of our own inner self-leadership system.

We are likely to do a better job if we like what we do.

In the ideal self-leadership situation, followers spend a large proportion of their time on naturally motivating tasks. After all, we are likely to do a better job if we like what we do. But self-leadership also enables us to motivate and structure ourselves to do work that must be done, even though the task may not be naturally motivating. In fact, our original views on self-leadership several years ago were focused on actions and behaviors that are intended to aid a person to structure the short-term work environment in productive ways. We might think of these as near-term behaviors and actions. Many times, these actions help us to accomplish something that we might otherwise not want to do. These actions mainly consist of self-managing behaviors—sort of a self-behavior-modification approach (see the next chapter). We sometimes call this a *push strategy*.

A more comprehensive view of self-leadership, however, includes behavior and thinking concerned with a longer-term outlook—more of a superordinate self-influence system. More often than not, these viewpoints are more concerned with structuring ourselves and the situation so that we want to do the tasks that are required for us to perform well. We think of these approaches as more of a *pull strategy*.

The unique aspect of a pull strategy is that it seems to take on a life of its own. The reason for performing the tasks leading to high performance seems to create a special joy that comes from the process of performing, not the results or consequences of the achievement.

A pattern of high performance seems to create a special joy that comes from the process of performing.

In the next few chapters, we will review various self-leadership strategies. In Chapter 8, we articulate behavioral-focused self-leadership: actions and behaviors that help us establish self-discipline (to "push" ourselves) to accomplish difficult or unattractive but necessary tasks. We label this approach to self-leadership *the Grind*.

In Chapter 9, we look to the task itself as a source of self-leadership. An effective self-leader always attempts to redesign his or her own work to find intrinsic fulfillment from performing the task itself. We think of the task as a source of natural rewards that are built into the job itself and enable it to become motivating for its own value (to pull us to high performance). Discovering and adopting naturally rewarding activities are keys to this approach. We label this approach to self-leadership as *Smelling the Roses*.

In Chapter 10, we consider patterns of thinking as a source of self-leadership. Most of all, an overall approach that focuses on opportunity thinking rather than obstacle thinking is articulated. A primary purpose is to enhance one's own sense of self-efficacy. Cognitive strategies include mental imagery, self-talk, and mental rehearsal to develop constructive thought patterns. An effective self-leader tends to avoid and/or control excessive self-recrimination and guilt. We label this approach to self-leadership *the Opportunity Thinker*.

Finally, in Chapter 11, we define some overall strategies like self-initiative, self-problem solving, and active teamwork and networking. We place special emphasis on striking an appropriate balance between the various self-leadership strategies. The chapter ends by articulating how a *Master Self-Leader* combines and integrates all four approaches to self-leadership.

THE IMPORTANCE OF LONG-TERM ORGANIZATIONAL SUPPORT

Self-leadership can never be maximized and amplified throughout an organization without organizational support. Certainly some employees are capable of exercising significant self-leadership in the absence of organizational support, even for substantial periods of time. Over the long run, however, organizational reinforcement of self-leadership is a must. Later, we revisit this issue and reflect on the question of how organizational cultures can help or hinder self-leadership. Clearly, long-term support is critical if an organization is to build a company of heroes. A lone self-leader is much less effective than the synergy that derives from a total company of self-leaders.

Even self–control is ultimately subject to some external control.

In actuality, the self-leadership system of each employee is subject to higher-level standards and reinforcement; that is, even self–control is ultimately subject to some degree of external control. But one could become overly immersed in metaphysical arguments about the nature of self-control. The important point is that external organization support for self-leadership is crucial. However, we'll save our viewpoints on how leaders and organizations can provide this support until later chapters. For our next step, let's try to understand the real nature of self-leadership in some detail.

BEHAVIOR-FOCUSED SELF-LEADERSHIP STRATEGIES

The Grind

From time to time, we all seem to stumble in our quest to meet a goal or deadline. No matter how important, no matter our overall dedication, we just seem to have trouble either starting or finishing a specific task or project. We say to ourselves, "I need to get this job done, and I recognize I'm having difficulty. What can I do to break this barrier?"

In this chapter, we attempt to answer this question by concentrating on behavior-focused self-leadership strategies. Recall that self-leadership is the deliberate influence we exert over ourselves for the purpose of performing better. One class of self-leadership strategies are specific actions that we undertake to enhance our own performance. Note that behaviors are action oriented. That is, these strategies are things that we do *to* ourselves or *for* ourselves that help us perform.

I'm having difficulty. What can I do to break through?

Many behavioral strategies are routine; they are the small actions we do day by day. If your daily practice is to make a "to-do" list in the morning, you are performing a common self-leadership behavior. Most effective self-leaders are habitual list makers, but the timing and form can be quite different. Many people construct a new list every morning. Some (like the first author) make a weekly to-do list (typically on Sunday night but also supplemented by a Friday night weekend to-do list). Whatever your own practice, list making is a self-leadership behavior that is a form of short-term goal setting. We can think of the more routine behavioral strategies as a form of day-to-day self-discipline—the repetitive actions that help us focus on tasks that need to get done.

Other behavioral strategies are anything but routine—for example, an action that is somewhat special or radical. A writer we know had writer's block and was unable to meet her goal using her usual procedures. Finally, in order to induce a radical change, she left her home, drove for an hour, and checked into a motel with her portable computer and a briefcase full of notes. She resolved not to leave until the block was broken.

After watching TV for three hours, Paula opened the briefcase and turned on the computer. Going through the notes, she began to write notes at random, with no discernible organization. After a few hours, she realized that some themes were emerging from her random notes, and she reviewed them, grouping the ideas by clusters. The clusters became somewhat coherent paragraphs and pages, and eventually a structure and pattern emerged. Paula realized that she had made a breakthrough. She stayed in the motel for about 48 hours, and when she finally checked out, she took with her about 80 percent of a first draft. The block had been broken.

Paula had invoked a type of *cuing strategy* (using the environment to cue desired behavior) to help get her report written. By changing the place and setting of her work, she found the self-discipline necessary to get the job done. Of course, we hope that this issue is not a recurring one with Paula. In the long term, she needs to find ways to write with considerably less self-imposed stress. But most of us can sympathize with Paula. (On occasion, we've also been afflicted by the dreaded "writer's block" virus!) We've all experienced incidents of short-term difficulty in accomplishing a particular task.

Action-oriented self-leadership strategies are especially helpful for accomplishing a task we are finding difficult. For some reason, often without explanation, we just can't seem to get a particular task finished. So we grit our teeth, try to use a trick or two, put our nose to the grindstone, and force it through. In essence, we grind it out. That's why we characterize our first general type of self-leader as the *Grind*: someone who uses action–oriented self-leadership strategies to accomplish tasks that are difficult or not attractive or motivating in themselves.

We've all experienced incidents of short-term difficulty in accomplishing a particular task.

Sometimes it's useful to think of behavior-oriented strategies as a "push" type of approach to self-leadership. That is, these are actions that are intended to help us push through tasks that we find difficult or challenging, and not particularly intrinsically motivating. We might think of push strategies as a type of self-discipline. Of course, we don't recommend dependence on push types of strategies as the predominant form of self-leadership; after all, there is a limit to how long or how intensely we can continue to push. Nevertheless, in the short term, push self-leadership strategies can be helpful and effective.

Behavior-focused self-leadership strategies are a form of self-behavior modification.[1] That is, we deliberately modify the environment around us so that it stimulates and reinforces performance-oriented behaviors. A classic example of self-behavior modification is withholding a reward from ourselves until we accomplish a particular task.

In this chapter, we classify and discuss different types of behavior-focused self-leadership strategies as follows: self-goal-setting, self-observation and self-evaluation, self-reward (and self-punishment), cuing strategies, and rehearsal.

SELF-GOAL-SETTING

Perhaps the most important self-leadership strategy is self-goal-setting. A goal is a desired end state—that is, a state or event that we wish to achieve at some time in the future. Sometimes goals can be assigned by others (a supervisor, for example), but here we discuss goals that are self-assigned as a way to influence our own behavior. We can also think of goals as a level of performance to which we aspire. Quotas, performance standards, deadlines, budgets, to-do lists, and project objectives are examples of aspired performance levels.

High performance is almost always driven by goals.

Goal setting is one of the most thoroughly researched areas of human behavior. The main reason that goals are important is that a flood of evidence confirms that *people with goals perform at higher levels than do people without goals.* When investigating in detail why high performers do so well, we typically find a goal-oriented philosophy and practices. Different people may have their own idiosyncratic ways and methods of actually doing goal setting, but one way or another, high performers are almost always driven by goals.

Goal setting has a significant history of development in management and organizational circles. For example, management by objectives (MBO) was at one time a leading management fad that became the inspiration for a certain way of leading others. But many found the formality of an MBO system to be overwhelming or controlling, and, as a result, distortions of the system began to appear. Also, many MBO training programs placed an obsessive emphasis on quantitative goals. As a result, some important areas that deserved goal setting were omitted because of the difficulty of quantification. To be truly effective, goal setting should be a self-oriented interpersonal process to help an individual lead himself or herself. Most important, individual managers and employees can use goal setting without a formal MBO system. Today the legacy of MBO is that it has passed from a formal organizational bureaucratic system into a commonsense personal strategy of most successful managers and professionals.

Certain attributes of goal setting facilitate the process. For example, goals are not only important for establishing efficiency but also in the pursuit of effectiveness. In essence, this distinction relates to the domain in which goals are set. From a work viewpoint, if goals are set in areas that are important to the organization, then these goals relate to "doing the right things"—that is, effectiveness—choosing the right domain. Efficiency refers to "doing things right"—that is, setting the goal within the chosen domain. From an organizational viewpoint, effective goals support the vision of the organization.

People with goals perform better than people without goals.

Another attribute that facilitates goal setting is the notion that specific goals are more effective than vague or ambiguous goals. Goals work best when they are stated in a quantitative manner. Also, setting a goal that is specific will permit a judgment to be made at a later time as to whether the goal has actually been achieved. When setting a goal, it is important to ask whether the goal is as precise as it could possibly be. Also, a goal should have a specific time deadline or should be accomplished over a specific time span. The following list shows the difference between vague goals and specific goals:

Vague Goals	Specific Goals
To improve profitability.	To achieve an increase in annual net income of 22 percent.
To improve market share.	To achieve 43 percent of market share for the first half of the next fiscal year.
To maintain high air quality standards.	To reduce sulfide emissions to 25 parts per million.
To improve employee relations.	To achieve a 20 percent improvement in annual employee attitude survey.
To complete the project as soon as possible.	To deliver the project report by June 1.

Another important question is how difficult goals should be. Generally research has shown that the more difficult the goal is the higher is the performance—provided the person psychologically accepts the goal. In more practical terms, we believe that one should define challenging yet attainable goals. If a person sets an easy goal, then performance is likely to be lower because the ardent pursuit of a meaningful target (the goal) will diminish once the goal has been attained. On the other hand, if a goal is impossible to attain, the individual is likely to drop out of the race at an earlier moment. The pursuit of the impossible dream may work for a few rare individuals, but for most of us, pursuing an impossible dream as a goal is a myth. When a goal becomes so difficult that goal acceptance is lost, performance will suffer.

Of course, difficulty is a relative matter; a goal that is difficult for one person may be easy for another. That's why goal setting works best when it's attuned to the individual. To stimulate high performance, the goal must be challenging for that particular individual.

Goal setting works best when the goal is challenging for that particular individual.

Goals also work best when some sort of feedback and reward system is in place. That is, for a system of goal setting to be consistent and useful over time, a person must know how he or she has actually performed in relation to the goal. Also, goal setting is more likely to be sustained when goal attainment is rewarded. We discuss both of these aspects of goal setting in more detail later in this chapter.

The important point is that if goal setting is to be maximized as a system of self-leadership, then a system of goal setting, feedback, and reward is necessary.

Most of the time when we think of goals, we mainly consider job-oriented goals—that is, what we want to accomplish in regard to job responsibilities over the next immediate time frame. But goals are also useful in regard to professional and personal development. For example, anyone who has ever persisted through the challenges and rigors of attaining an academic degree has been strongly influenced by a goal. For many people, this professional goal setting continues at least to some degree at later stages in life, perhaps by pursuing an advanced degree at night school or setting out to learn a new computer software system. Given the rapid deployment of technology, no professional can thrive without an active goal-oriented system of lifelong professional development.

We also use goals in personal life. What do we want to achieve in terms of family pursuits? Financial goals? Personal relationship? Consider the following exercise, which we sometimes use in our executive development programs. You might want to work through it yourself as a means of personal development. By thinking long term—that is, *very* long term—we can hopefully achieve a desired balance of personal goals, professional goals, and job goals.

WRITE YOUR OWN
OBITUARY

The time is the future—hopefully, decades away. The sad truth is that you have passed away, and tomorrow your obituary will appear in the newspaper. This obituary won't be limited to your business and professional accomplishments but will address the many varied aspects of your life. This obituary is written in a creative and interesting way.

1. Compose your own obituary. How will *you* want it to read when all is said and done?
2. Do an evaluation of your life and circumstances today. How do these circumstances contribute to and detract from whatever your obituary says?

In addition, it's useful to think of different time horizons for goals. We can have very short-term goals, such as the to-do lists that so many of us use. We can have shorter mid-range goals, such as completing a project report within the next two months. We can have longer mid-range goals, such as, "I *will* complete this book sometime this year!" Finally, we can have very long-term goals—the new graduate who says to herself: "I intend to be a corporate vice president before I am fifty years old."

Personal goal setting can be an extremely powerful mechanism of self-leadership. Goal setting focuses our attention on what we want to accomplish and often can serve as a positive motivator. Goal setting can also help us push ourselves to achieve a task that we are finding difficult to complete. Following are some tips that can help guide the use of goals for effective self-leadership practice:

- Set the domain for goal setting. *Job-oriented goals* should be tied to organizational vision. *Personal-oriented goals* should be tied into long-term life and career strategies.

- Goal setting works better when goals are written. Undertake some training on how to write goals effectively.

- Make goals as specific as possible. Look for quantitative outcomes or time deadlines.

- Choose a challenging but achievable level of difficulty. Easy goals mean low aspirations; impossible goals are difficult to really accept.

- Create a feedback and review system for reviewing progress toward goals. Establish specific review dates.

- Establish a reward for yourself when you do achieve a goal.

SELF-OBSERVATION AND SELF-EVALUATION

Have you ever kept a diary or a personal budget expense ledger? Studied your performance on an activity such as your golf swing or your piano technique to look for ways you could improve? Tracked your progress on projects on a wall chart? All of these strategies and other related techniques represent the general self-leadership category of self-observation.

In order to perform better, each of us must be able to answer the question, "How am I doing?" The key is to *deliberately* seek opportunities and systems to monitor our own behavior and performance. Effective self-observation requires asking for and obtaining feedback. It means designing systems and events so feedback is automatically provided to us. It means *not* waiting for others to deliver feedback to us but instead pursuing active and intentional feedback-seeking behavior.

Our own empowerment and autonomy is increased when we undertake active self-observation. We are less dependent on others and so don't have to wait for others to provide us with the information we need to improve our performance. This is very important in an empowered work setting. In fact, self-observation that enables self-evaluation can be thought of the life's blood of the self-leadership process. It provides the information and substance for systematic effective management of self.

More specifically, self-observation involves determining the why, when, and under what conditions certain behaviors occur. If the behaviors are positive, the information obtained can help to guide continued positive performances in the future. If the behaviors are negative, the information may provide the insights to eliminate this problem in the future.

When we generate our own feedback, we are empowered because we are less dependent on others.

For example, let's assume that you want to increase the number of times you reinforce the good performance of the people you work with. By keeping a pen and a note card in your pocket, you can record whenever you deliver a compliment to a coworker. Then at the end of the day you count how frequently you used this positive behavior. By tracking this behavior for a week, you can study your trend in this activity. Adding information on who you complimented, for what reason, and where you were when you communicated your approval provides a great deal of information to help guide you in the future. In fact, we recommend that you try this simple note card and pen system to track a personal behavior that is important to you. Often the very act of observing a behavior for a while can produce positive results because of increased awareness.

Overall, self-observation can provide a solid foundation for effective behavior-focused self-leadership. The key is to develop a system that fits your personal style and needs. Then target important behaviors and track them over time. The information you gain can make all the difference in your pursuit of effective self-leadership practice. When you've mastered this skill, you will have personal insight that you can use to help others to do the same for themselves.

SELF-REWARD AND SELF-PUNISHMENT

Once we have a better sense of how we are doing based on our self-observations, we can use this information for creating self-motivation. The most straightforward way to accomplish this is through the self-administration of consequences. That is, we can make certain outcomes available to ourselves based on our evaluations of our own performance. This forms the basis for two self-leadership strategies, *self-reward* and *self-punishment*.

Self-reward and self-punishment are really two sides of the same coin because both involve providing ourselves with objects, thoughts, or events that are significant to us in some way. Usually we think of rewards and punishments as being restricted to what we receive from others (e.g., the boss), but this need not be so. Self-leadership frees us to use many management techniques in dealing with our own behavior and performance. The key is to target a certain behavior and make our self-administration of consequences contingent on our performance of that behavior.

Self-reward is used to strengthen and increase behaviors that we see as desirable. If we are trying to increase the quantity of calls we make on potential new clients, we can reward ourselves when we make progress in this area—perhaps a fine dinner at our favorite restaurant, buying something we've been wanting, or simply a coffee break. All qualify as potential self-rewards if you find them of value. The key is to find something *you* value and then provide that item for yourself when you accomplish something worthwhile. Self-rewards can also be mental. For example, you can imagine your favorite vacation spot or indulge yourself with some internal self-praise: "I did a great job this time. Man, am I good!"

Self-reward gives us a moment of reinforcement when we do something well.

Significant evidence has been gathered indicating the effectiveness of self-reward for creating motivation to meet a variety of personal challenges. The evidence for self-punishment, on the other hand, is not very supportive. In fact, the challenge for most people is to try not to be too self-critical. Self-punishment not only focuses on the past but dwells on what we did poorly rather than ways to improve. Even if self-punishment were effective, it could be freely avoided since it is self-administered, and because it is unpleasant, we would have a difficult time applying it consistently. In general, we are better off self-rewarding what we do well and using other strategies (e.g., self-goals for improvement) to deal with past failures.

A simple exercise that we suggest you try is to identify a specific behavior you would like to strengthen or increase and then target a level of performance that you would like to achieve. When you make progress toward this objective or perform notably positive behaviors, reward yourself with something you value. Above all, get in the habit of deliberately thinking about rewards for yourself. Empowered work environments with more people reporting to a single boss are perfect for self-reward strategies. A wait for someone else to pat you on the back for your accomplishments may be a very long wait. Self-reward is a proven strategy with the capability to produce a great deal of personal motivation.

Overall, self-reward can be an important part of a comprehensive self-leadership system. Self-punishment, on the other hand, is better left reserved for the occasions when we have been obviously dishonest or destructive. In the long run we are likely to be well served by focusing on how to improve in the future rather than our shortcomings of the past.

CUING STRATEGIES

When we deliberately set out to control the environment that immediately surrounds us, we are undertaking a *cuing strategy*. Cuing strategies enable us to influence our own behavior through the powerful effect of our work context. Frequently, opportunities exist for us to undertake a change in the physical environment that will have an influence on our behavior or performance. For example, something as simple as the placement of our office door can send a signal to others about our receptiveness. Want to be totally alone so you can finish that report that is due tomorrow? Close the door. (The signal is, "Don't disturb me unless it's really important.") Are you available for task-oriented conversations? Leave the door partially open. (The signal is, "I'm available for conversations if you need me.") Want to increase your networking and informal knowledge about what's going on? Leave the door wide open. (The signal is, "Come in and talk to me about anything.") Each of these choices will influence the cues that affect us. A busy office with lots of colleagues visiting will cue a different kind of behavior from a quiet, solitary one. Depending on the immediate behaviors you hope to accomplish, the cues that you choose will differ.

The main point is that the physical environment should support the task that we want to accomplish. Take the case of Betty, the internationally known novelist.

CLEARING THE DECKS
FOR WRITING

"I know that many of my readers take my writing for granted, but the fact is, I do get writer's block," said Betty, the internationally known novelist. "So there are several things I do to keep myself on track."

"For example?" asked Steve, the newspaper reporter who was conducting the interview.

"Well, for one thing, I can write better when I have tranquil surroundings. That's why I had this glass room built on the back of my house. Notice the way the room juts into the forest behind my house. Although I'm indoors, I have the sensation of sitting in the middle of a quiet forest. It's beautiful in both summer and winter, and I appreciate it. It relaxes me, and I can write much better when I'm in a quiet mood."

"What else?" prompted Steve.

"Another thing," Betty continued, "is that the time of day is important. I generally write better in the morning. I'm definitely a morning person, so I schedule my writing from 7 A.M. to 9 A.M., take a break for a light breakfast, and then I'm back to work until noon. I can turn the telephone off in this room, and switch it to the recorder in the front of the house. I schedule all my telephone calls and meetings for the afternoon, and I work on my background research in the afternoon and evenings. I also like to get out and feel physically active in the afternoon. I seldom write after noon, but I really clear the decks for my morning output. It really works for me. This is my eighteenth novel!"

By arranging her physical environment in a particular way, Betty plays to her strengths and helps to overcome her weaknesses. The arrangement of her office and her writing schedule is a cuing strategy that is effective in enhancing her own performance.

Actually, cuing strategies are quite common. We might write a reminder note for ourselves. Our daily schedule book is a type of cuing strategy. The airline pilot who routinely goes through a checklist for the nine thousandth time is using a cuing strategy. When we use call waiting, or deliberately turn it off, we are structuring our environment to manage the cues that influence our behavior.

Social occasions can also be used as a cuing strategy. Consider the story of Dr. Laura Sims and her bagel brunches. These informal and nonagenda meetings are an effective application of a deliberate cuing strategy designed to increase her information base about her agency. In fact, the brunches are a combination cuing strategy and self-observation strategy that helps her to obtain feedback and check out how she is doing in her work.

THE BAGEL BRUNCH

Dr. Laura Sims, director of the Human Nutrition Information Agency, walked into the conference room. The bagels, cream cheese, orange juice, and hot coffee were ready. Standing around the table were eleven employees of the agency, all from different levels and departments. She smiled, sat down, and greeted the group with a cordial "good morning."

"Would you pass the orange juice and bagels?" she began. "Why don't we go around the table and briefly introduce ourselves. I don't think everybody knows everybody else here. Most of you know me. I'm Laurie Sims."

Later, she discussed the event: "I have no agenda for the meeting. I usually go around the table and ask them to tell us all about something interesting that is happening in their own departments. Or I ask them to tell me about one thing in their work that they most enjoy doing. It gives me a chance to hear viewpoints without having them filtered through the chain of command. It provides them with an opportunity to talk and an opportunity for me to listen. It also sends a signal that I'm approachable. They get to know me—at least a little bit. I learn a lot from these sessions. I try to do about one each month."

REHEARSAL

Rehearsal or practice is another powerful self-leadership strategy. By going over an activity before we do it, when it really counts, we can significantly contribute to our performance. Have you ever found yourself practicing something that you have to say that is either very important to you or that you don't feel completely comfortable about? Or perhaps you've noticed that you go over in your mind a difficult challenge you will soon face. Both of these examples are a form of re-hearsal—one physical and the other mental.

Physical rehearsal can be used for a wide range of activities. Practicing your golf swing at the driving range and working on your tennis serve at the courts are both basic forms of rehearsal. In fact, rehearsing physical activities, such as the skills required in a wide range of sports, is usually viewed as a commonsense way to improve performance. World-class athletes have been practicing for years; after all, that's how they got to be world class.

A variety of activities at work lend themselves to practice as well, though we often overlook this useful self-leadership strategy. For example, rehearsing an important upcoming presentation for the boss or going over a sales approach we plan to use on a potential new customer should improve our eventual performance. Similarly, practicing some sensitive performance feedback we need to give to a subordinate or what we plan to say to a coworker with whom we have an ongoing conflict fit well with a rehearsal strategy.

"For 37 years I've practiced 14 hours a day . . . and now they call me a genius."

—Pablo de Sarasate[2]

Mental rehearsal is essentially the same process except that we engage in it in our minds. Have you ever noticed Olympic athletes standing with their eyes closed, perhaps bobbing their heads and even shifting their bodies in different ways, just before their event? They are using mental rehearsal to work through their performance before it is their turn to compete. Olympic gymnasts, skiers, skaters, high jumpers, and many others are frequent users of this self-leadership technique. Instead of physically working through the steps in their performance, they picture and mentally experience them.

The keys to successful physical and mental rehearsal are fairly straightforward:

1. Identify a significant activity that you will soon be performing that lends itself to practice.

2. Identify the key components that need to be completed for a successful performance.

3. Work through these components physically or mentally, or both, in detail, paying particular attention to any areas that you expect that you might have difficulty with. In addition, it can be helpful to pair your practice with expected rewards. For example, picture a positive outcome in your mind resulting from your successful performance.

Rehearsal can be a very helpful self-leadership strategy if we simply make use of it. They say that practice makes perfect. We're not sure that perfection is achievable, but we are confident that practice can help you to do better. We encourage you to make a regular practice of practicing. We wager that about the only thing you will risk losing is poor performance.

THE BIG PRESENTATION— GETTING READY

Before Bob made his annual report to the board, he scheduled some time in the boardroom.* He hadn't finished collecting and analyzing all of the financial information, but specific numbers were not his concern at this moment.

In the boardroom, he positioned the overhead projector farther away from the wall; too many times he had seen people annoyed by the small images projected on the screen. He tested to see if he could work without the microphone, and then he dimmed the lights to make sure he understood the switches. If the lights were too low, he might lull his audience to sleep; too high, and the screen would be hard to see. If his voice didn't

---

*This story is from Henry P. Sims, Jr., and Peter Lorenzi, *The New Leadership Paradigm* (Newbury Park, Calif.: Sage, 1992).

carry, that would irritate board members. He made a note to himself to check the sound system early in the morning of his actual presentation.

He placed one of his transparencies on the overhead projector and then walked to the back of the room. Could the text be seen clearly from the back of the room, or should he increase the font size? He decided that the text size and clarity were more than adequate.

On the way out, he remembered that he needed to check to be sure the copy center had his handouts in time; he wanted his executive summary to be included in the three-ring binders the board members received the day before the meeting.

THE GRIND

The practical, behavior focused self-leadership strategies covered in this chapter are especially suited for helping you successfully complete difficult, unattractive but necessary tasks—or for dealing with what we call the Grind. For better or worse, we all face some important tasks that are not much fun. In the next chapter we will address some strategies for making tasks more naturally enjoyable. Nevertheless, some tasks lend themselves more to a self discipline approach that helps us to maintain our motivation as we try to get them over with. Strategic use of self-set goals, self-observation, cues, self-administered consequences, and rehearsal can help us maintain the push we need to complete the rough parts of our jobs.

FINDING NATURAL REWARDS IN THE TASK

Smelling the Roses

> The only thing that really matters is the love of the game.
> —*Charles Barkley, NBA All-Star Player*

Is work something we like to do, or something we hate to do? Do we perform better if we like the work we do? These are the issues of this chapter. Doing work—that is, performing the work task itself—presents certain consequences that are either pleasant or unpleasant. We believe that performing a task has natural rewards or punishers that are inextricably linked to the task. In this chapter, we explore how we might intentionally manage these natural rewards as a deliberate self-leadership strategy. First, consider the case of Henry.

IS HENRY WORKING?

Henry stretched slowly as the morning sun streamed through the window. It was shortly after 6 A.M., the time that Henry, a habitual early riser, normally awoke. He lay in bed for a few minutes, enjoying the comforting feeling of early morning. His wife, Laurie, a late riser, was sound asleep beside him. In a few minutes he was in the kitchen, and starting on his routine: brew the coffee (Vienna roast, special blend), put the dog out, bring the newspapers in. In a few minutes, the coffee was done, and Henry sat down in his favorite chair on the back deck overlooking the woods (no deer in sight today).

This was Sunday, so the newspapers—The *Washington Post*, the *Washington Times*, and the *New York Times*—were especially fat. Henry is a professor of business administration at the state university. Leisurely, he continued his routine: First opening the *New York Times* and removing the business section, then the sports section, placing both sections on top of the first section containing the main news. He then did the same with the *Washington Post* sections and placed the *Washington Times* aside for (perhaps) a later review.

He took his first sip of coffee and savored it. Now he picked up the business section and began to scan the headlines. He took another sip of coffee—again looked out over the woods—and thought to himself, "It's a great morning!" Within a minute, he was intensely involved in an article about the automobile industry, which he followed closely.

This story is true. Henry normally begins his Sunday mornings as described. We pose this question to you for consideration: *Is Henry working?*

At first, using conventional logic, you might laugh and say, "No. Of course not." He's home rather than at the office. It's Sunday morning, before 8 A.M., and normal working hours begin at 8:30 A.M. on Monday. Most of all, Henry is actually *enjoying* what he's doing. He savors the coffee. He relishes the view of nature from his deck. And he enjoys learning more about the automobile industry, which he follows closely. One person we know put it this way: "If you enjoy it, it isn't work!" So, according to these criteria, we might conclude that Henry is *not* working.

But think about it for a minute. Henry is a professor of *business*. If we ask Henry's dean whether he would want Henry to read the business section of the *New York Times* as part of his job, we suspect his dean would say, "Yes, of course!" After all, Henry is supposed to keep up with current business news. It makes him a better teacher and researcher. So by these criteria, Henry *is* working when he reads the *Times* business section on Sunday morning.

THE NATURE OF WORK

We'll leave it to each reader to decide whether Henry's Sunday morning routine is work or not work. The answer is a matter of judgment, and it does depend on one's own personal definition of work.

The traditional view of work stems from the historical view of it as physical labor. Certainly at one time, most humans accomplished their work through physical labor. But, at least in the United States, this is no longer true. The story does raise interesting philosophical issues about the nature of work. Furthermore, these philosophical issues are not merely idle speculation; the answers have real practical meaning for each of us. Certainly the story of Henry points out the different conclusions we might derive if we take a conventional-historical view of work versus a more modern interpretation.

Traditionally, work has been equated with physical labor. But today in the United States, most of us work with our mind.

Let's get to the point. Our own personal opinion is that work is not restricted to any particular time and place. A person can work at 6:30 A.M. on Sunday morning at home as well as 8:30 A.M. on Monday at the office. Work is what one does in order to fulfill the mission and objectives of the job. We are finding a considerable trend toward more and more people in the United States fulfilling their work requirements while at home under the control of their own schedule. In fact, we suggest that generally people are likely to be more effective at performing their work if they can do it at a time and a place of their own choice.

Interestingly, the converse is also true. We all know of instances where a person was at the right place—the office—during so-called working hours and yet was *not* performing work. We believe that time and setting do not define whether one is working.

Second, we think the setting in which one does the work can also influence performance. In Henry's case, the hot coffee and the deck overlooking the wooded park were important parts of his Sunday morning enjoyment of his work. Also, Henry had the unusual capacity to consciously reflect on the nature of what he was doing.

But most of all, we believe that overall long-term performance is likely to be better if we are able to do tasks that we enjoy. With Henry, his job tasks definitely do include reading the *Times* business section, which he does with a great deal of enjoyment. (Not everyone enjoys the same tasks. Henry's wife, Laura, a biological scientist, prefers reading the health section of the newspaper.)

DEFINING NATURAL REWARDS

We normally think of a reward as something provided by someone else; receiving a reward thus is an external event. However, there is a second type of reward, generally less recognized and less understood but no less important. This type of reward—a *natural reward*—is so closely tied to a task or activity that the two cannot be separated. For example, a person who enjoys reading a novel or playing a game of tennis is usually engaging in an activity that could be described as naturally rewarding (worded another way, intrinsically rewarding). No externally administered incentives are required to motivate this behavior. The incentives are natural; they come from the task itself. There is an embedded joy in performing the task.

An important point is that natural rewards are idiosyncratic to the person. That is, what is naturally rewarding to one person may be punishing to another. One person loves the challenge of setting up a complex computer program. Another person can't stand this task. One person prefers tasks that involve a high interaction with others. Another person prefers to work alone. An interesting extension of this point is that different people who have the same objective or the same task may have a very different preference structure regarding how to get to the objective. The optimal route to the desired end result may be quite different for different people. There may be no such thing as one best way. One example is the difference between a night person and a morning person. Some people prefer to work at night, some to work during the day.

ARE YOU A MORNING OR A NIGHT PERSON?

Juanita and Amy were deep in conversation. As newly acquainted freshman roommates, they were engaged in finding out about each other. At the moment, they were discussing the use of the computer. The university provided one computer for their suite, and they had to share it.

"I'm a morning person, myself," said Juanita. "I like to work before breakfast, and I do most of my computer work then. I do hardly any work at all after dinner."

"Well," replied Amy, "I'm a late sleeper myself. I'm hardly ever up before 9 A.M. I'll be doing all of my computer work in the evening and late at night. I guess we won't have any trouble over using the computer."

The joy that comes from performing our work task is an important source of motivation and sustenance that helps us to maintain effective performance over the long run. We call this *finding natural rewards in the task*. That is, we enjoy doing the task itself, whether it's "work" or not. The metaphor that we use to describe this effect is Smelling the Roses, a phrase everyone is familiar with. By Smelling the Roses, we mean deliberately experiencing the joy and satisfaction that come from performing the task itself. Henry experiences a natural enjoyment that comes from reading and keeping current on business. As a professor, he also finds joy in fulfilling his teaching responsibilities. He gets a kick out of engaging a class of intense M.B.A. students. All in all, Henry has a distinct advantage in his job because he finds satisfaction in a large part of his normal job duties. Not everything about Henry's job is roses, however. He dislikes long, rambling committee meetings and faculty politics. He does, however, make it a point to take the time to smell the roses.

We're more likely to do a good job if we like the work we do.

Natural rewards can also come from the immediate context or surroundings in which the work is done. Some of Henry's enjoyment of his Sunday morning routine comes from the pleasant wooded setting. Similarly, a runner is likely to enjoy running through a beautiful wooded area or along a breath-taking ocean beach more than around and around an oval track. The point is that we should seek out the natural rewards in our work that come from both the setting and the task.

By now you're saying that it's great for Henry to work on Sunday mornings outside by the woods, but *I* have to work in the office starting at 8 A.M. on Monday, and *I* don't have the luxury of choosing my time or place as Henry does. This point is well taken; we can't all keep our schedule the way Henry does. Most of us can't work whenever and wherever we want to and not work whenever we want to. Clearly there are limitations in how much one can redesign one's own job. We can't all work at home as a personal choice. Most of all, we all have some part of our job that we just don't like to do but must. There's not always a clear, intrinsic satisfaction with all parts of our work, and relying on push self-leadership is sometimes our best choice. But we've seen too many people who begin by focusing on and accepting the negative aspects of their job. A more productive and effective approach is to look for the simple, small next step of trying to do something in an enjoyable way. Over the long run, step by step, it is possible to build enjoyment into work by seeking out desirable work settings and activities that provide some satisfaction and joy.

Here's the fundamental thesis that we believe to be true: The more we like the work we do, the more we are likely to do a good job over the long run. The follow-up to this logic is: If we want to sustain high performance over the long run, we should try to move toward jobs, tasks, and assignments that provide opportunities to do the kind of work we like to do.

In the short term, this may not be possible at all. The young woman who wants to earn money for college tuition may not get a great amount of satisfaction from making french fries at the local fast food restaurant for eight hours a day. However, in the long term, we have more control over our work activities. In Henry's case, his opportunity to enjoy reading the Sunday *Times* is a direct result of a decision he made many years ago to leave his engineering job and return to graduate school. This decision, made at considerable short-term sacrifice, led to the long-term job flexibility that Henry now enjoys. But we can also shape our current job, whatever it is, to some degree. Consider the following case of Karen, who is most adept at exerting some control over the tasks she is expected to perform at work.

SELF-REDESIGN OF TASKS

When Karen reported for work as the new office receptionist, she brought with her qualifications and abilities well beyond her narrow job description.* In a tight job market, though, a paycheck was important, so she had to take what she could get. But over a period of weeks and months, her job changed dramatically until she had become a professional writer and assistant project director for a major project in the firm. She accomplished all this step by step by taking initiative and tackling challenges outside her normal job responsibilities. She carefully identified and voluntarily pursued specific opportunities where help was needed, asking her work associates if she could assist them.

Gradually the managers began to realize that Karen could be depended on to undertake and accomplish tasks that were falling between the cracks. Most of all, she did not act like a receptionist but rather like a key organizational employee ready to do whatever needed to be done. As Karen later explained, "I simply redesigned my own job."

Through hard work and initiative, she had taken it upon herself to change her own work to provide opportunities for feelings of competence, self-control, and purpose. It wasn't too long before Karen's title, salary, and official responsibilities changed to reflect what she was actually doing. She knew the transition was complete when a new receptionist was hired.

Karen is effective at self-leadership. More specifically, she is adept at finding natural rewards from the task itself and using those natural rewards to sustain her performance. Effective self-leaders always try to do at least some redesign of their own work to find intrinsic fulfillment from performing the task itself. They seek out natural rewards and add them to the task mix, so that the job becomes more

---

*Source: We originally reported this story in *SuperLeadership: Leading Others to Lead Themselves* (New York: Berkley Books, 1990).

motivating for its own value. Discovering and adopting these naturally rewarding activities as a part of the work are key to this powerful part of self-leadership. Karen's case is admittedly a bit extreme in that she essentially created a new position for herself. A key element in her success was taking on small chunks of greater and greater responsibility over time. Gradually her initiative became obvious to her superiors, and she reaped the natural reward of doing work that was more enjoyable to her. And she enhanced her value as an employee of the firm.

Clearly, there are limitations on how far people can redesign their own jobs. On occasion, it might even be necessary to implement the ultimate self-generated job redesign: resigning and going to work somewhere else. But we've seen too many people who begin by focusing on the reasons why it can't be done. This negative thinking is dysfunctional. A more productive and effective approach is to look for the simple, small next step by doing something in a more enjoyable way. Over the long run, step by step, it is possible to build enjoyment into work by seeking out desirable work contexts and activities that provide a sense of competence, self-control, and purpose.

We propose that employees are responsible for seeking out the naturally occurring rewards that stem from the task itself. Instead of depending on management or someone else to do it, every employee typically can find opportunities to redesign his or her own tasks.

Sometimes the connection between our job responsibilities and tasks that we enjoy can be an extremely powerful motivator. Consider the following story of Bill Gore, who founded and built a multimillion dollar company. Gore's development and introduction of extremely innovative products was inspired by his own personal experience of activities that he enjoyed.

HAVING FUN THE BILL GORE WAY

Frank Shipper

> *To make money and have fun.*
> —*Bill Gore, founder and past president*
> *of W. L. Gore & Associates*

This quotation captures the way Bill Gore and a number of other successful leaders view their work. Bill Gore was an avid outdoorsman who liked to have fun as part of his work. A story told about Hans Selye, the father of stress research, in his retirement illustrates this point. One day a friend was visiting in the Selye household. The friend proceeded to tell Hans that he needed to slow down and find a hobby like raising flowers. Hans listened politely. After the visitor finished, Hans took him into the study and casually waved his arm in the direction of some bookshelves containing many of his studies. He told the visitor, "This is my garden, and those are my flowers."

Bill Gore was a leader in the same vein. He loved to tinker and test his products and the unique structure of W. L. Gore and Associates. He especially achieved significant breakthroughs while enjoying his favorite outdoor activities. For example, Bill and his wife, Vieve, did the initial field-testing of Gore-Tex fabric during the summer of 1970. Vieve made a hand-sewn tent out of patches of Gore-Tex fabric, and they took it on their annual camping trip to the Wind River Mountains in Wyoming. The very first night in the wilderness, they encountered a hailstorm. The hail tore holes in the top of the tent, and the bottom filled up like a bathtub from the rain. Undaunted, Bill Gore stated: "At least we knew from all the water that the tent was waterproof. We just needed to make it stronger, so it could withstand hail."

The company's second largest division began while Bill Gore was enjoying the ski slopes of Colorado. Bill was having a good time skiing with a friend, Dr. Ben Eiseman of Denver General Hospital. As Bill Gore told the story: "We were just about to start a run when I absentmindedly pulled a small tubular section of Gore-Tex out of my pocket and looked at it. 'What is that stuff?' Ben asked. So I told him about its properties. 'Feels great,' he said. 'What do you use it for?' 'Got no idea,' I said. 'Well give it to me,' he said, 'and I'll try it in a vascular graft on a pig.' Two weeks later, he called me up. Ben was pretty excited. 'Bill,' he said, 'I put it in a pig and it works. What do I do now?' I told him to get together with Pete Cooper in our Flagstaff plant and let them figure it out." Not long after, hundreds of thousands of people throughout the world began walking around with Gore-Tex vascular grafts.

Bill also had fun tinkering with his organization's structure. The Gore structure is probably the world's flattest organizational hierarchy for a large company. There is a president, a secretary/treasurer, and all others are associates. Bill referred to it as a lattice organization. Roles are defined in the organization in terms of leadership. *Management* and *manager* are taboo words. Bill wanted to avoid smothering the company in thick layers of formal management because he felt that hierarchy stifles individual creativity. Bill once explained the structure this way: "Every successful organization has an underground lattice. It's where the news spreads like lightning, where people can go around the organization to get things done." An analogy might be drawn to a structure of constant cross-area teams—the equivalent of quality circles going on all the time. When a puzzled interviewer told Bill that he was having trouble

understanding how planning and accountability worked, Bill clearly enjoyed thinking about it. He replied with a grin: "So am I. You ask me how
it works? Every which way."

Bill liked to tell people about how quickly this unorthodox organizational structure can respond to problems and how productive the organization is. For example, it took Bob Gore, Bill's son, and the organization
one month to develop a second-generation Gore-Tex when a problem
was discovered with the first version. In addition, Bill estimated the year
before he died that "the profit per associate is double" at Gore to that of
employees at du Pont.

Perhaps the overriding secret to his success was Bill Gore's obvious
commitment to the two parts of his company's slogan: "To make money
and have fun." He clearly enjoyed both.

NATURAL REWARDS AND CORPORATE CULTURE

Sometimes the notion of finding natural rewards from the task itself can become
embedded in an organization's culture. In Silicon Valley, south of San Francisco,
the late Friday beer bust has become an institution at many companies; it helps to
enhance the informal communication that is so necessary for a fast-moving, flexible organization. Also, these events are an important stress reliever that helps to
counteract the natural tension of working in a high-velocity environment.

Of course, this focus on enjoyable aspects of work is not restricted to Silicon
Valley. For example, in AES, an independent power producing company that we
describe in detail in Chapter 16, natural rewards evolved into a central part of the
organization's core values. In describing the AES culture, chairman Roger Sant
says, "It just isn't worth doing unless you're having a great time." CEO Dennis
Bakke adds, "By fun, we don't mean party fun. We're talking about creating an
environment where people can use their gifts and skills productively, to help meet
a need in society, and thereby enjoy the time spent at AES."[1]

DEVELOPING NATURAL REWARD STRATEGIES

Each of us can take specific actions to develop and enhance natural rewards in our
tasks. The objective is to create a positive identification with work that pulls us to
high performance because we are committed to, believe in, and enjoy the work
for its own value.

Remember that natural rewards vary and are unique for every individual. What is naturally rewarding for you may be drudgery for me. (Rose enjoys weekend gardening; Mary wouldn't be caught dead on her knees in the dirt.) To identify the kinds of tasks that are naturally rewarding for you, examine the activities that you already naturally enjoy—activities where the rewards stem from performing the task itself rather than being distinct from or external to the task. Also, try to identify the places where you derive satisfaction from the setting itself. In general, your search will be most fruitful if you look for activities and places that help make you feel competent and provide you with a sense of self-control and purpose. The evidence indicates that these three ingredients—a sense of competence, self-control, and purpose—seem to drive natural rewards for most of us.[2]

Each of us can develop our own self-leadership by building more enjoyable features into our work activities and by focusing on the naturally rewarding aspects of our work. To build natural rewards into your tasks:

- Identify contexts (places) where you could perform your work (or at least some of your specific tasks) that would make it more pleasant and appealing.
- Identify activities that could be built into your tasks (different ways of accomplishing the same things) that you like to do—that make your work naturally rewarding.

The key to this approach is to redesign your tasks by working in the contexts and building in the activities that make them more naturally enjoyable. In essence, to the extent you can, redesign your own job.

We can enhance our own self-leadership by assertively trying to design natural rewards into the work we do.

The way we think about our tasks is an important factor in this self-leadership strategy. There's a sort of self-fulfilling prophecy here. If we think we don't like performing a particular task, it's likely we really won't like it when we actually do it. Conversely, if we think we will like performing a particular task, then it's more likely we will experience that task positively when we actually do it.

Clearly this part of self-leadership overlaps with cognitive self-leadership strategies, which we cover in some detail in the next chapter. The main distinction is that the focus is on the way we think about our task. Also, this kind of thinking is, to some degree, under our volitional control. Here are some specific ways to enhance your thinking process about tasks:

- Identify the pleasant enjoyable aspects of your tasks.
- Focus your thoughts on the pleasant rather than the unpleasant aspects of your tasks while you work.
- Focus your thoughts on the pleasant rather than the unpleasant aspects of the surroundings in which you perform your tasks.

Concentrating on the naturally rewarding aspects of tasks can provide motivational and emotional benefits, especially when we must deal with problems and concerns that are part of the job. The idea is to not avoid or ignore the difficult or distasteful aspects of our jobs but rather to deal with them constructively.

Self-leadership based on natural rewards represents an important way to achieve higher performance. While the action-oriented behavioral strategies provide an effective short-term push to accomplish tasks that we may not like, it's not a good idea to become overly dependent on these behavioral strategies over the long run. For long-term high performance, it's important to be able to undertake tasks that we like to do (that pull us to high performance), and to do these tasks in places and settings that are appealing. As Norman Vincent Peale once said, "Do your job naturally, because you like it, and success will take care of itself."[3]

If we practice a self-leadership style that allow us to enjoy our job activities, we will stand a much greater chance of achieving the motivation we need to be successful. Organizations that make natural rewards a part of the total organizational environment are more likely to be successful. Most of all, for each of us as individuals, taking a moment to smell the roses will help us to be a more effective self-leader and can provide a significant boost to our long-term performance—another step along the way to a company of heroes.

COGNITIVE-FOCUSED SELF-LEADERSHIP STRATEGIES

The Opportunity Thinker

There is nothing either good nor bad, but thinking makes it so.
—*William Shakespeare*, Hamlet

We can lead ourselves in many different ways. One approach is to attempt to influence our own pattern of thinking because thoughts lead to action—to behavior. If we can influence our ways of thinking in desirable directions, we can enhance our own actions and behavior and, ultimately, our performance and effectiveness.

In this chapter, we focus on how individuals can deliberately attempt to control and enhance their own thinking in productive ways. We call techniques associated with this approach to self-influence *cognitive-focused self-leadership strategies* because they deal with the mind—with the way we think. We believe effective self-leaders can improve their own performance through the manner in which they control and influence their own thoughts.

If we can think better, we can perform better.

We characterize a person who is an effective cognitive self-leader as an *Opportunity Thinker*. This person uses positive and constructive thought patterns to create opportunities in work and life. The Opportunity Thinker tends to see the glass as half full and to view the world in terms of what might be rather than what might have been. Opportunity thinking is a critical element leading to creativity, innovation, and initiative. The Opportunity Thinker is an expert at cognitive focused self-leadership strategies.

WHY OPPORTUNITY THINKING?

The ultimate purpose of opportunity thinking is to amplify our personal productivity and effectiveness. In essence, if we can think better, we can perform better. One mechanism by which cognitive self-leadership works is by increasing one's sense of self-efficacy, which relates to our self-confidence in regard to carrying out a particular task. Self-efficacy is a concept from the field of psychology that concerns people's perceptions of their ability to perform specific tasks or activities.[1] When people's perceived self-efficacy is high regarding a specific activity, they will tend to exert more effort and to persist longer in their performance. Consequently, their likelihood of successfully performing is significantly increased. On the other hand, if their own self-efficacy is low, they will not tend to try as hard and will give up more quickly in the face of a setback. For example, how an individual who is about to make her first sales call on a potential customer perceives her ability to make the sale will influence her success or failure. Effort and persistence and ultimately the likelihood for success can be significantly determined by the self-perception she holds at the time of the meeting. Of course, leadership can significantly influence self-efficacy. In a later chapter, we will provide more details about the effect that different types of leadership have on an individual's self-efficacy and subsequent performance.

A man is what he thinks about all day long.
Ralph Waldo Emerson

Opportunity thinking can also be influenced by training. An example is the training program developed by Christopher Neck and Charles Manz to use principles of cognitive self-leadership to improve the job performance of flight attendants at America West Airlines.

MENTAL SELF-LEADERSHIP TRAINING: TEACHING EMPLOYEES TO BE OPPORTUNITY THINKERS

Christopher P. Neck

America West Airlines, an international commercial airline, employs approximately 12,100 people and is based in Phoenix, Arizona. Researchers from Arizona State University recently attempted to teach various employees of America West to use mental self-leadership strategies to enhance their work lives.

Just prior to their training, the airline had declared bankruptcy. It had laid off 2,000 workers and reduced its fleet of aircraft from 115 to 100 planes. Consequently, many of the employees of America West were fearful of losing their jobs.

Trainees received instruction in six two-hour sessions on the following mental strategies to enhance their performance: self-talk, mental imagery, managing beliefs and assumptions, thought patterns, and relapse prevention. Within each session, the training included definition and description of the mental self-leadership strategies, examples of real-life applications, specific and relevant on-the-job applications, and relapse prevention (personal strategies designed to ensure maintenance of the learned skills when faced with job pressure that might cause trainees to revert to old dysfunctional habits). Multiple training methods were used to help reinforce the learning of the mental self-leadership strategies: instructor lectures, video presentations, and individual and group exercises.

The first session focused on breaking the ice (to establish rapport and create interest) with the trainees and provided a general overview of the principles of thought self-leadership. The second session was directed toward describing the link between an individual's distorted thoughts and his or her beliefs and assumptions. Trainees were taught to identify their mental distortions and to replace them with more functional thoughts.

**With a bit of awareness and introspection, we can
significantly improve our own pattern of
opportunity thinking.**

The third session centered on self-dialogue. The primary thrust was replacing negative self-talk with self-talk of a more constructive and positive nature. The fourth session involved the concept of mental imagery; trainees were taught to follow specific mental imagery steps in order to complete assignments on the job and outside work more effectively.

In the fifth session, the training dealt with the concept of thought patterns. The thought pattern training involved individuals' examining their patterns of habitual thinking and then attempting to alter any negative thinking habits to more constructive ones. Finally, relapse prevention was the central theme of the sixth session. Trainees received instruction on a process designed to prevent them from forgetting to practice the mental self-leadership techniques learned when faced with a threatening situation.

At the conclusion of each session, the employees were instructed to apply the skills that they learned to situations on their job (specific application was one of the topics in each training session). Additionally, throughout the training, the employees were frequently reminded to consistently practice these newly learned self-leadership strategies in order to enjoy the full benefits of using these mental skills.

Did the training work? Indeed it did. A quantitative assessment indicated that the trainees liked the program, experienced better mental performance, utilized the principles in their daily lives, demonstrated enhanced thoughts under simulated conditions, and experienced improvements in job satisfaction, self-efficacy, and mood. The assessment also indicated that the training had an effect on employees' perceptions about how to accept and deal with the bankruptcy as a reality. In other words, after the training, the employees viewed the bankruptcy situation at America West in a more optimistic manner. Overall, this example suggests that employees can be taught to lead themselves through opportunity thinking.

We do not have a choice about whether our thought patterns will influence our behavior or not. The fact is, the behavior and actions of every human being are influenced by cognitions. The important issue is whether we want to be a victim of our thought patterns or want to use our thoughts deliberately in ways that are productive and constructive. The opportunity thinker is consciously aware of the power of productive thoughts and undertakes specific actions to use this powerful approach to self-leadership in a useful manner.

POP PSYCHOLOGY OR SOLID SCIENCE?

When we started our investigation of cognitive self-leadership over a decade ago, we had somewhat of a skeptical attitude, since the notion of cognitive self-leadership overlaps with many approaches to pop psychology.[2] One of the most popular sections in any bookstore is the self-help section, which mainly features popular psychology books attempting to help readers think right and feel good. Nevertheless, as we pursued this notion of cognitive self-leadership, we began to find solid grounding in fundamental psychological research.[3] We were especially inspired by the research showing that cognitive self-influence strategies can be helpful in developing high-performance patterns for a wide range of specific activities, perhaps most notably in sports performance.

Finally, we realized that cognitive self-leadership had achieved respectability when *Fortune* magazine ran a feature article, "Leaders Learn to Heed the Voice Within." This article describes how many large corporations have instituted training programs designed to help managers influence their own thinking in productive ways.

LISTENING TO THE VOICE WITHIN

The idea of talking to yourself might seem to be a notion from mainstream pop psychology.* Yet the idea of self-talk is well founded in psychological theory and research and has even invaded the venerable pages of *Fortune* magazine. According to *Fortune*, executives need to listen to their voice within to make sense of today's fast-paced world.

Perhaps the idea was best captured by Willow Shire, former vice president of Digital Equipment, who encountered a crisis in her life, in part stemming from the business difficulties at Digital. "If you need an answer," she said, "if you listen to yourself, . . . the answer will come." Shire is one of many stressed-out executives who are turning inward for answers.

---

*The ideas and quotations in this section were taken from "Leaders Learn to Heed the Voice Within," *Fortune*, August 22, 1994, pp. 92–100.

Not surprisingly, the trend is helped by sponsored management development programs such as those offered at AT&T, PepsiCo, and Aetna. Popular books such as Peter Senge's *The Fifth Discipline* and Steven Covey's *The Seven Habits of Highly Effective People* are important sources of inspiration and information on how to listen to the voice within.

According to Joseph Galerneau, head of executive training at AT&T, the goal is to help disciplined order followers become self-starting entrepreneurs. Galerneau says that "we need our people to act independently, to be responsible for managing their own piece of the business. It takes a certain amount of reflection to do that successfully."

Edward McCraken, CEO of Silicon Graphics, finds meditation to be helpful: "You have to go with your intuition without letting your mind get in the way. The most important trait of a good leader is knowing who you are."

Introspection can be extremely useful in moving from hierarchical leadership to a more empowering style. Erica Anderson, of Proteus International, says, "At first, it's hard to persuade leaders to let go of control. But once [executives become] actively self-reflective, they realize they don't know all the answers. . . . It makes others on their team feel useful and powerful." Clearly, this involves getting in touch with one's own emotions. The stoic Strongman leader is a figure of the past.

The most important trait of a good leader is knowing who you are.

Becoming more introspective does not require radical changes in personality. According to the article, most people can become more reflective provided they have some guidance and at least a bit of motivation. The training tools that can help this process have been around for some time. Srikumar Rao, professor at Long Island University and a creativity trainer, asks students to make a list of everything they hope to accomplish in their lives—sometimes as long as 500 items—and then pare the list down to as few as two or three key goals. Both of us (Sims and Manz) have used a "write your obituary" exercise to nudge executives to a more reflective and long-term perspective. Steven Covey asks managers to write down eulogies they would like given at their funeral—one by a family member, a work associate, a friend, and someone in their community.

One of the objectives of introspection is greater tolerance for ambiguity and paradox. Tony Smith, president of Vanlenti Smith & Associates, says, "We request that people commit to the future they want, even though they don't know how to achieve it, and then to create the know-how afterward."

All of these ideas are consistent with the notion of cognitive self-leadership strategies. Introspection—listening to the inner self—is largely a variation of the method of self-talk, where we look into the mirror and have a conversation with ourselves. This conversation can often be a critical contribution to unleashing the power of our own self-leadership.

CAN WE REALLY CONTROL OUR OWN THINKING?

Another issue is the question of whether we really can influence our own thought patterns. After all, isn't thought nonvolitional or spontaneous? Doesn't thought just "happen," and we have no deliberate control over what we think? If this is what you think, try the following test: *Do not think of a buffalo!*

For most of us, the image of a huge grazing animal—an American bison—immediately comes to mind. We are usually incapable of blocking such an image when prompted, no matter how deliberate we are.

Indeed, we can influence our own thought patterns.

Nevertheless, solid research demonstrates that we can develop certain habits and practices that truly do influence our pattern of thinking. Much of this research was originally undertaken in sports psychology, but the specifics of cognitive self-influence translate very well to work situations. We are strong believers in the power of individuals to influence their own thinking in positive, constructive ways. The first step is awareness that cognitive self-leadership is feasible—indeed, we *can* influence our own thought patterns

The next step addresses the issue of how thoughts can be influenced. Following are some practical suggestions that can help each of us develop more productive patterns of thought.

DESIRABLE COGNITIVE PATTERNS

Mental Imagery

We use mental imagery when we imagine ourselves engaged in important performance actions. We can also imagine the rewards and consequences that stem from performance. At first glance, mental imagery might seem like daydreaming or even idle thoughtfulness. It might appear to stem from a lack of concentration rather than focused attention. In fact, when used in the proper way, mental imagery intensifies concentration and can provide a purposeful mental focus on the task at hand. It is a way to gather confidence and self-efficacy and can help provide courage to persist in anxiety-provoking situations. Consider the case of Sharon, a systems sales representative with a history of apprehension about public speaking occasions.

SHARON'S PRESENTATION

As Sharon waited in the lobby, she noticed her hand trembled slightly. She had been promoted to systems sales representative about six months ago and had been pleased with a significant raise in salary and status. Sharon Faulkner, Systems Leader! Most of all, she liked the technical part of the work. Putting these systems together was a real challenge, but she was confident she had the ability to do it.

When she had accepted the promotion, she hadn't thought much about sales presentations. Moreover, for the first six months, she had always been somebody else's backup while she learned the job. Now, this was her first potential account where *she* was the systems leader. In ten minutes, she would begin her first live sales presentation before a potential client. She felt sick to her stomach, her head ached, and she watched her hand shake a bit more.

She remembered back in high school when she had been required to deliver a speech as class treasurer before the entire student body. She had been nervous then too. All in all, it had been a miserable experience, and she had avoided public speaking events as much as she could through college. She was much better at the technical side. She remembered with pride that she had no trouble competing in her engineering class.

She realized she had to get control of herself. Slowly she thought of the sales presentation training she had participated in a few months ago. She deliberately thought about the preparation she had done for this presentation. She recalled the physical rehearsal she had done before her office colleagues on three occasions. She mentally went through the transparencies that she had meticulously reviewed one last time last night. She knew they were all there, and in the proper order. She didn't have to memorize anything. She knew she merely had to let the transparencies be the driver of her presentation.

She let her mind visualize . . .

Next, she thought back to the training. The training always started with some breathing exercises, so she took a deep breath, closed her eyes, and began her relaxation breathing pattern. Then she let her mind visualize the conference room where she was to do the presentation. Step by step, she used the mental imagery that she had been taught to go through the presentation. She saw herself standing tall. She realized she looked good—dressed conservatively but still fashionably. This made her feel good. She saw herself smiling from time to time. She remembered to pause at strategic intervals, and she saw herself answering the impromptu questions with confidence and knowledge. She saw herself conclude the presentation with a big smile. Most of all, she saw the pleased responses on the faces of the clients and their eagerness to go forward with the system.

Suddenly, she got the call: "Ms. Faulkner, you can go in now. They're ready for you." She arose and confidently entered the conference room. She knew she would be okay. It would be great!

Imagining the rewards that stem from good performance can also be a useful strategy. "I can see myself going up to the stage to accept the award at the annual sales meeting," said one manager. If we can look ahead and imagine the pleasant consequences that stem from our performance, we can use imagery as a powerful motivating force.

Mental Rehearsal

In a previous chapter, we discussed physical rehearsal as a useful action to help self-leadership capability. But rehearsal need not be confined to physical rehearsal; it can also be mental. That is, we can gain much of the same benefit of physical rehearsal by training ourselves to go through a work performance in our mind, step by step.

Rehearsal has the capacity to instill confidence in our performing a task. When we practice, we can learn from feedback and mistakes, and we develop the confidence that's required when we actually carry out the task. Mental rehearsal is a well-developed technique useful to many activities—notably sports and drama but work situations as well.

Mental rehearsal enhances one's self-confidence for performing.

Undertaking mental rehearsal can create cognitive scripts that give us step-by-step knowledge and confidence on how to carry out a particular performance event. We know that experts have very well-developed cognitive scripts, and we also know that deliberate cognitive rehearsal can be especially helpful in developing mental scripts at the earlier stages of learning.

Try mental rehearsal when you find a moment to yourself. (If you have difficulty finding an opportune moment, you can create one. One person we know creates this moment by retreating to a men's room and sitting in a stall for a few minutes before an important presentation.) Training in controlled, relaxed breathing is helpful. The main point is that the mind is not allowed to wander but is intently focused on the task at hand. Carefully, step by step, the mind goes through the various stages of the performance. The actual performance is anticipated through imagination in the mind. A person adept at mental rehearsal can develop imagery that is remarkable in the degree of detail and vividness. Mental rehearsal, an appropriate self-leadership strategy, enhances one's self-confidence for performing.

Cognitive Self-Talk

We tend to think of people who talk to themselves as mentally unstable. "You're talking to yourself again, Joe. Are you going crazy or something?" is a typical reaction. However, research has shown that self-talk, both out loud and at a mental level, can be a powerful mechanism for influencing one's self.

We were especially interested to read a quotation by Mike Tyson, the former heavyweight boxing champion. Speaking from jail while being interviewed by Larry King, Tyson said, "I cheer for myself a hundred times a day."[4] Normally Tyson is not someone we would hold out to be a role model, but we found this statement on his coping behavior while in prison to be interesting. In our own terms, we would classify his statement as a cognitive self-leadership behavior.

Sometimes we have to act as our own cheerleader.

The reality is that we all talk to ourselves though usually at a silent, mental level. Think of a time when you made a comment in front of others that you know you shouldn't have said; you really put your foot in your mouth. Afterward you probably continued to engage in quite a bit of talking but to yourself in your mind: "What a stupid thing to say! I don't believe I said that! Now everyone thinks I'm an idiot!" As this example of internal dialogue indicates, we are typically much more sensitive and careful about what we say to others than we are concerning what we tell ourselves. Unfortunately, when we use excessive negative self-talk, we adversely affect our perceptions of our own self-efficacy and ultimately our performance, so the challenge is to master our use of self-talk.

First examine and better understand your current self-talk patterns. Is it critical and destructive? Or do you more frequently engage in positive confidence-building self-talk that helps create the motivation and self-efficacy you need to perform well on tasks? Self-observation techniques can help you to gain this useful information for improving the way you talk to yourself. For example, make it a point to observe your self-talk tendencies as you confront and deal with important and challenging tasks. If possible, keep a simple diary of these personal dialogues. Then after a few days, study the patterns in your diary, looking for possible problems in your self-talk tendencies and consciously trying to change these patterns. You may even want to write down a new set of phrases (a new positive constructive script) that you can use when you face similar problems in the future.

Another useful technique is to try talking to yourself as you would a valued colleague or friend. For the sake of discussion, let's call this person Chris. What if Chris is struggling with an important task? What would you say when Chris is feeling down and out, when Chris is not sure he (or she) will be able to persist and successfully meet the challenge? If you value your relationship with Chris, you would likely choose your words very carefully to try to give needed support for Chris to get over the top. It seems logical that we should treat ourselves just as well, that we should be our own supportive colleague and friend, that we should take the time and effort to talk constructively to ourselves.

Most of us would admit that the old saying, "Sticks and stones may break my bones but names will never hurt me," is not true. When others are critical of us, it does hurt. We can try our best to cope with unkind words, but they have a negative effect, and that effect accumulates over time. Unfortunately, we are even more vulnerable to self-criticism and self-abuse because we typically do not put up our guard to protect ourselves. Consequently, we can become beaten down from within. On the other hand, constructive self-talk can have tremendously beneficial effects if we work to develop the skill to have it work to our advantage. The key is to practice and develop the habit of using constructive self-talk. We can then draw upon this source of inner strength when we face difficult and anxiety-producing challenges. Perhaps it's time you had a talk with yourself about your own self-talk habits! We suspect that you will not find a better listener for what you have to say.

Beliefs and Assumptions

Mental imagery and self-talk is largely driven by beliefs and assumptions. What we believe is fundamental in determining what we do and how we perform. Years ago, a study was done with weight lifters. The subjects were divided into two groups. One group was given accurate information regarding how much weight they were lifting, and the other group was told they were lifting less than they actually were. What happened? Those who were told they were lifting less subsequently lifted significantly more, many breaking their own personal records. These findings present some interesting insights. Throughout history, there has been a tendency for people to accomplish more when they believe they can do it. In the case of the weight lifters, when they believed they were capable of lifting, they simply lifted, even though it was actually more than they had ever lifted before.

Unfortunately, many of us engage in dysfunctional thinking founded on unrealistic and destructive beliefs. Some of the more notable research in this area was done by Albert Ellis and Aaron Beck.[5] Later, David Burns developed a set of common categories of dysfunctional thinking that reflect unrealistic beliefs.[6] These include *all-or-nothing thinking*—the tendency to view a lack of complete perfection as total failure (one bite of ice cream means the diet is totally blown and therefore I might as well eat the whole half-gallon)—and *jumping to conclusions*—negative conclusions drawn despite having incomplete information (Sally challenged my request for her to perform a task, and therefore I know she is personally out to undermine my authority and effectiveness at work). The unrealistic beliefs and assumptions that underlay this dysfunctional thinking will trigger a variety of negative mental activities. Specifically, negative mental imagery and self-talk will result that contribute to self-defeating thought patterns.

Our most important belief is our belief in ourself.

The first step is to learn to recognize these dysfunctional thinking tendencies. Observing and even writing down your thoughts as you find yourself struggling with troubling issues, and especially when you believe you are not being very effective can provide you with useful information. Learning to challenge your beliefs and assumptions can be a very useful skill. For example, if you find yourself reacting in the same dysfunctional way whenever you encounter a particular situation, examine the beliefs that underlay your reactions. Is Sally really trying to undermine your authority and effectiveness, an assumption that would naturally trigger a negative reaction? Perhaps she is simply trying to help you develop an even better way to complete the task, to use her creativity and knowledge of the job. This new assumption would likely trigger a much more positive reaction.

In summary, much of our mental activity is driven by the immediate beliefs and assumptions we hold. By becoming more aware of these beliefs, learning to challenge them, and, when appropriate, replacing them with more constructive ones, we can take an important step toward more effective self-leadership.

COGNITIVE PATTERNS TO AVOID

The antithesis of effective self-leadership is excessive self-recrimination and guilt. Guilt poisons one's sense of self-efficacy and ultimately leads to a loss of performance. Guilt erodes the self-confidence that we need to perform.

Sometimes, perhaps, a small amount of guilt can be used in a productive way. When people work together (for example, coauthors on a book!), both parties typically incur a sense of mutual obligation. Each partner recognizes and accepts a commitment to the other. When mutual goals are agreed upon, both parties incur a sense of obligation to achieve the goal. If one of the partners does not follow through, a guilt response is not unusual. In the short term, this guilt can be used in a productive way to motivate performance. Nevertheless, research shows that over the long term, guilt can degenerate into self-recrimination and degrade motivation to perform, sometimes resulting in action paralysis and even severe depression. Most of all, guilt wears away at one's confidence to produce what is required.

**A little self-guilt might help our motivation.
Excessive self-guilt can paralyze our performance.**

To avoid (or extract yourself from) excessive guilt, practice self-observation, which will lead to self-awareness. Make it a priority to pay attention to your thoughts as you deal with daily problems, and especially attend to self-criticism and guilt. You'll achieve even greater effectiveness if you write down your self-observations. Do your thoughts reflect constructive, rational thinking, or are they symptomatic of unrealistic, destructive beliefs, such as the "all-or-nothing" thinking that we mentioned earlier?

Generally avoid self-guilt and recrimination because they are detrimental to effective self-leadership. Those who are prone to frequent excessive guilt will find specific actions useful in avoiding this scourge of self-leadership.

SUMMARY: THE OPPORTUNITY THINKER

Overall, the use of a variety of cognitive-focused self-leadership strategies creates the type of employee we like to call the Opportunity Thinker. This person is future oriented, confident, and excited about what will come.

In contrast, we have the Obstacle Thinker, who has negative and destructive cognitive self-leadership practices. This person sees shadows around every corner and often protests, "We can't do that because . . ." The Obstacle Thinker is fearful of the future. Consider the case of the following professors—one an opportunity thinker, one an obstacle thinker.

THE OPPORTUNITY
THINKER

Professor Antonio Sanchez casually walked into the faculty lounge. After the hectic schedule of the first week of classes, he was ready for a midmorning coffee and some schmoozing with colleagues. After pouring his coffee, he sat down at a table with his colleagues, Jennifer White and Peter Longworth, and listened as they talked about their students.

"I have a terrible class this semester," confided Peter. "They are stupid and dumb. I don't see how I can teach them anything."

Antonio was a bit taken aback. He had just finished his morning class and had felt very positive about the potential of his students. "I guess I'm lucky," he joined in. "I have a bunch of terrific students. I'm really looking forward to this semester."

Continuing, he asked Peter, "What section do you have?"

Peter replied, "Section 2 of the M.B.A. program. They're a lousy class."

Antonio knew the M.B.A. program was organized into a lockstep structure, so that the same students were in each section and took different classes together. This seemed to help esprit de corps. He also knew about the stringent selection qualifications to be admitted to the program. The class consisted of top students who had proven records of high performance.

"That's interesting," he replied in a laconic manner. "I have Section 2 also. I guess we're talking about the same students!"

Antonio and Peter stared at each other.

Antonio is an Opportunity Thinker. He sees the glass as half full. He sees the potential of the students and welcomes the challenge of working with them. Peter is an Obstacle Thinker. He sees the glass as half empty. He sees how much the students have to learn. Interestingly, if the self-fulfilling prophecy holds true, Professor Sanchez will probably have an exciting and interesting group of students—and Professor Longworth will indeed have his group of dull and uninteresting students.

The Opportunity Thinker deliberately uses cognitive-focused self-leadership strategies such as mental imagery and mental rehearsal, cognitive self-talk, and self-management of beliefs and assumptions as mechanisms to meet the future with a constructive and optimistic outlook. Opportunity thinking, an important part of becoming a master self-leader, can take us through difficult times. As an ending to this chapter, we recount for you Ronald Reagan's amazing responses after being the target of an attempted assassination. Reagan was indeed a never-ending unreconstructed Opportunity Thinker.

RONALD REAGAN: OPPORTUNITY THINKER

On March 30, 1981, President Ronald Reagan was wounded in the chest by an assassin's bullet.* The horror of the situation was a shock to millions around the world. Logically, one would think President Reagan would condemn the violent act and display a negative outlook in the wake of the atrocity. Instead, the president was said to have smiled through his surgery. Numerous optimistic and humorous quotations from the president reached the public, which gradually helped relieve the mass tension. The victim seemed to be trying to reassure onlookers rather than appeal to sympathy for himself.

> To his wife: "Honey, I forgot to duck."
>
> To his doctors: "Please say you're Republicans."
>
> To his daughter: "He ruined one of my best suits."
>
> To the medical staff: "Send me to LA where I can see the air I'm breathing."

Clearly, President Reagan's vaunted sense of humor did not desert him in this time of crisis. The result? The president's popularity subsequently soared. A short time after the incident, the president achieved his first major political accomplishment: Congress approved his budget.

P.S. We definitely don't recommend getting shot to improve your standing in the polls!

---

*This story is from Charles C. Manz, *Mastering Self-Leadership: Empowering Yourself for Personal Excellence* (Englewood Cliffs, N.J.: Prentice-Hall, 1992), p. 88.

BALANCING AND INTEGRATING SELF-LEADERSHIP STRATEGIES

The Master Self-Leader

> So many deeds cry out to be done. . . .
> Seize the day. Seize the hour.
> —*Mao Tse-tung*

The issue is not whether to lead ourselves. In fact, to at least some extent, we all exercise self-leadership. Unfortunately, many of us are not as good at it as we would like to be. Most of use would desire to significantly improve our self-leadership practice. The master self-leader can balance both behavioral and cognitive approaches to self-influence. In earlier chapters, we presented the parts to self-leadership. Here, we explore a more integrated, balanced view of self-leadership that combines the various behavioral and cognitive strategies.

THE STRATEGIES OF A MASTER SELF-LEADER

Previously, we focused on the details or pieces or a larger self-leadership puzzle:

Self-Discipline Behavior-Focused Strategies (The Grind)

- *Management of cues.* Arrange and alter cues (e.g., sights, sounds, wall displays) in the work environment to facilitate your desired personal behaviors. Eliminate negative and increase positive cues. Use cues to remind you, and focus your attention on positive behaviors.

- *Self-observation.* Observe and gather information about specific behaviors that you have targeted for change. Keep a record of your observations for later study.

- *Self-goal-setting.* Set goals for your own work efforts and areas for personal improvement. Set both long-term and short-term goals. Your goals should be specific and challenging but achievable. Write them down.

- *Self-punishment.* Punish yourself for behaving in undesirable ways. (Note that this strategy is not very effective and should not be overused. We recommend that you use other strategies instead.)

- *Rehearsal.* Practice work and personal activities both physically and mentally before you actually perform them. Use practice to refine your approach and help you prepare for effective performance.

Strategies for Building Natural Motivation into Work (The Rose Smeller)

- *Redesign your work* to increase the level of natural rewards in your job.

- *Search for and discover natural rewards* that are part of rather than separate from the work (the work, like a hobby, becomes the reward). Natural rewards result from activities that cause you to feel a sense of competence (that you are good at what you're doing), a sense of self-control (that you "own" and can take pride in your task performance), and a sense of purpose (a reason for doing your job—like helping others—that goes beyond its immediate performance).

- *Build natural rewards into your work* by choosing to do your tasks in naturally rewarding ways. Increase your naturally rewarding activities.

- *Focus thinking on the naturally rewarding features* of your work (rather than dwelling on what you don't like) to increase your motivation.

Strategies for Establishing Effective Thinking Patterns (The Opportunity Thinker)

- *Establish overall constructive and effective habits or patterns in your thinking* (e.g., a tendency to search for opportunities rather than obstacles embedded in challenges) by combining the next three strategies.

- *Manage your beliefs and assumptions.* Challenge your existing beliefs and replace destructive ones with constructive ones.

- *Mental imagery.* Mentally picture realistic positive performance with positive results before you perform a task.

- *Internal self-talk.* Study your existing self-talk and learn to talk to yourself in a constructive, positive way.

These strategies are organized according to the three self-leadership approaches described in chapters 7–10: action or behavioral strategies for doing necessary tasks, tapping the power of natural rewards, and redesigning our psychological worlds. Note that beliefs, imagined experiences, and self-talk interact to create constructive thought patterns. Thought patterns, stimulating tasks, and behaviors integrate into a repertoire that together form an overall comprehensive framework. Together, these three approaches to self-influence form the framework for becoming a master self-leader.

First, our own behavior is the central focus of self-leadership. Our behavior affects our personal effectiveness (our success in achieving our goals as well as our satisfaction with our work, ourselves, and our lives). But each of the three parts of self-leadership has an impact on our behavior and ultimately our personal effectiveness. Our behavior and our mode of thinking each in turn acts on one another.

The combination of thought and action makes a master self-leader.

Overall, this framework suggests a comprehensive, systematic approach to self-leadership. It's the *combination* of self-leadership that contributes to real improvements in overall performance and achievement. For example, by effectively applying self-discipline techniques of the Grind approach (such as self-goal-setting and self-reward), indirect benefits, such as increased enjoyment of our work (natural rewards) and improved, more beneficial patterns of thought, will be encouraged. The combination of these strategies can help us become master self-leaders. A vivid example of the use of a combination of strategies from these approaches is provided by the story of Rudy, whose experience at Notre Dame University inspired a major popular motion picture. Indeed, Rudy's persistence and ultimate achievements were due to the integrated self-leadership that he always applied to himself. He never lost confidence in himself, never allowed himself to think he could not succeed.

RUDY! RUDY! RUDY!
DREAMS DO COME TRUE

Christopher P. Neck

Rudy Ruettiger, better known as just Rudy, provides an inspiring example of combining the various self-leadership components. Rudy, best known as the focal character of a popular movie, vividly demonstrated how effective self-leadership skills can pay off in the game of football and the game of life.

While growing up, Rudy had a dream: he visualized himself playing football for Notre Dame University. But when he graduated from high school, he found himself with no money for college. He spent four years working in a power plant and as a navy yeoman on a communications command ship, never losing sight of his important long-term goal.

Finally, after saving some money, Rudy applied to Notre Dame. He was strongly disappointed when he was rejected. Did he quit? Complain about how unfair life was? No. After receiving the rejection, he drove in the middle of the night to Notre Dame. Upon his arrival he met a priest who sympathized with him and counseled Rudy to enroll at Holy Cross, a community college within a stone's throw of Notre Dame. Holy Cross was not Notre Dame, but Rudy viewed succeeding there as a short-term goal toward reaching his long-term goal of playing for Notre Dame.

Rudy, already in his early twenties, entered Holy Cross in 1972. During his first three terms there, he reapplied for admission into Notre Dame and was rejected each time. He never gave up. He believed he could make it at Notre Dame, and, he already visualized himself as a Notre Dame student. He started working as a groundskeeper at Notre Dame Stadium and boxed in campus charity fights. He took advantage of the natural motivation he gained from being involved with the campus of his dreams. In 1974, Rudy applied one last time for admittance into Notre Dame and was finally accepted.

Once enrolled, he told the head football coach that he would make the team. Thus, he not only told himself he could do it but voiced his intention to the coach. Rudy did not have an athletic scholarship, but he made the team as a walk-on after a demanding tryout. His fighting spirit and ability to take punishment from larger and stronger players earned him a spot on the practice squad. Each week, he helped the team prepare during practice sessions, although he sat in the stands during the games.

Rudy played on the practice squad for two years. As his second season neared its completion, Rudy, now twenty-six years old, had yet to play in a game. Finally, as a reward for his persistence and diligence, he was allowed to suit up for the last game of the season and stand on the sidelines with the rest of the team. As an honor from his teammates, he was allowed to lead the team on to the field.

Finally, with seventeen seconds left and the Notre Dame team leading comfortably, his teammates and fans shouted, "Rudy, Rudy, Rudy!" Everyone wanted to see Rudy play. Even more, Rudy wanted to get in there and live his dream. The coach got the message and sent Rudy in the game. Was Rudy prepared for this opportunity? Indeed. On the next play, he sacked the opponent's quarterback for a five-yard loss. When the time ran out, his fellow teammates carried him off the field on their shoulders—an expression of honor that has not been bestowed on any other Notre Dame player since.

Rudy's experience demonstrates what can happen to effective self-leaders.

Rudy was successful in achieving his dream because he demonstrated many of the qualities of a master self-leader.

- He gave direction to his life by setting long-term goals and shorter-term goals to achieve these bigger ideals.
- He took advantage of the natural rewards of his achievements along the way.
- He visualized his success, continuously maintained a positive mental pattern, and, most of all, exercised self-initiative.

Rudy became a colorful example of self-leadership and tirelessly persisted in making his dream come true. Master self-leaders will enjoy personal excellence in their lives.

GENERAL SELF-LEADERSHIP STRATEGIES

Now consider one last set of more general strategies that can complement the more specific ones that we have already presented. This final set includes self-initiative, self–problem solving, proactive teamwork, and networking. These general self-leadership strategies serve as an overall guide to help us find our own heights of achievement in both work and life.

Self-Initiative

Self-initiative is a very important ingredient of overall effective self-leadership. After all, a primary advantage of a self-leadership-based approach to organizing is that many individuals learn to stand on their own two feet with confidence. As a consequence, the organization benefits from a wider range of backgrounds, experiences, perspectives, and creativity. The possibility for synergy is enhanced when self-initiative from many individuals is combined into a focused direction. Each individual becomes a pillar of strength for the organization and reduces the vulnerability that stems from overdependence on a single strong leader.

It has been said that getting started is like being half finished. By mastering the art of self-initiative, the potential for actually accomplishing worthwhile tasks is enhanced. This idea is consistent with what Peters and Waterman called a "bias for action" in their landmark book, *In Search of Excellence*. Before anything gets done, someone has to get things started. This is not to say that everyone should run off in all directions in an uncoordinated manner. On the other hand, doing *something* is usually better than doing nothing.

Before anything gets done, someone has to get things started.

The key point, however, is that a master self-leader learns the important skill of self-initiative, of initiating progress toward established goals. Every self-leadership strategy depends on self-initiative for implementation. This skill is largely founded on an action–oriented mental attitude mixed with a healthy dose of self-efficacy concerning the task at hand. Perhaps FDR captured the essence of this general strategy best when he said, "But above all try something."

Self–Problem-Solving

Too often organizations have placed virtually sole power for solving important problems in the hands of a few powerful leaders or experts. In this book, we have repeatedly noted that each person contributes an important piece of the overall puzzle. We believe that the person who performs a specific job day in and day out typically becomes the organization expert on that job. If a particular problem affects that job, then the person who performs it should be involved in the decision.

Ultimately, many—perhaps most—problems should be solved by the person who delivers the actual service or determines the actual quality. If a production process isn't working as expected, the persons performing the process can fix the problem most quickly before too much wasted effort and resources are expended. Similarly, future sales potential can be preserved by on-line adjustments to meet the specific needs of a customer.

All this implies that a certain skill level needs to be established. Rather than reserving problem-solving skills in the hands of a few, this capability needs to be widely distributed. Sound training and guidance during skill development are needed. Ultimately each person needs to learn how to size up a problem, identify alternative solutions, and make an appropriate choice from among the alternatives. Again, once one masters this skill, it can be demonstrated to others.

Proactive Teamwork

Proactive teamwork is the art of working with and through others to accomplish important tasks. One of the keys to developing this ability is to learn how to think in terms of "we" instead of "I." Many issues affect and involve multiple people, especially if the organization is based on teams. Thus, it is important to consider the perspectives, concerns, and contributions of others. Some team-based organizations discourage self-focused words like *I* and *me*, instead encouraging words like *us* and *we*.

Another helpful and timeless guide is the well-known but frequently ignored Golden Rule of treating others the way we would like to be treated. By using empathy to walk in the shoes of others, a stronger bond is promoted. By combining skills, experience, and ideas with those possessed by others, we create the potential to accomplish more than one person can do alone.

Think in terms of "we" rather than "I."

All this suggests the importance of acting from a win–win stance. If you can learn to act in ways that promote the benefits of others as well as yourself—that is, to look for ways for everyone to win—effective teamwork is encouraged. The key is to think beyond independence (which, of course, we advocate) to interdependence. Others do not have to lose in order for us to win in most situations. Unfortunately, internal battles put the organization at a disadvantage before it even enters the competitive marketplace. By practicing proactive teamwork and encouraging it in others, you can make a significant contribution toward rising above this kind of self-defeating thinking and behaving.

Networking

Networking is significantly related to proactive teamwork but implies a broader and even more action-oriented kind of stance. If we can think of everyone in the organization as a kind of teammate, a potential source of help when we need it, a great deal of positive potential is established. Of course, networking is a two-way street. Someone who works in a very different kind of functional area or product or service line may have a unique spin on a current problem. By establishing good working contacts with others in different areas of the organization, we create a potential mutually beneficial crossover of ideas and resources.

Once we take a proactive stance about networking, a different perspective is established for what we might otherwise see as wasted activities. For example, all those boring committee meetings or corporate retreats take on a new importance. These gatherings can be good opportunities to expand a personal network for mutual benefit. Clearly understand that we are not advocating meetings for the sake of meetings, nor are we suggesting that we become political animals driven to establish self-serving power coalitions. We are suggesting that constructive positive networks are the foundation for higher performance.

Perhaps this strategy can be best summarized by suggesting that we think of ourselves as part of an ever-changing extended team. By sharing and benefiting from the combining of skills and knowledge of this broad team, we are unleashing the potential for complementary and synergistic work performance. The main message is, "Think teamwork." And to have teamwork, we must have a team. By working to establish networks of useful contacts, we are in fact creating a positive team for ourself and others.

The main message is "think teamwork": create a positive team for yourself and others.

Ultimately, beneficial application of the various specific and general self-leadership strategies should contribute to a changed, more effective, and more rewarding lifestyle and outlook. Ideally this new pattern of self-leadership will be tailored to the specific values and needs of each of us. That is, each of us needs to find the right combination of strategies and practical ways of applying them that are suited to our own unique situations.

To illustrate the comprehensive self-leadership system represented by the master self-leader, we present the story of Randy to show how one person can put together a number of specific self-leadership strategies.

RANDY:
LEARNING TO BE A
MASTER SELF-LEADER

Randy squinted slightly as he performed the suturing. The sailor stirred slightly; the drug Randy had administered had calmed him, but he wasn't quite asleep. Randy continued with the suturing, which he performed with expertise. (He had practiced suturing many times, on animal subjects during training and later on cloth mockups.) The puncture wound was located just below the sailor's rib cage; the skin had been penetrated, but fortunately, there was not much further damage. The repair was mainly a suturing job—challenging for Randy but within his capabilities. His training had been extensive, and Randy felt good about his capacity to deal with this emergency.

The young sailor now being stitched up had been engaging in horseplay with a buddy when he inadvertently ran into the tip of a missile located in the storage room. His buddy had covered the wound with towels and rushed the wounded man to Randy's cubicle. Randy was the ship's corpsman—the medical technician who provides the front-line medical care to the men and the officers of the guided missile cruiser.

After Randy finished with the sailor, his thoughts wandered back to his sophomore year in high school. He remembered how close he had come to dropping out and how he had stayed for his high school diploma only because of the influence of his uncle. But he hadn't liked high school, and he hadn't thought much of himself as a student. He had little self-confidence and virtually no life goals.

Somehow, the navy had saved him. Despite his poor high school academic record, Randy had done well on the navy aptitude tests and found some satisfaction with the discipline that was imposed on him in boot camp. Later, he was assigned to a destroyer, where he became an orderly in the ship's medical department. Here, he came under the influence of Doc Iverson, the chief medical corpsman. (Iverson was not a medical doctor but was affectionately called "Doc" by the crew because of his seemingly immense practical medical knowledge.)

Randy began full of self-doubt. Eventually he became a master self-leader.

Over the course of a few months, Randy gained immense respect for Iverson. In the course of his duties, Randy found himself continually looking over Doc's shoulder. In turn, Doc seemed to accept the curiosity of the young, unskilled orderly. Eventually Doc encouraged Randy to apply to the corpsman training program, and Randy took the tests, although he was plagued by doubts. All during the tests, Randy kept saying to himself, "I *am* passing this test!"

He made it. Randy was selected to enter naval medical corpsman training. At first, Randy was doubtful about his potential to complete the training, but Doc's confidence propelled him ahead. In fact, he was surprised at how much he enjoyed the challenge of the corpsman training course. Most of his instructors were knowledgeable and patient, and as Randy got further into the training, the intensity of his study and self-discipline improved tremendously. He came to love the work. In the end, he graduated in the top 50 percent of his class. He was first assigned as an assistant corpsman, where he gained valuable experience. Most of all, Randy learned to be confident of his own abilities. He especially appreciated the fact that corpsmen frequently serve without direct medical supervision and must be confident about their work. He knew that he had developed into a top-notch corpsman. Later, after more training and experience, he had been assigned to the cruiser.

By now, Randy had tremendous confidence in himself as a corpsman. Despite his enlisted rank, he knew he was better at *his* job than any of the officers on the ship. He knew they all depended on him, and he continued to work hard to improve his knowledge and skills.

In fact, Randy was planning to begin college premed studies on his next shore assignment. He knew it would be a long haul before he could call himself an M.D., but he was confident he could do it. He established this goal as a central part of his life. He visualized the M.D. certificate framed and hung on his wall. On this ship, the crew even began calling him Doc, and he accepted it as he recalled the encouragement of Doc Iverson. Most of all, he was determined to earn the official title.

RANDY'S STORY IN PERSPECTIVE

Over time, Randy became a strong master self-leader. In fact, the role of the navy corpsman has emerged over the years as one where the corpsmen have a particularly high degree of self-regulation of their own behavior. Despite relatively low rank, they have exceptional decision-making discretion. For Randy, the extraordinary self-efficacy that he experiences about himself derived from the extensive training he received, plus the opportunity to undergo mastery experiences. As a group, navy corpsmen are self-managed individuals with a high degree of self-efficacy perceptions about themselves.

Randy's story illustrates how an overall pattern of self-leadership strikes an effective balance among various self-leadership strategies. Randy is exercising effective self-leadership by applying many of the strategies and techniques that we have suggested. Most of all, he is doing so in a way that is consistent with his own situation and personal makeup. For example, he uses goals to guide and direct his life, and he recognizes the value of rehearsal in performing his tasks.

A primary strength in Randy's approach is his overall constructive and positive orientation to thinking and behaving. For example, he tries to build in, focus on, and otherwise experience the natural rewards of his work. Randy loves his work, and he especially loves the autonomy and discretion that are part of it. He is very strong at self-initiative and self–problem solving.

Finally, and perhaps most important of all, Randy has adopted a desirable pattern of thinking. He uses visualization to look ahead and see the achievement of his goals. He has a very strong belief in himself. He has developed the ability to see through the often obstacle-laden exterior of challenges and to be especially responsive to opportunities. His orientation is to strive forward, even under difficulties, rather than flounder and retreat from formidable problems. His course of action is founded more on advancing toward existing opportunities rather than retreating from obstacles. Randy has established a positive psychological world in the way he does his work and lives his life.

Randy's course of action is founded on advancing toward opportunities rather than retreating from obstacles.

IS THAT RANDY IN THE MIRROR?

Perhaps you see a little of Randy in yourself when you gaze into the mirror, but if you're like most of us, you would like to see more. The point is, each of us has choices about the way we choose to think about things and the way we choose to behave. The ideas represented by the philosophy of self-leadership offer a framework to help us choose and act wisely and efficiently.

If we want to lead others to lead themselves, we first need to look in the mirror and examine our own self-leadership practices. Once we master the important art of leading ourself, we can help others to do the same. In time, a company of heroes will result, filled with master self-leaders.

Part III

Creating Heroic Self-Leaders Through SuperLeadership

SUPER-LEADERSHIP

Leading Others to Lead Themselves

In this chapter we address in detail some of the more important leadership themes involved with the practice of SuperLeadership: (1) how self-leadership serves as the central driving process of SuperLeadership, (2) some of the fundamental changes implied in this shift from an external influence focus to a more internal self-leadership driven process, and (3) practical tips on how you can begin to put SuperLeadership into practice to empower others to lead themselves.

The notion of using empowerment to develop the capabilities of followers is not new. Consider the case of the McCormick Spice Co., where decades ago, Charles McCormick developed the concept of the junior board to empower and develop key middle management employees.

AN EARLY USE OF MULTIDISCIPLINARY INNOVATION TEAMS: THE MCCORMICK MULTIPLE MANAGEMENT SYSTEM

Stephen J. Carroll

The McCormick Spice Company was founded in 1889 by Willoughby McCormick in the basement of a Baltimore, Maryland, row house. The strategy of the firm was to sell premium-quality spices at a premium price. The company soon became the largest of its type in the world. In 1932, Willoughby McCormick died suddenly. Charles McCormick, his successor, was only thirty-six years old and regarded by many in the company as quite different from his rather autocratic uncle. The younger McCormick shortly initiated a new team-oriented system of management called multiple management.

The heart of this system is a board, typically composed of fifteen middle-level managers, who are charged with identifying improvement possibilities, conducting analyses, and making recommendations for changes to the senior board of directors. This group was originally called a junior board of directors, but today it is described as a multiple management board. C.P. McCormick indicated in his writings that several considerations went into his decision to establish this first board. One was his concern about his own inexperience in managing and his need for help and ideas.

McCormick believed individuals of high ability were frequently overlooked and not utilized.

Further, he wanted to identify competent individuals who had not been previously connected with running the company. McCormick's prior experiences left him with the belief that ability and competence could be found at all levels of the company, and individuals of high ability were frequently not fully utilized. McCormick saw this approach as an excellent way to train and prepare young managers for future top management positions. Those who served on a board gained experience in dealing with company-wide problems. Moreover, the board itself could help the company identify talent.

The initial junior board of directors performed so well that McCormick soon added a sales board and a production board. The sales board was composed of field salesmen and sales managers who would be brought together twice a year to discuss competitive marketing issues and to recommend solutions. Their field and customer experience were invaluable. The production board was composed of production workers, foremen, and production management personnel who attempted to improve the efficiency of their production plants. In a study of their multiple management system a few years ago, I found that the company had eighteen boards, some in recently acquired firms that initially had quite different cultures from the parent McCormick. Over the years, the procedures under which these boards operate have changed as the company has gained experience.

An invitation to join a board is usually based on recommendations from current board members, but service is voluntary. Board members carry out their assignments in addition to their regular job assignments, although they do receive some extra compensation for their board work. There are annual openings on the boards, since board members rate each other's performance each year. Those receiving the lowest ratings must leave.

The McCormick boards were an early example of a philosophy intended to tap and unleash the creative powers of ordinary employees.

Projects for the boards are chosen from a list compiled by the board chairs from recommendations by board members, other managers, other employees, and customers. Usually a few study projects are chosen at the beginning of the year, assignments are made to various board members, and the boards meet periodically to evaluate progress and make suggestions. Under the multiple management system, the organization is encouraged to cooperate and help board members obtain the information and assistance they need. When projects are completed, they are discussed by the entire board, and changes may be made at this time. The board's recommendations are then presented to higher management levels at meetings.

This McCormick multiple management system was eventually copied by at least one hundred companies. It is still used in McCormick today, with variations used in a number of other U.S. companies such as Motorola and the Lincoln Electric Company.

Most of all, the McCormick boards were an early example of a philosophy intended to tap and unleash the creative powers of ordinary employees. It was a form of empowerment—an early way of creating a company of heroes—before the term *empowerment* was known.

SELF-LEADERSHIP: THE HEART OF SUPERLEADERSHIP

It should be clear by now that SuperLeadership is a paradigm shift from traditional management control and direction. The main difference is the emphasis on followers, and especially the notion of developing followers who are effective self-leaders. The variety of self-leadership issues and strategies already addressed in this book reflect the core of this distinction. SuperLeadership is first and foremost based on self-leadership. This approach views each person as his or her own ultimate best leader. The SuperLeader's primary task is to help others to develop their own customized self-leadership influence system that will enable them to optimize their own effectiveness in work and life.

First and foremost, SuperLeadership creates self-leadership.

To accomplish this, the SuperLeader must achieve mastery of his or her own self-leadership. This achievement enables the SuperLeader to serve as a model and guide for others as they seek their own effective self-leadership approach. Serving as a model is not meant to imply that the SuperLeader strives to have others copy in every detail his or her own approach. Rather, the SuperLeader serves as a general example of a balanced self-directed and self-motivated person who has discovered how best to interact with work and life. Self-leadership skill and knowledge enable the SuperLeader to serve as a resource to help others pursue their own growth and transition toward greater independence and interdependence. A primary objective is to deemphasize external management direction and control.

Following are some important self-leadership principles for guiding the practice of SuperLeadership:

- Helping others to master a self-leadership system that is best suited to their own unique qualities is the ultimate goal of SuperLeadership.
- Effective self-leadership combines and balances self-discipline, natural enjoyment and motivation, and effective thinking habits and patterns.
- Learning and development of self-leadership skill has considerable value that is worth short-term costs (e.g., temporary failures, extra time).
- Facilitating the development of others' confidence in their self-leadership capability is an important foundation for effective self-leadership practice.
- With patience and persistence, almost everyone can become an effective self-leader and be of benefit to the organization.
- Self-leadership is a logical and effective basis for influence in a civilized, educated world and will provide the best outcomes over the long run.
- Self-leadership is an ethically sound basis for organizational leadership as long as it is pursued with the resulting benefits to the individual as a first priority (which will benefit the organization as a natural consequence).

These principles are mainly commonsense ideas about how to treat others so that they become more effective and work with you, not against you. Following these principles can help build a strong foundation for creating a company of heroes. Employees are not just *allowed* to be self-leaders; they are *expected* to become self-leaders.

SHIFTING FROM EXTERNAL TO INTERNAL INFLUENCE

In one sense, SuperLeadership is an advanced form of participatory management, yet in another sense, it goes well beyond. SuperLeadership does not view organizational influence as a management prerogative that can be shared with employees if management chooses. Employees participate in management-centered influence and, indeed, become the central focus of the influence process itself.

Employees are not just *allowed* to be self-leaders, they are *expected* to become self-leaders.

Clearly leadership is viewed in a radically different way from the past. Optimal employee empowerment through the facilitation of self-leadership skill development and effective practice is the key. Nevertheless, it is not enough simply to state and then pledge allegiance to this philosophy. For SuperLeadership to produce full benefits, it must be based on a series of consistently practiced strategies and behaviors. Perhaps the best way to provide insight into this different form of leadership is to identify some central themes of the transition to SuperLeadership.

The list that follows sets out some primary themes involved in shifting from traditional external-based leadership influence to SuperLeadership. Scan the entire list to get a sense of the kind of shifts that are identified:

From	*To*
External observation	Self-observation
Assigned goals	Self-set goals
External reinforcement for task performance	Internal reinforcement plus external reinforcement for self-leadership behaviors
Motivation mainly based on external compensation	Motivation also based on the natural rewards of the work

From	To
External criticism	Self-criticism
External problem solving	Self–problem solving
External job assignments	Self–job assignments
External planning	Self-planning
External task design	Self–design of tasks
Obstacle thinking	Opportunity Thinking
Compliance to the organization's vision	Commitment to a vision that the employee helped to create

The list can serve as a kind of road map for aspiring SuperLeaders. Making this transition involves some very fundamental shifts in the way influence is carried out. SuperLeaders abhor followers' dependence on external direction. Creating a company of heroes is achieved through an overall shift from external leadership influence to the development of self-leadership throughout the organization.

GETTING STARTED: PUTTING SUPERLEADERSHIP INTO PRACTICE

Following is a list of practical tips for getting started with SuperLeadership:

- Develop an understanding of the new, challenging management/leadership role (coach, facilitator, coordinator).
- Ask questions rather than giving answers.
- Listen!
- Allow people to make mistakes in the spirit of learning and progress.
- Require teams to solve their own problems.
- Require teams to do things their own way.
- Provide guidance and teaching in the beginning. Then back off.
- Be open and honest. Share all the important information that affects the employees.
- Provide key learning and training opportunities.

- View your own success through the success of followers.
- Personalize and apply the key strategies for SuperLeadership.

The list is not intended to be exhaustive, but it does represent a useful starting place for beginning to lead others to lead themselves. When any or all of these simple tips are consistently applied, the SuperLeadership process will move along.

Each tip offers a different yet complementary contribution to the development of follower self-leadership. Asking good questions that stimulate others to think through and solve their own problems, for example, is a powerful way to encourage self-leadership. Of course, it's tempting to answer followers' questions when we know the answer (or at least an answer), and will reinforce our own sense of value and importance by stating it. But if people are to become effectively empowered, they need to learn how to answer their own questions. Supplying an answer is a useful short-run strategy for providing traditional leadership influence; asking good development-oriented questions, however, is more challenging and helps build for a better future in which followers are better able to contribute their full capabilities.

Another critical SuperLeadership behavior is listening. SuperLeaders are adept at engaging in a dialogue, with both parties contributing. Traditional leaders, normally in the power position, must make a special effort to involve followers in dialogue.

Similarly, allowing people to make honest mistakes in the spirit of learning and progress is essential. As people are learning to do things on their own that they have not done before, it stands to reason that they will make mistakes. Of course, it's important that these mistakes are not too large (e.g., threaten the survival of the company) or the result of indifferent carelessness. Nor should a customer bear the brunt of an employee mistake. Nevertheless, when people initiate actions on their own with good intentions and sincere effort, learning, not recrimination, should be the focus when mishaps occur.

The idea of empowerment is to get people to solve their own problems. It may be difficult at first to stand by and leave unpunished employee failures. Nevertheless, mistakes are a natural part of human performance, especially during learning. Again, taking a long-term view is a key; relatively low-cost mistakes today can help develop a very valuable employee who knows well what to do and what not to do in the future.

When people initiate actions on their own, with good intentions and sincere effort, learning, not recrimination, should be the consequence when mishaps occur.

SUMMARY

In the end, SuperLeadership is deeply rooted in the philosophy and assumptions of the leader. Are people capable? Will they respond if given the opportunity? SuperLeaders are optimistic about the basic capability of people, and this optimism extends across different times and different places. Consider the following story of a national hero whose writings sound curiously like SuperLeadership.

LEADERSHIP ACCORDING TO KI HADJAR DEWANTARA: CREATING A NATION OF SELF-LEADERS

John S. Tabor and Waskito Tjiptosasmito

This brief account tells the story of how one man transformed himself and others through leadership. The setting is Indonesia. Ki Hadjar Dewantara was born Raden Mas Suwardi Astroningrat of Javanese nobility in 1889, during the period of Dutch colonial rule. Although he was well born, his family was not wealthy. His youth was characterized by incomplete education and then frequent moves from one type of work to another, including pharmacist, reporter, and school teacher. He ultimately became one of several key leaders of the revolutionary struggle against the Dutch.

Upon the declaration of independence in 1945, he was appointed the first minister of education and culture of Indonesia. He articulated a model of leadership that guided his efforts to attain independence and to educate Indonesian youth to contribute to that result. Most of all, his philosophy emphasized individual and collective self-responsibility as vital to national independence. This philosophy of self-reliance was deeply rooted in the historical culture of Java (the principal island of Indonesia).

Suwardi was very aware of the subordination of his people by the Dutch and from an early age sought to mobilize the people to attain their independence. He cofounded the Indonesian party, wrote frequent essays to point toward independence, and—after a lengthy exile, first on a prison island and then in the Netherlands—founded an independent school, Taman Siswa. Later he even changed his name to Ki Hadjar Dewantara, meaning "one who exalts the people through education." His intention was to separate himself from his feudal origins and to focus on the struggle for independence through education. The school was to educate Indonesian children in ways that would imbue them with knowledge, self-confidence, self-leadership, and a sense of mutual obligation to their family, community, and the people of Indonesia. The school was challenged several times by the Dutch authorities but was ultimately allowed to continue and to expand to other parts of the colony.

The person in front leads by giving examples.

Ki Hadjar developed the Taman Siswa schools and educational philosophy over a thirty-year period. Leadership was foremost in mind in his formulations for teaching, learning, and character development. Teachers were not to be controllers but guardians (*Pamong*) of the students. The system of education was to be "guided development of students" (*Among*). The *Pamong* were to be guided in their own work by three fundamental principles:

1. Ing Ngarsa Sang Tuladha—"The person in front leads by giving examples," or modeling the roles and behavior the followers should learn. The *Pamong* were to exemplify supportive leadership and to lead the study of the lives of Indonesian heroes and myths.

2. Ing Madya Mangun Karsa—"The person in the middle leads by developing efforts," or inspiring and encouraging followers to attain their objectives. The *Pamong* lived with their students in *ashramas* and gave them continuing encouragement and reinforcement for achievements.

3. *Tut Wuri Handayani*—"The person leads from behind," by providing opportunities for followers to develop themselves, giving assistance only when necessary, and intervening only when followers are at risk.

It is the last principle to which Ki Hadjar returned frequently in his writing about Taman Siswa. He clearly expected that leaders would move expeditiously from leading by example, to encouragement of others to lead themselves, finally to providing opportunities for self-leadership. The emphasis in *Pamong* leadership was on leading others from behind. *Tut Wuri Handayani* was later adopted as the motto of the Ministry of Education of Indonesia.

Ki Hadjar Dewantara's vision was to develop through a learning process the natural strength of Indonesians into a disciplined, determined, and capable force for achieving independence and founding a nation. The core of the learning process was the development of self-leaders, who became leaders of their family, community, and people. The leadership of others was mutual and shared; together they led themselves to achieve the vision.

Ki Hadjar Dewantara was a SuperLeader who worked to build a nation of heroes.

THE TRAUMA OF TRANSITION

Learning to Lead Others to Lead Themselves

SuperLeadership is accomplished neither overnight nor without challenge. In this chapter, we discuss the realistic difficulties of meeting the challenge of transition to an empowered system of self-leadership and tackle the question of individual change: How does the individual manager become a SuperLeader? In later chapters, we address the transition to empowered team leadership, as well as the complex and difficult challenge of organizational transition. Changing individuals, changing teams, and changing whole organizations are all part of negotiating the demanding road of creating a company of heroes. This is a tough challenge. As James O'Toole puts it, "Ninety-five percent of American managers today say the right thing. Five percent actually do it."[1]

THE INDIVIDUAL JOURNEY: BECOMING A SUPERLEADER

Consider the middle manager dilemma in the following story. What is expected of the manager today? How should he or she behave as a leader? Many managers are indeed confused by this question.

MIDDLE MANAGER DILEMMA: MANAGER OR VISIONARY LEADER?

Leadership used to be a simple thing. You were born with it, or you were not. You had charisma, or you didn't. You had the power of your position, or you didn't. The amount of power from one's position in the hierarchy was relatively clear. You had the authority to impose your will, or you didn't. You knew when you could kick ass and take names, and knew when you couldn't.

But then all this turned upside down. Someone told you there was a difference between being a manager and being a leader. The implication was that being a manager was inadequate; you had to be something more. Until then, you had always taken pride in being a manager. Management was something to which you aspired early in your career, and you were proud when you received your first appointment that carried the title "manager." You didn't see any jobs on the career ladder that had the title "leader."

All this didn't make much sense to you. You thought, "Of course, I'm supposed to be a leader as a part of my management role. What's the big deal about that? Am I supposed to stop being a manager?"

Then you heard you were supposed to be "visionary." At age forty-two, running a division of thirty-eight people, you had a difficult time understanding just what this meant. You had your own ideas of how the so-called vision of the corporation should be revised, but you weren't receiving any invitations from the CEO soliciting your opinion. From your viewpoint in the middle management ranks, the notion of vision was not something that was useful on a daily basis.

Oh, yes, there was a corporate mission statement, and when you read it the first time, you were pleased with the ideas it represented. You were also hopeful that there might be some real changes that would bring actual corporate practices more in line with what the mission statement really said. But time passed, and you realized the mission statement didn't have much effect on what really happened day to day.

Somehow, being a manager is no longer sufficient.

Most of all, you were having a problem understanding how you were really supposed to behave as a "visionary" leader. You thought your CEO should certainly be a visionary, but what should *you* do differently in your own division?

Your sense of accomplishment deriving from your achievements as a manager seemed to dwindle. If you were no longer to take pride in being a manager, and you didn't really know what it meant to be a "visionary," then just what were you supposed to do? It was all very confusing.

Three basic assumptions underlie our ideas on self-leadership:

1. Everyone practices self-leadership to some degree, but not everyone is an effective self-leader.
2. Self-leadership can be learned and thus is not restricted to people who are "born" to be self-starters or self-motivated.
3. Self-leadership is relevant to executives, managers, and all employees—that is, to everyone who works.

Few employees are capable of highly effective self-leadership the moment they enter a job situation. Especially at the beginning, the SuperLeader must provide orientation, guidance, and direction. The need for specific direction at the early stages of employment stems from two sources. First, the new employee is unfamiliar with the objectives, tasks, and procedures of the new position and undoubtedly has not fully developed tasks capabilities. Second, and more pertinent, the new employee may not yet have an adequate set of self-leadership skills. For the SuperLeader, the challenge lies in shifting employees to self-leadership. Thus, the role of the SuperLeader becomes critical: he or she must play the pivotal role of leading others to lead themselves.

Overall, SuperLeadership means encouragement of followers to exercise initiative, take on responsibility, and use self-leadership strategies in an effective way to lead themselves. One other feature is very important: *guided participation*. This concept facilitates the gradual shifting of followers from dependence to independent self-leadership through a combination of initial instruction, questions that stimulate thinking about self-leadership (e.g., what are you shooting for? What is your goal? How well do you think you're doing?), and increasing participation of followers.

Guided participation involves the gradual shifting of followers from dependence to independence.

Consider the goal-setting process as an example of how the transition to self-leadership unfolds. Teaching an employee how to set goals can be a straightforward procedure: First, an employee is provided with a model to emulate; then he or she is given guided participation; and finally, he or she assumes the targeted self-leadership skill (in this case, goal setting). Modeling is an especially important element in learning this skill. Because of their formal position of authority, SuperLeaders have a special responsibility to demonstrate goal-setting behavior that other employees can emulate. Furthermore, goals need to be coordinated among the different levels of the hierarchy. Subordinate goals, even those that are self-set, need to be consistent with superior and organizational goals.

A SuperLeader takes into account the employee's time and experience on the job, as well as the degree of the employee's skill and capabilities. For a new employee, whose job-related and self-leadership skills may be undeveloped, an executive may wish to begin with assigned goals while modeling self-set goals. Shortly, the SuperLeader endeavors to move toward interactive goals. Usually the best way to accomplish this is by guided participation, which includes asking the employee to propose goals. At this stage, the SuperLeader still retains significant influence over goal setting, actively proposing and perhaps even imposing some of the goals. Usually, this is the give and take that is typical of the traditional MBO (management by objectives) approach.

Finally, for follower self-leadership to truly flourish, the SuperLeader will deliberately move toward employee self-set goals. In this situation, the SuperLeader serves as a source of information and experience, as a sounding board, and as the transmitter of overall organizational goals. In the end, in a true self-leadership situation, the employee is expected to establish his or her own goals.

Sharing goal setting with subordinates is frequently one of the most difficult transitions for traditional leaders to understand and accept on their road to effective SuperLeadership. Often an executive is reluctant to provide the full opportunity for a subordinate to lead himself or herself because it seems the executive is losing control. Consider the following case of Joe Paterno, coach of the national champion Penn State football team, who clearly recognizes this struggle. Paterno is an interesting mixture of Strongman, Visionary Hero, and SuperLeader. Most of all, he clearly has the intellectual capacity to be seriously introspective about his own leadership.

TALES OF TRANSITION FROM JOE PATERNO AND OTHERS

Many managers struggle with the challenge of managing the way they think they should versus their own natural style. One of the most interesting of these individuals is Joe Paterno, the well-known coach of the national champion Penn State Nittany Lions football team. In a personal interview, we found that Coach Paterno had a special ability to be intro-spective about this dilemma of overcontrol and undercontrol.* "It's diffi-cult," he candidly admits, "for me to handle people in the way I think they want to be handled . . . because I have a tendency to want *complete* con-trol. . . . In the early part of my career, . . . I would plot every offensive and defensive move we would use in a ball game and try to devise the game plan by myself. . . . I felt that I had to have input on everything that went on every minute of the day and every day of the week."[†]

Paterno also recognizes the benefits of getting others involved in the action, especially assistant coaches: "I'm cognizant that people will not work two extra hours at the film projector if they're going to come in the next day and be told exactly what to do . . . that's not going to work . . . you destroy any ingenuity . . . any satisfaction they get out of the job it-self. I'm aware of that. . . . I have to fight like hell to constantly remind myself of it."

On the practice field, Paterno is a well-known screamer, cajoling his players to higher intensity. A casual observer would classify Paterno as a classic Strongman leader. But behind the scenes, Paterno also reaches out in a unique way to his players. During the season, an informal group of representatives from the players meet each Wednesday morning at 7:15 in a cafeteria for "Java with Joe." They have an open discussion of what is happening on the team and why.

Paterno started these meetings after a frustrating 1992 season that ended with five defeats, a low in his coaching career. "I thought I had lost the squad," said Paterno.[‡] He realized he needed a new avenue of com-munication with today's new breed of player. Paterno characterized these meetings as "the culmination of talking and getting things out in the open, and understanding we're all in this together." In these meetings, Paterno seemed to behave like a SuperLeader, asking, "What's going on? Is there something you want me to address with the coaches? How do you feel?" In the end, the team responded with an undefeated season in 1994, capped by a victory in the Rose Bowl.

They have open discussions of what's happening, and why.

---

*Unless otherwise noted, Paterno's quotations are taken from a personal inter-view. Some of this material was originally published in Charles C. Manz and Henry Sims, Jr., *SuperLeadership* (New York: Berkley Books, 1990).

[†]Mervin D. Hyman and Gordon S. White, Jr., *Joe Paterno: Football My Way* (New York: Collier Books, 1971), pp. 266–267.

[‡]Malcolm Moran, "Scream Machine at Penn State," *New York Times*, October 10, 1994, p. C3.

This type of behavior has a way of catching on without the players' really realizing it. Senior All-American quarterback Kerry Collins was quoted as saying, "It's funny, I'll be talking to people and I'll start saying things that he has said for four years. And I'll think, 'What am I doing?' "§

According to Paterno, having the opportunity to fail—to make mistakes—is part of the learning process. "You can't grow [if you don't make mistakes]. . . . I've got to give them a chance to do some things [on their own]." Paterno recognizes the value of mistakes in his own development. "[My former coach] allowed me to make a lot of mistakes. . . Many times, I would go in there with the 'greatest idea in the world' [when] it may have [already] been tried three different times, [and] it didn't work. . . . I do the same thing. . . . [An assistant coach] will come in with a 'great idea'. . . . I saw the same thing 12 years ago. . . . [They] do some things I'm sure are not going to work."

Paterno seems to be destined to fight with himself over the classic dilemma between his natural hands-on activist Strongman leadership style and the behaviors required of a SuperLeader. This seems to be a conflict between his emotional self, which has a strong desire to control (perhaps overcontrol) the situation, versus his intellectual self, which realizes the necessity and benefit of providing more opportunity for his assistant coaches. The natural self says, "Hey, I gotta get in there and do it myself," while the intellectual self says, "I have to stand back and give them an opportunity to do it." In the end, he says, the important thing "is still keeping control but knowing when you don't have to have control."

Paterno remains an intriguing combination of many of the leader behaviors we have described in this book: practice-field Strongman, university Visionary, and behind-the-scenes SuperLeader. Perhaps it is his complexity that makes him so appealing.

Others Tales of Transition

Like Paterno, others struggle with this challenge of moving down the road to SuperLeadership. In his book, *Reengineering Management*, James Champy talks about Rick Zaffarano of Hannaford Brothers Company. He describes Zaffarano as struggling to hold back while employees organize their own work and goals. According to Zaffarano, the temptation to weigh in and provide the answer is almost irresistible.

Martin Berger, a corporate executive vice-president described what happened to him as he made his journey along the road to SuperLeadership.* One of the first steps is to recognize one's overinvolvement, com-

---

§Ibid.
*We originally told Berger's story in *SuperLeadership*. Berger's quotations are from "Learning to Slow Down," *New York Times Magazine,* September 16, 1984, p. 106.

pulsiveness, and unwillingness to let go. "I'm involved in a great many projects in my company, and I can't do them casually."

Berger is candid about his own motivation. "I am sure that at least part of my problem is that I am still seeking 'stroking'. . . . approval. . . . I'm still anxious that my bosses know when I do something well. I get especially upset if someone gets credit for something that I believe I did." But Berger talks about his own transition. "Now I'm attempting to become a person who makes things happen without appearing to be there. . . . I work hard at making myself invisible. . . . My way of dealing with it is to think of myself as a combination coach-spectator. What that means is that I spend a lot of time listening before I do anything. When someone describes a plan of action that I think is incorrect, I don't take the plan apart and substitute my own. I let the speaker finish and wait to hear what others have to say. Usually, if I see something wrong, someone else will too."

Berger goes on to say that "this approach has its risks. I may hide myself so successfully that people will start to wonder what I'm doing and decide I'm not necessary." But he also realizes the benefits: "[I have] learned a great deal. . . . I gather information that I don't think I could have gotten any other way. I was [actually] more involved in what was [really] going on."

"I realized this change begins with me."

Another transition story is told by Thomas Dunn, an army colonel, who describes his transition as an "epiphany."[†] Dunn began his change in the way he leads as he started a new assignment as commander of the Red River Army Depot in Texarkana, Texas. He had been inspired by contact with innovative changes in the private sector, including Cadillac and the Saturn plant of General Motors. Observing the changes in the private sector, he came to believe that the only way to survive was to build an extraordinarily creative and innovative organization. He captures the essence of the change: "I realized that the change begins with me. You can't impose your will on someone else."

This process was also described by Dennis Longstreet, CEO of Ortho-Biotech, a Johnson & Johnson subsidiary. "You start asking them [employees] to describe their ideal productive workplace, and you give up a lot of control. I was used to standing up on a stage behind a podium with slides and rehearsed scripts. Now, everything is done in a town meeting fashion, with them doing most of the talking and me doing the

---

[†]Dunn's quotations are from "Brave New Leadership," *Government Executive* (July 1994): 22–30.

listening. When you start something like this, you give up a lot of ability to make firm, hard decisions, and you take a chance that employees may lead you someplace you don't want to go. But then you learn that most of them want the same things you want. Everyone wants to succeed."‡

Good leaders intuitively understand the importance of knowing where they are going. However, during subordinate employees' critical transition from traditional external leadership to self-leadership, some of the previous dependency on superior authority needs to be unlearned. In its place, employees must develop a strong sense of confidence in their own abilities to set realistic and challenging goals on their own.

Frequently this transition is not very smooth, leaving the employee wondering why "the boss" is not providing more help and the executive biting his or her lip to avoid telling the employee to do the "right thing." The leader's reputation with followers may take a temporary downturn because of the follower's perception of a loss of guidance. Employees need to have some latitude in making mistakes during this critical period.

Employees develop a strong sense of confidence in their own abilities.

Reprimand takes on special importance during the critical transition phase, when the superior–subordinate relationship is very delicate. Careless use of reprimand can seriously set back the employee's transition to self-leadership. The issue becomes especially salient when employees make mistakes—sometimes serious mistakes. In our experience, during the transition to self-leadership, some mistakes are inevitable and should be expected as an employee reaches out. The way the SuperLeader responds to the mistakes can ensure or thwart a successful transition.

In a book about the 3M Corporation, *Our Story So Far,* former CEO William McKnight viewed the issue this way: "Mistakes will be made, but if a person is essentially right, the mistakes he or she makes are not as serious in the long run as the mistakes management will make if it is dictatorial and undertakes to tell those under its authority exactly how they must do their job. . . . Management that is destructively critical when mistakes are made kills initiative and it's essential that we have many people with initiative if we're going to grow."[2]

Andrew Grove, CEO of chip maker Intel Corporation, discussed the issue of

---

‡J. Huey, "The New Post-Heroic Leadership," *Fortune,* February 21, 1994, pp. 42–50.

how to respond when an employee seems to be making a mistake. Reacting too soon or too harshly can result in a serious setback in efforts to develop employee self-leadership. According to Grove, the manager needs to consider the degree to which the error can be tolerated. If the task is an analysis for internal use, the experience the employee receives may be well worth some wasted work and delay. However, if the error involves a shipment to a customer, the customer should not bear the cost of boosting the employee further down the learning curve.

The most difficult time is when a follower makes a decision that the leader believes is wrong.

As strange as it may sound, sometimes the SuperLeader might *deliberately* hold back on decisions that at other times, in other places, he or she would be more than willing to provide. The most difficult time is when a leader has given authority to a follower, and the follower makes a decision that the leader believes is wrong. What should the leader do? If allowed to stand, the decision may be costly or damaging. If the leader overturns the decision, then the so-called empowerment or self-leadership will be thrown out the window. In practical terms, the answer to this question depends on balancing the costs and negative consequence of a potentially bad decision with the notion of thinking of the decision as a learning investment. There will be times when a SuperLeader grits her teeth, bites her tongue, and allows what she thinks is a bad decision to stand. At some point, self-led employees must stand on their own.

The good news is that after this critical transition phase, the effects on the self-led employee's performance can be remarkable. Effectively leading themselves produces a motivation and psychological commitment that energizes employees to greater and greater achievements. Leaders become SuperLeaders when they have successfully unleashed the power of employees to lead themselves.

LEARNING THE BEHAVIOR OF SUPERLEADERSHIP

Training is an important ingredient to help individual managers work through the trauma of transition. We especially endorse the use of role plays or behavioral simulations that deal with the difference between traditional managerial roles and a SuperLeader role. These activities, which typically revolve around a scenario or task assignment, are especially useful in working out the language that exemplifies the day-to-day behaviors of SuperLeadership. In a case describing the leadership transition in an empowered team environment at the Charette Corporation, Manz, Keating, and Donnellon vividly describe the type of verbal behavior that takes place in these simulations.[3] For example, one manager was quoted as saying, "I'm not here to solve the problem. I'm here to assist *you* in solving the problem." In another episode, one manager exclaimed, "That's not up to me; it's up to you." Later, in a critique, he was reminded by a colleague that a leader is still part of a team: "You should have said, 'It's up to *us!*'" Manz, Keating, and Donnellon also set out four stages that managers are likely to experience as they make this transition:

Stage 1: Initial suspicion, uncertainty, and resistance.

Stage 2: Gradual realization of the positive possibilities offered by teams.

Stage 3: Understanding of their new leadership role.

Stage 4: Learning a new language.

This last stage, learning a new language, is particularly important. First, terms are important. In reality, abstract words like *empowerment, self-leadership,* and *teamwork* must be translated into day-to-day practices at the location. Furthermore, the specific forms of verbal behavior that make up a leader's pattern of language must change. There will be less instruction and command and more questions. Most of all, there will be less talking in general, and much more listening.

HOW FAST? FACTORS INFLUENCING THE CHANGE

What are the factors that play a role in how fast a manager can move followers toward self-leadership? What are the elements in the present situation that bear on the speed of transition to SuperLeadership?

Any empowering behavior used out of pretense, rather than a genuine appreciation of subordinate ideas and contributions, is likely to be of limited effectiveness. Leading others to lead themselves needs to be done in a genuine, honest, and respectful manner in order to be of any lasting benefit. We have encountered managers who have learned to "talk the talk" but either don't know how or do not sincerely desire to "walk the talk." In one case, the CEO of an independent insurance firm preached the philosophy of employee empowerment and self-leadership but in reality used teams to exercise tighter control over team members.[4] Employees quickly saw through this inconsistency, and they resisted and undermined the whole empowerment system. Trust is probably the most important foundation for a transition to SuperLeadership, and the only dependable way to establish trust is through honest application of the SuperLeadership principles.

The place to begin is significantly influenced by the task and the social skills of the followers. A critical issue is the identification of the needed skills and abilities necessary for followers to become empowered. What behaviors will followers need to acquire in order to be effective self-leaders?

Another factor that can influence the specific actions appropriate for leaders to take is the amount of time available. Developing self-leadership takes time and should be done in an evolutionary manner. However, follower self-leadership should not be thought of as a low priority. Leader behavior focused on developing follower self-leadership should be thought of as an investment that will result in future payoffs for the organization.

A critical issue is the identification of the skills and abilities that enable followers to become empowered.

In a related vein, the appropriate SuperLeader behavior and the effectiveness of that behavior will be influenced by the general cultural orientation of the organization in regard to self-leadership. An individual manager who is undertaking the transition to SuperLeadership needs the support of the organization. A leader who genuinely tries to encourage and facilitate self-leadership in followers will find his or her efforts undermined if the wider work system does not endorse and support (or even discourages) real self-leadership. Without such support, the leader's behaviors are likely to be of considerably lesser potency (and perhaps even confusing or frustrating) in fostering highly committed, motivated self-leading employees.

When working with groups or teams, the stage of the team's development is another important factor. Early in its development, a team's capability to manage itself will be limited. Thus, the appropriate combination of leader behaviors will consist of a mix of SuperLeader behaviors and more traditional external leadership patterns. As the team increases its self-management capability, more leadership authority can be transferred to the work team itself. The main role of the external leader is to facilitate team self-management. Thus, the work team's area of decision making widens relative to that of the leader's as the team develops. The level of autonomy that the work team possesses at a particular time will influence the appropriate mix of subsequent leader behaviors.

As the team develops, the team's decision making widens relative to that of the leader.

Another element that will affect appropriate leader behavior is the nature of the technology (fundamentally, the way people interact with one another and equipment to transform inputs into product or service outputs). The type of technology employed at the work site initially may place limits on the extent to which a leader can facilitate and allow teams to exercise self-management. Over time, however, the design of the technical system and the social system must be balanced to promote employee discretion. After all, technology can be designed or changed to enhance or retard self-management potential. The same set of tasks can be organized in quite different ways, thus creating organizational choice regarding possible control orientations (e.g., reliance on self-managing teams).

A successful transition requires support from the existing organizational context, particularly the human resources system. A hospitable work context that provides for the material, informational, and technical expertise needs of followers is essential.

Finally, we believe that the most important factor of all is the individual manager's attitude toward followers. Indeed, this is closely correlated with one's own personal philosophy about the nature of people at work. One of the biggest hurdles is changing one's own fundamental beliefs about the capability of employees to respond well if given the opportunity. Consider the following case, where at least one manager considers his own followers to be fools.

CAN THE FOOLS WHO WORK FOR ME REALLY LEARN TO LEAD THEMSELVES?

Gregory Stewart

The training session had been great. Jan was thinking back over how much she had learned. However, her pleasant thoughts were interrupted when she heard Tom say, "Employee empowerment and SuperLeadership sound nice, but these practices are just impossible given the lazy slobs who work for me."

Jan was stunned. Up to now, Tom had seemed to support the idea of leading others to lead themselves. Why was he sounding so negative now?

During the next break Jan made a point of asking Tom what he meant by his statement.

"Well, you know," replied Tom, "this stuff works great for businesses with professional workers, but I'm stuck working with a bunch of idiots. My workers are just too stupid and unmotivated to lead themselves."

Jan didn't know how to respond. She wanted to believe in self-

leadership, but maybe Tom was right. Perhaps some employees are incapable of leading themselves.

That evening Jan was having dinner with Paula, another training participant who worked in the same office as Tom. Jan remembered Tom's comment and decided to ask Paula what she thought about the idea of leading others to lead themselves.

Paula answered, "I think it is a powerful concept. Over the last year I have been trying to get my employees to take personal responsibility for their work. I can already see much improvement. With the principles we learned today, I am sure that I can do even better." Paula then went on to recount several examples of how her employees were already leading themselves.

Jan listened carefully to Paula. Then, as they were paying for the meal, she asked Paula to explain how her workers were different from Tom's. "Oh, they are really the same. We both hire employees from the same applicant pool," stated Paula. "It's just that Tom starts out with a pessimistic viewpoint about new employees right from the very beginning."

As the training concluded the next day, Jan heard Tom belittle the trainer and point out how silly the training concepts were. She also heard Paula praise the trainer and eagerly list ways that she was going to use the new ideas to become a better leader.

Jan was confused. Why had Tom suddenly changed? Why did he and Paula seem to have such different perceptions of workers who were essentially the same? Can ordinary line workers really lead themselves?

This scenario is based on actual experience and illustrates some common problems we've encountered when training managers in SuperLeadership skills. Many managers agree that allowing workers to lead themselves is a great idea—until they begin to think about actually doing it with the people who work for them. Also, the attitude that a manager initially starts with has considerable impact on how he or she receives training. Clearly, managerial beliefs can be difficult to change.

Managers usually agree that empowerment is a great idea—until they think about actually doing it with the people who work for *them*.

Managers usually agree with the general idea of leading others to lead themselves, but when they think about changing their own behavior, they fear that their own leadership power and status will be diminished. They worry about their employees being motivated enough to lead themselves. They even wonder about the self-leadership ability of some of their workers. Taken together, these feelings cause many managers to resist accepting what they learn during training sessions.

In contrast, other managers fundamentally believe followers are capable of empowerment. These leaders accept new ideas. They look forward to trying the principles that they learn during training and they seek opportunities to help others learn to lead themselves.

The beliefs that managers bring with them to training play an important role in their own learning and future behavior. Managers with positive beliefs readily accept and apply empowerment principles. Managers with negative beliefs, however, must first be convinced of the benefits of leading others to lead themselves. They must then be convinced that the people working for them are capable of becoming self-leaders.

The transition from negative to positive beliefs is often slow. Core beliefs concerning leadership must change. Transformation is facilitated by clearly showing managers the benefits of developing self-leaders. Trainers should not underestimate the effort required to foster new leadership concepts. Top-level managers must commit to long-term efforts. When possible, supervisor selection should also be based on beliefs related to empowerment.

As skeptical managers see their peers succeed at empowering workers, they will begin to change their own beliefs. Rewarding managers for developing self-leaders (while not punishing them for initial failures) will also encourage them to try new leadership approaches. It isn't easy, but managers like Tom can be converted to believe that leading others to lead themselves is possible.

Managers frequently find a change to SuperLeadership threatening, they view it as a perceived loss of their power and control. On the one hand, they have lots of experience and training to lead in a way that is consistent with the concept of "boss," but now they are expected to change. Managers have to unlearn being bossy and believe their followers can be mature and responsible enough to handle the change.

When followers are effective, the leader is effective. When followers lead themselves, the leader becomes a SuperLeader. As a SuperLeader, it's not the leader's shining and taking the spotlight that's important but rather the pride the leader takes in seeing followers develop as mature problem solvers on their own.

When followers are effective, the leader is effective.

Overall, the unique process of leading others to lead themselves depends on finding the appropriate balance during a transition to employee self-leadership. This is a major challenge. It is not unusual for leaders in this transition to report a tempo-rary decrease in satisfaction with their work. However, the long-term rewards are substantial. Indeed, as one's followers become empowered self-leaders, the leader experiences a unique sense of achievement and satisfaction, mainly through the achievements of others. As followers become accomplished self-leaders, the strength and power of the leader increases—until that leader becomes a true SuperLeader. Many leaders moving along this road together can create a company of heroes.

TEAMS AND TEAMWORK
Creating Heroic Teams

The leader looked out at the eyes around the campfire. Slowly he picked up a stick and snapped it in a second. Next, he picked up a bunch of sticks together and attempted to break them. They bent but did not break. "A stick by itself," he said, "can be broken easily. But if all the sticks stay together, they will not break." Slowly he smiled. "The same is true of us."[1]

Fundamentally, self-leadership is an attribute of an individual. That is, each person in an organization has both an opportunity and a responsibility to develop his or her own self-leadership capabilities. Also, leaders have the responsibility of developing and encouraging individual self-leadership. Essentially, developing individual self-leadership is a form of employee empowerment. In fact, our original formulation of the concept of self-leadership was pointed mainly to the individual follower.

In today's complex environment, the lone wolf is gone.

But few of us work in isolation. For most of us, our work has some interdependence with others. In fact, in today's increasingly complex environment, the opportunity and requirement for working together are stronger than ever. The lone wolf is gone. Much of our work involves working together, and today, working together means teams and teamwork.

Teams, the focus of this chapter, have become the most common vehicle through which self-leadership is expressed. Empowerment typically relies on team structures. Thus, teams are a critical element of the organizational self-leadership system. For many organizations, teams are the springboard to self-leadership. In this chapter, we address the idea of self-managed and empowered professional teams and how these teams can contribute to productivity and innovation. And most of all, we emphasize how the SuperLeader can encourage self-leadership through empowered teams. The team becomes the unit of self-leadership.

TEAMS: WHAT THEY ARE AND WHAT THEY DO

Work designs based on self-management tend to give employees a high degree of autonomy and control over their immediate behavior. Teams are one of the many forms of employee participation that have emerged in the United States. Not all teams are empowered, however. Indeed, the traditional sports team is seldom a participatory unit. In fact, a team can function well under the thumb of a strong-minded leader. We think of the late Vince Lombardi (coach of the champion Green Bay Packers) as an example of a successful boss-type coach who demanded compliance from his players. His teams were definitely not self-managed. But teams in today's contemporary business sector in the United States are not like the Lombardi teams.

In contemporary empowered teams, employees are typically organized into units that complete a whole or distinct part of a product or service. They make decisions on a wide range of issues, often including such traditional management prerogatives as who will perform which task, solving quality problems, settling conflicts between members on the team, and selecting team leaders. The story of the Fitzgerald Battery Plant of General Motors Corporation is an example of the many activities that self-managed teams have taken on in many work organizations.

TEAM ROLES AND RESPONSIBILITIES AT FITZGERALD

The self-management practices we describe here are from the Fitzgerald Battery Plant of General Motors Corporation.* We derived this

---

*These roles are from C. C. Manz and Henry P. Sims, Jr., *Business Without Bosses: How Self-Managing Teams Are Building High-Performing Companies* (New York: Wiley, 1993). A training case based on the Fitzgerald story is available under the title of "The Greenfield Case" and is available from Organization Design and Development, 2002 Renaissance Blvd., King of Prussia, Penn. 19406. (231) 279-2002.

information from interviews and observations that we conducted several years after start-up, when the plant was at a relatively mature stage. Following are some specific details, in no particular order, that describe how the teams handled responsibilities that in other organizations are typically performed by traditional bosses.

Establish relief and break schedules. Teams had great discretion in establishing their own schedules. Since most of the teams were buffered by short-term in-process inventories, breaks could be scheduled at their own volition. Teams handled this authority in a responsible way. Often they scheduled breaks to facilitate production. For example, a short tool or process change might be undertaken while the team was on its break.

Select and dismiss the leader of the group. Teams elected their own leader from among the team members. Elections were conducted whenever a leader resigned or was challenged by another team member. A few teams had had the same team leader since the start-up of the plant; others had experienced several team leaders over the years. At first, popular individuals tended to be elected team leader. However, teams soon found that the leaders who had organizing and planning skills, plus interpersonal and conflict resolution skills, were more effective. So-called popularity diminished as a criterion for election to team leader.

In addition, management appointed people to fill the role of coordinator, a leadership role external to the team. That is, the coordinator was not a team member. In other plants, this person might be called a facilitator or a counselor. Each coordinator had responsibility for from one to three teams. While the coordinator filled the space in the organizational hierarchy typically occupied by a foreman or general foreman, their behaviors were quite different. Many of the coordinators at Fitzgerald had previously served as team leaders.

Finally, although teams technically had the authority to dismiss a team leader, this was virtually never done. Instead, an ineffective team leader might be encouraged to resign or might be challenged by another potential leader.

Initiate minor and major equipment and machinery repair. Overall, team members might carry out minor repairs themselves in order to keep production flowing. Major repairs were carried out by the maintenance department but were frequently initiated by team members. We recall the statement of a team member in a weekly team meeting: "They better get that bearing replaced this weekend, or that machine will break down next week, and we'll lose a day's production!" Most of all, team members seemed to take an unusual degree of psychological ownership in their production equipment. They were very concerned about making the equipment work in the right way.

Make specific job assignments within the work group. Each team made its own job assignments, and the practices were quite different across teams. One team might rotate jobs every hour, while another team would make assignments strictly on seniority. Overall, teams seemed to find a way to satisfy individual preferences within the team without compromising productivity goals.

Train new members of the work group. This responsibility was carried out by all teams. Occasionally the external coordinator would pitch in or conduct some special training. Of course, more formal training programs were also conducted for the team members. Training was also important in terms of developing the wide range of skills required for each new member to advance along the pay scale.

Make sure needed production materials are available. In many traditional plants, workers will allow a production material to deplete in order to take an unauthorized break. At this plant, responsibility for ensuring production materials were available was vested in the team itself. Team leaders spent a great deal of their time ensuring that proper materials were available to meet production requirements.

Keep a record of hours worked for each group member. Each team member kept a record of his or her own number of hours worked, the plant had no time clocks. Weekly time records were turned in to their team leader and then to the coordinator. When asked, "Don't they cheat?" one team member replied, "Who do they cheat? Other team members! You may be able to get away with it once or twice, but that's all. You can't fool your teammates."

Make sure spare parts are available. Team members accepted the responsibility for keeping track of minor spare parts required to run their own operation.

Perform quality control inspections and compile quality control data. For the most part, teams did their own quality inspections and compiled their own quality statistics. One team member might typically be assigned this responsibility. A separate quality control inspector did not exist. However, occasionally, team quality data were audited by a small, central quality control department.

Prepare material and labor budgets. Once a year, teams undertook a planning exercise in which they prepared a budget for their team. Budgeting was also done independently, in parallel, by accountants from the office. In general, team budgets were at least as demanding and as stringent as the accounting budgets. Differences were discussed and reconciled in order to arrive at a final budget. Of course, team members required training and appropriate information to carry out this planning exercise.

Prepare a daily log of the quantity produced and the amount of in-process inventory. For the most part, teams compiled their own in-process inventory records, subject to occasional auditing from production scheduling. Teams knew their own production schedule and kept their own records of how much they produced and the quantity of their in-process inventory.

Recommend engineering changes for equipment, process, and product. As they worked with equipment, teams occasionally requested changes that would lead to significant process or product improvements. One engineer at the division level expressed a preference for placing new or experimental equipment at Fitzgerald. "They *make* it work!" he exclaimed.

Select new members for group. Dismiss members from group. Teams had considerable but not total discretion over who would join or leave a group. Most intergroup mobility was facilitated by the coordinator, who used interpersonal skills to explore new assignments to different groups. Great effort was made to match the preferences of individuals with teams. Employees moved from one team to another for any of several reasons: to earn higher pay, to do a different type of work, or because of personal preferences.

Evaluate group members for pay raise. The plant used a "pay-for-knowledge" system: employees were paid according to the tasks they were qualified to do rather than being paid a rate for a particular job that they were performing at the moment. To gain the highest pay rate, an employee had to pass performance tests for all tasks on two different teams. These performance tests were conducted by a coordinator, team leader, and senior team member. Thus, part of the evaluation of whether an employee could perform a specific job was performed by a teammate.

Conduct safety meetings. Safety meetings were conducted on a scheduled basis, normally by the team leader, or perhaps by a coordinator or other technical person. During the early stages of the start-up of the plant, the plant's safety performance was poor. However, the safety record had continuously improved, and during the time of our visits, Fitzgerald's safety performance was in the top quartile of all General Motors plants.

Shut down the process or assembly if quality is wrong. Stop production to solve process or quality problems. Teams had the authority to stop production without necessarily asking permission from a representative of management. Typically, this authority was exercised rarely, and almost always to solve a serious quality or process problem. This authority was used with great discretion, since a shutdown decision might have ramifications for other teams.

Conduct weekly group meetings. Usually a weekly half-hour meeting was conducted on company time. In addition, shorter meetings would be conducted almost daily. And on occasion, a more lengthy problem-solving meeting might be conducted to work on special production or quality issues.

Review the quarterly performance of the company, plant, and group. Each quarter, the plant manager met separately with each team and reviewed company, plant, and team performance with the team. These occasions provided an opportunity for an exchange of communication between the plant manager and team members. The communication exchange went both ways.

Discipline group members for absenteeism or tardiness. Theoretically, this authority was vested within each team, but some teams used the authority, and others did not. Coordinators said this was the most difficult responsibility to get the team to undertake.

Select new employees for the plant. Employees were selected into the plant through an assessment center process. An evaluation team observed employee candidates during interpersonal exercises and provided ratings and final judgments. The plant evaluation team consisted of one manager, one coordinator, one team leader, and two members of different teams.

Of course, all of these responsibilities are appropriate to the specific site of the Fitzgerald Battery Plant. Other sites will undoubtedly be different in the specifics of the roles and responsibilities expected of each team. In each case, however, roles and responsibilities must be specified in advance, with a sequenced timetable of implementation and a substantial degree of flexibility to take advantage of the learning as team implementation proceeds.

Team designs have varied across companies, and it's difficult to find a single commonly accepted definition of the team approach. It seems to be more of an overall philosophy and approach than a tightly defined set of rules. In fact, part of the essence of teams is to encourage each set of employees to find their own way, their own kind of group self-leadership, that best fits their own situation and team members. Most of all, the team approach represents an attempt to utilize the organization's human resources more fully—especially those at the lowest levels.

A typical objective of an empowered team system is to *improve productivity for the organization as well as the quality of working life for employees.* Sometimes the dignity and freedom workers receive is especially publicized, but the drive toward productivity and competitiveness is always there, whether stated openly or not.

Typically, teams have some common characteristics: a distinct recognizable task that employees can identify with; members with a variety of skills related to the group task; discretion over such decisions as work methods, task scheduling, and task assignments; and compensation and performance feedback for the group as a whole.

The drive toward productivity and competitiveness is always there.

The early days of team systems in the United States were heavily influenced by a concept known as sociotechnical systems (STS) theory. STS emphasizes the need to design both the social and technical aspects of work. Typically, an STS analysis results in a shift to performing work in groups, with the technology and people matched together in clusters, which are sometimes known as autonomous work groups (teams). The main rationale is that teams can more effectively apply resources to deal with the variances (changes and unpredictable events) in work conditions than can individuals acting on their own.

Today, the formal analysis techniques of STS are less commonly employed, but the philosophy of matching the technical system and the social system remains and is an important part of successful team design. Another issue that is particularly salient to higher-level teams such as cross-functional or concurrent engineering teams is that of specialization versus generalization. How much of their own specialized skill should each member retain, versus how much generalized skill should each member develop?

MULTISKILLED TEAMS: JACK OF ALL TRADES, MASTER OF ONE

Janice A. Klein

A hallmark of empowered teams is multiskilled team members who are capable of being assigned to perform most any team task.* There are many benefits to multiskilling, including flexibility and enriched jobs, but there are also some costs. Here I explore the challenge of finding an appropriate balance between specialized skills and generalized skills in empowered teams. This issue is especially salient in lower-level self-managed teams and midlevel professional teams such as cross-functional teams, concurrent engineering teams, and new product development teams.

Many of the early applications of self-managed work teams made

---

*Source: Janice A. Klein, "Maintaining Expertise in Multi-skilled Teams," in *Advances in Interdisciplinary Studies of Work Teams,* Michael M. Beyerlein and Douglas A. Johnson, eds. (Greenwich, Conn.: JAI Press, 1994), pp. 145–161.

the assumption that all team members should be able to rotate through all team tasks. But where team members are required to perform a wide range of tasks, there is a risk that they may become jacks of all trades, masters of none. What is needed is to have jacks of all trades with sufficient knowledge and skills to perform the work of the team proficiently and continuously improve the overall operation. The essential question is, To what extent do individual team members need to be multiskilled in the tasks of the team?

To some degree, the extent of multiskilling depends on the type and depth of knowledge or expertise required to perform various tasks or activities. Within each type of expertise on a team, there are different levels of knowledge, which influence the extent of multiskilling. For routine activities, it might be feasible to have every member of the team be a bit of a generalist—a jack of all trades—but for activities that require significant training, it is typically preferred to have specialists—master of one—who can apply specialized knowledge across various team activities.

Typically, the routine aspects are required of all team members to provide coverage in the event of absences. Activities requiring craft, specialized, or expert knowledge are reserved for those who have specialized in a particular task. Also, expert or craft knowledge is often required to handle nonroutine occurrences.

There is a difference in the mix of specialization versus generalization when comparing traditional organization of work with an empowered team. In the empowered team, specialization is still maintained, but a significantly higher level of multiskill capability is required of each team member. Each team member develops sufficient knowledge of others' functions to integrate their skills better. The idea is not to dilute specialized expertise but to enhance it by incorporating integrative knowledge.

The object is not to reduce specialized expertise but to increase integration among the specialties.

Multiskilling is attractive to managers for a number of reasons. The integrative feature leads to greater team flexibility in task assignment, which translates into reduced idle time and enhanced productivity. Broader knowledge also facilitates continuous improvement suggestions. Most of all, faster and better decision making is possible within the team rather than being vested in a management hierarchy. The most important consequence is significantly reduced cycle time.

Too much of a good thing, however, can turn sour. Training costs might become excessive. Team members who constantly rotate between jobs may never have the time to become proficient. Efficiency may suffer because many tasks require building up a rhythm. Team members may not have time to move down the learning curve before moving on to another task.

Multiskilling is perceived both positively and negatively by the workforce. It can lead to less boring jobs, provide an opportunity for learning new skills, enhance future employment opportunities, and give the workforce some control over their daily work environment. Nevertheless, some individuals would rather stay in narrowly defined jobs.

In essence, if a team comprises highly skilled or professional employees, there is a limit on the extent of multiskilling across areas of expertise. Many professional jobs typically require years of schooling to perfect expertise. It may be unreasonable and impractical to expect highly skilled professionals to acquire expertise in multiple disciplines. In addition, multiskilling may be viewed as an affront to professional or craft pride.

Despite the difficulties of finding an appropriate balance, empowered teams typically move toward a higher degree of multiskilling than traditional organizations do. In essence, the whole becomes greater than the sum of the individual parts. Synergy is created by bringing together the expertise of individual team members. At times individual team members might use their unique competencies to perform solo tasks, while at other times they might work collectively or collaboratively.

Most of all, empowered multiskilled teams have clearly demonstrated a stronger propensity toward creativity and innovation, flexibility, and, especially, significantly reduced cycle time. All of these outcomes, however, are dependent on each team's finding an appropriate balance between generalization and specialization.

The team concept has emerged as a distinctly Western phenomenon (teams have been used in the United States, Canada, Europe, and Mexico, to name just a few locations) although it's frequently confused with so-called Japanese management. Both are often associated with the idea of participatory management, but each approach is targeted at a quite different population, with distinct cultural values. In our attempts to understand the team system, we have traveled to Japan and read extensively about Japanese management systems, but teams in Japan are quite different from U.S. teams.

Our main conclusion is that we would be better served by attempting to learn from successful experiences with empowered teams in the West rather than looking to the Japanese for innovative organizational philosophies. The rationale for and early successes with team designs originated in the United States and Europe and better fit Western cultures. The unique defining characteristic of U.S. teams is that they promote a high degree of initiative and a sense of responsibility, creativity, and problem solving from within. When teams live up to these ideals, they are uniquely self-reliant.

WHY TEAMS?

The challenge of competitiveness is here. The emergence of the global market-place has placed a new premium on productivity and quality. Business organizations around the world are struggling to find ways to deal with increasing interdependence, complexity, and uncertainty. In the face of these pressures, the team concept is beginning to show potential for improving productivity, quality, and employee quality of work life, among other payoffs. It is an approach that is designed to take advantage of the strengths of Western culture and history.

Teams have emerged as a potent weapon in the competitiveness wars. In fact, we suspect that the notion of teams has reached the stage of the recurring management fads that we often encounter in the United States. Therefore, some team applications are being undertaken simply because "it's the thing to do," with little thought given to how the approach fits the needs of the organization. We deplore this justification and strongly believe it's a sure recipe for failure. Nevertheless, there are some solid reasons that teams make good sense.

Teams have emerged as a potent weapon in the competitiveness wars.

From a management viewpoint, productivity and quality are the main reasons to implement a team system. Teams are a way to undertake "continuous improvement" to enhance productivity. Today, teams are often seen as a critical element to a total quality management (TQM) program. And, of course, the real issue is whether teams actually work as well as they're supposed to.

ARE TEAMS EFFECTIVE?
THE BOTTOM LINE

Do self-managing teams really produce superior results?* *Business Week* claims teams can increase productivity by 30 percent or more and can also substantially improve quality. Other examples reported in the press include an Alcoa plant in Cleveland where a production team came up with a method for making forged wheels for vans that increased out-

---

*This section is adapted from C. C. Manz and Henry P. Sims, Jr., *Business Without Bosses*: How Self-Managing Teams Are Building High-Performing Companies (New York: Wiley, 1993).

put 5 percent and cut scrap in half. At Weyerhaeuser, the forest products company, a team of legal employees significantly reduced the retrieval time for documents. A thousand clerical workers at Federal Express divided into "superteams" of five to ten people and helped the company reduce service problems by 13 percent in 1989. At Rubbermaid, a multidisciplinary team from marketing, engineering, and design developed the "auto office" in 1987, and sales exceeded projections by 50 percent in the first year.[†]

Corning Glass eliminated one management level at its corporate computer center, substituting a team adviser for three shift supervisors, producing $150,000 in annual savings and increasing quality of service. Perceptions of autonomy and responsibility among workers increased because they felt they experienced more meaningful and productive work. In an insurance firm, change to automation led to a shift from functional organizational design to self-managed teams. A twenty-four-month follow-up found improved work structure, flows, and outcomes.[‡]

In our previous book, *Business Without Bosses,* we described several organizations that have enjoyed impressive payoffs with teams in both the long and short term. We tell a more detailed story of the mature General Motors automobile battery plant organized around teams that company officials reported had productivity savings of 30 to 40 percent when compared with traditionally organized plants. We tell how teams helped Lake Superior Paper Company enjoy possibly the most successful start-up in the history of the paper industry. We describe the beginning adjustments of management to the team approach that a few short months later was credited with productivity improvements of 10 percent per year, cost savings of 10 to 20 percent of earnings, and customer service quality levels of over 99 percent.

Considerable data indicate the effectiveness of teams, but before you blindly jump on the teams bandwagon, be aware that not all the evidence is completely supportive. More rigorous academic research has produced mixed findings. Perhaps the difficulty of evaluating the team concept in terms of any hard scientific data was best expressed by Miner:

> *The results are often positive. It is hard to predict whether the outcomes will be greater output, better quality, less absenteeism, reduced turnover, fewer accidents, greater job satisfaction, or what,*

[†]John Horr, "The Payoff from Teamwork," *Business Week,* May 7,1989, pp. 56–62; Brian Dumaine, "Who Needs a Boss?" *Fortune,* May 7, 1990, pp. 52–60.
[‡]Madeline Weiss, "Human Factors: Team Spirit," *CIO* (July 1989): 60–62; Lee W. Frederiksen, Anne W. Riley, and John B. Meyers, "Matching Technology and Organizational Structure: A Case in White Collar Productivity Improvement," *Journal of Organizational Behavior Management* (Fall-Winter 1984): 59–80.

but the introduction of autonomous work groups is often associated with improvements. It is difficult to understand why a particular outcome such as increased productivity occurs in one study and not in another, and why, on some occasions, nothing improves. Furthermore, what actually causes the changes when they do occur is not known. The approach calls for making so many changes at once that it is almost impossible to judge the value of the individual variables. Increased pay, self-selection of work situations, multiskilling, with its resultant job enrichment and decreased contact with authority almost invariably occurs in autonomous work groups.[§]

Perhaps the most revealing scientific study of the bottom-line effect of teams is contained in a paper by Barry Macy and associates at the Texas Center for Productivity and Quality of Work Life (Texas Tech University). Their analysis contrasted the success of various changes involving human resources, work structure, and technology (e.g., training, reward systems, work teams). Very strong effects, especially in terms of financial outcomes, were observed with team applications. The Macy study is one of the first rigorous scientific efforts that shows the clear financial effect of the team approach.[*]

**The most revealing scientific study shows the clear
financial effect of the team approach.**

Are teams always successful? No. In *Business Without Bosses*, we reported on a team implementation at an insurance company that was clearly a failure. Indeed, we believe that team success depends much on implementation. For example, we continue to hear tales of companies' removing a supervisor and precipitously declaring that a work group is a "team." We call this the "team-alone" syndrome, where a group of employees suddenly finds itself with much larger responsibility but without the necessary training and resources. As Ed Lawler has said, "Teams are . . . like the Ferraris of work design. They're high performance, but high maintenance and expensive."[†]

Those close to the self-management movement informally report

---

[§]John B. Miner, *Theories of Organizational Structure and Process* (Hinsdale, Ill.: Dryden Press, 1982), pp. 110–111.

[*]See Barry S. Macy and Hiroaki Izume, "Organizational Change, Design, and Work Innovation: A Meta Analysis of 131 North American Field Studies—1961–1991," in *Research and Organizational Change and Development* (Greenwich, Conn.: JAI Press, 1994), 7:235–313.

[†]Brian Dumaine, "The Trouble with Teams," *Fortune,* September 5, 1994, p. 86.

substantial productivity gains and cost savings that typically range from 30 to 70 percent when compared with traditional systems. Clearly, self-managing teams have the potential to exert substantial effects on the bottom line. Perhaps the notion was captured best by Charles Eberle, a former vice president at Procter & Gamble, who speaks with the advantage of years of practical experience:

> *At P&G there are well over two decades of comparisons of results—side by side—between enlightened work systems and those I call traditional. It is absolutely clear that the new work systems work better—a lot better—for example, with 30 to 50 percent lower manufacturing costs. Not only are the tangible, measurable, bottom-line indicators such as cost, quality, customer service and reliability better, but also the harder-to-measure attributes such as quickness, decisiveness, toughness, and just plain resourcefulness of these organizations.*[‡]

On occasion, the implementation of teams is motivated by a humanistic ideology. That is, teams are seen as an important way for people to find satisfaction and dignity in their work—in essence, an enhanced employee quality of work life. Other reasons are also occasionally cited: better innovation and adaptability and reduced turnover, absenteeism, and conflict.

We are sympathetic with all of these reasons, yet we believe that issues of productivity and quality—the important elements of competitiveness—are the more important drivers. In the end, more teams will be adopted only if teams truly work.

Recent years have brought many challenges for Western organizations: intense international competition, a workforce that demands more than simply making a living, and the increasing complexity of technical knowledge and information flows. As a result, companies are pressured to explore more effective ways of using human resources. Among the more noteworthy and promising is the concept of empowered teams.

For a time—when international competition was not strong, when employees were more accepting of no power and fulfillment—top-down control was sufficient for organizational success. More recently, however, employees have changed; they expect growth, fulfillment, and dignity from their work. Most of all, the emergence of the global marketplace has forced organizations to consider alternative ways of dealing with the competitive challenge. Flexibility, speed, quick response, and short cycle time have become extremely important perfor-

---

[‡]Quoted by Kim Fisher in "Are Your Serious About Self-Management?" a paper delivered at the International Conference on Self-Managed Work Teams, Dallas, Texas, October, 1991.

mance criteria. Many organizations are moving toward flat, flexible organizations (see "The Virtual Team" in Chapter 18.)

After more than a dozen years of studying teams, we are convinced that teams do work. Moreover, there is something exciting about the challenge of bringing a group of people together to combine their abilities and coordinate their efforts to excel.

THE HISTORICAL EMERGENCE OF TEAMS

According to a recent study by the Center for Effective Organizations at the University of Southern California, 68 percent of the Fortune 1000 companies use self-managed or high-performance teams.[2] However, the study also shows that only 10 percent of workers are in such teams. In essence, there's a whole lot of experimentation going on, but it has touched only a minority of employees. In the early 1980s, Edward Lawler, director of the USC center, estimated that about 150 to 300 work sites were using teams. Clearly the number of companies using teams has grown considerably. We believe that nearly every major U.S. company is trying or considering some form of empowered work teams somewhere in their organization.

Procter & Gamble is generally considered an important U.S. pioneer in applying teams to its operations. It began work with teams in the early 1960s, although these efforts were not publicized and virtually escaped media attention. P&G saw the team approach as a significant competitive advantage, and up through the 1980s, it attempted to deflect attention away from its efforts. The company thought of its knowledge about the team organization as a sort of trade secret and required consultants and employees to sign nondisclosure statements. Other companies have had team-oriented plants for years but have also considered their team approaches to be proprietary.

Despite its view toward secrecy, Procter & Gamble's successes with teams received considerable off-the-record attention from a small group of consultants across the country who were inspired by its experiences and learned techniques through an informal network. Many of them originally worked at P&G and were attracted to other companies by lucrative job offers because of their unique knowledge and expertise.

Through the 1970s and 1980s, General Motors was a locus of active experimentation with teams and was significantly less secretive than Procter & Gamble. Many of the GM team implementations have been very successful and have served as models for other changes around the country.

General Motors remains an enigma, however; it is a textbook case of how success with teams at one location does not necessarily transfer to another location. (Further, teams are not the sole answer to the competitiveness challenge.) We suspect the "not-invented-here" syndrome to be rampant at GM. Also, while specific GM manufacturing plants have been on the cutting edge of employee self-management, many suggest that the corporate level has maintained a more traditional top-down, control-based management mentality. Despite the problems of diffusion of its successes with self-management, General Motors should be credited with its leadership in active exploration of the team concept.

Teams that are successful at one location do not necessarily lead to adoption at another location.

Other prominent companies have been active with teams as well: the Gaines dog food plant in Topeka, Cummins Engine, Digital Equipment, Ford, Motorola, Tektronix, General Electric, Honeywell, LTV, Caterpillar, Boeing, Monsanto, AT&T, Texas Instruments, and Xerox, to name just a few. In manufacturing, we now have extensive experience with self-managing teams, starting in the 1960s. Today teams in manufacturing are a proven system. It's no longer a question of why, but now only a question of fine tuning to specific sites.

In the past few years, the use of teams in the service sector has been the most exciting area of application. Service teams are well past the experimentation phase, although we still have much to learn. Teams in government are the most rapidly changing area of application. Until two or three years ago, there was very little interest in empowered teams in government agencies. Now, however, driven by the thrust for "reinventing government" and the stark reality of government downsizing, experimentation with teams seems to be active indeed. It remains to be seen, however, whether teams in government will attain the same success seen in manufacturing and service.

Perhaps the most promising area of team development now is in the professions and middle management. These include teams like concurrent engineering teams, cross-functional teams, product improvement teams, task force teams, ad hoc teams, and new venture teams.

After our years of studying teams had convinced us of their tremendous potential, we were gratified that finally, at the beginning of the 1990s, the topic of teams had reached front pages. *Fortune* magazine featured a cover story—"Who Needs a Boss?"—about teams in the May 7, 1990, issue. *Business Week* featured a cover story about teams in its July 10, 1989 issue. And, even Dan Rather has spoken about "self-directed" teams on the evening newscast.

Until recently, teams were generally ignored by the popular media.

Although it has taken some time, the topic of teams has clearly reached the stage of becoming a popular fad, with all the accompanying advantages and disadvantages, but we believe they will pass the test of time and prove to be enduring. We think that teams are here to stay and that they constitute a fundamental change in the way Americans go about work. We suspect the label and approach will evolve and perhaps pass—like all other fads—but the fundamental ways that teams do business will remain with us for a long time, mainly because teams are effective. Teams may represent a whole new management paradigm. Perhaps they reflect a new business era as influential as the industrial revolution and are destined to revolutionize work for decades to come.

SUMMARY

Self managing and empowered teams are a natural extension of self-leadership. Teams are a type of collective or group self-leadership. The SuperLeader makes it happen by initiating, encouraging, and supporting empowered teams. Indeed, teams are a critical ingredient in creating a company of heroes.

TEAM LEADERSHIP

Team leadership is the key to team success. It comes in all forms, starting with the traditional Strongman, who exercises power through authoritarian behaviors. But in this chapter, we focus on self-managed or empowered teams. The fundamental question we wish to address is what type of leadership is most appropriate for empowered teams that are vested with a higher degree of power, authority, and self-responsibility. Consider the following story about team leadership at the Fitzgerald plant. How would you define the roles and responsibilities of these team leaders? How should these "coordinators" behave?

TEAM LEADERSHIP AT FITZGERALD

You are the production superintendent at the Fitzgerald Battery Plant and report directly to Ed Green, the plant manager. The plant started up about six months ago, now employs about 260 people, and is one of the many manufacturing plants of a large, multinational corporation. The plant produces sealed maintenance-free batteries for trucks and cars. It uses up-to-date but traditional manufacturing equipment to produce battery parts and then assemble the parts into a finished product.

When Ed asked you to help him start up the Fitzgerald plant, he stated rather firmly his commitment to the team concept, in which small work groups were formed to carry out the work. According to Ed's ideas, the work group would have the primary decision-making responsibilities for itself. A team is supposed to be self-managed. You recognized this concept as radical and risky, but you were willing to give it your best try. You and Ed had visited a few plants using this concept. In addition, you had excellent support from the corporate organizational change staff, essentially a group of applied psychologists who were instrumental in helping groups learn to communicate with themselves.

The coordinators will want to know what you expect.

After six months, you are convinced that the team concept will work, but you have been having problems. The plant is somewhat behind its start-up schedule. According to the way you are now organized, you have 24 "self-managed" teams, each with an internal elected team leader. The fact is that the teams have not been able to maintain the technical progress that is necessary, and you have been running yourself ragged in trying to put out fires. The division general manager has insisted that you install some general foremen to supervise the groups. You and Ed reluctantly realize that the teams do need some kind of leadership, but you refuse to call them foremen, general foreman, or supervisors. Instead, you call them coordinators.

The coordinators have been selected, and you are about to have your first meeting with them. They will want to know about their responsibility and authority and what you expect them to do. What will you tell them?

TEAM LEADERSHIP: ROLES AND STRUCTURES

Before we consider the behavior of team leaders, we should first consider the structure of team leadership: how the leader is appointed (and, perhaps, unappointed), whether the team leader is a member or co-performer of the team, and the degree of formal authority that is vested to the leader versus the team itself.

As part of this discussion, we also raise the philosophical issue of whether formal leaders are really necessary. After all, if teams are really to be self-managed, then do they need a leader? Occasionally one hears the term *leaderless teams*, which usually means that a team does not have an appointed leader. This is somewhat of a paradox, because, in reality, no team—at least no effective team—is ever truly leaderless. Some form of leadership is always necessary for a team to function (for example, team member self-leadership will exist within the team). In the absence of some form of formal external leadership, then at least some degree of emergent leadership will always be present. Thus, so-called leaderless teams really do have leadership, but it typically is exercised by leaders who emerge into a position of leadership without being assigned this role by upper management.

No team is every truly leaderless.

In general, we are not in favor of trying to create leaderless teams. Most of the time, particularly in organizations, some type of recognized leadership should be established, especially at the inception of the team. However, a team leader certainly need not be a traditional Strongman, and a high degree of empowerment of the team itself rather than primarily relying on the leader is typically most effective over the long run.

Among the various structural alternatives through which team leadership can be expressed, the most common and well known is the traditional external supervisor or foreperson. This person, typically appointed by management, has traditional powers that stem from the position itself—usually, the authority to make job assignments, give instructions and commands, and allocate some rewards and reprimands. Control over the team's activities is mainly vested in this appointed leader rather than the team itself. We think of this person as a boss. Usually this person is not a team member and is at least one step removed from carrying out the work tasks.

Interestingly, a natural pattern of leadership of an external appointed leader is often to act as a Strongman leader who directs and commands compliance from the team. Other leadership options, however, are more appropriate. Indeed, even within a traditional system, a supervisor might voluntarily choose to act as a SuperLeader and encourage considerable self-leadership-based empowerment in the group. The main point, however, is that often situations are structured via an external leader appointed by management, who retains a high degree of control and decision making that is typical of a formal appointed position.

Other types of structures are possible. For example, leadership maybe expressed through an appointed external leader, often called a facilitator (or coordinator, counselor, or coach) who is purposefully intended to facilitate empowered workers. A facilitator is usually not part of the team; he or she does not carry out team tasks, but rather offers advice and counsel on how the team itself might perform their duties. A facilitator is usually appointed by management, similar to a supervisor, but the expected behavior or role of the facilitator is quite different. Whereas a supervisor retains a high degree of control and decision making, a facilitator typically attempts to encourage a team to undertake self-control activities such as self–job assignments or self–goal setting. In other words, the expected role and pattern of leadership of an external facilitator is to assist a team to become empowered.

The actual behaviors of this role might vary from person to person; however, generally, the role of an external facilitator is consistent with SuperLeader-type behaviors that facilitate and influence team members and the team itself to act more as self-leaders. Strongman-type behaviors are quite incompatible with this facilitator role.

The expected role of a facilitator is to assist a team to become empowered—that is, to lead itself.

An internal elected team leader is another type of structure that might be utilized for team leadership. This type of leader is usually a team member and engages in most of the typical day-to-day activities of the team in addition to carrying out leadership responsibilities. This leader frequently comes to the position as a result of some type of team election (or even team leader rotation) and thus might be considered more of an emergent leader. Of course, if there is an election of the team leader, there must be some method of replacement to deal with turnover of the leadership role. This might be accomplished by invoking a specified term of office, at the end of which the leader may or may not be reelected. Other mechanisms might include a runoff to choose between alternate candidates or a vote of confidence in which a leader might be unelected or deposed. (We have found this to be quite unusual. Typically, an elected team leader in difficulty with the team will voluntarily step down before an "unelection" is necessary.)

A fellow worker who is also a team leader will have advantages and obstacles in terms of group norms, interpersonal relationships, and so forth that are not shared by external team leaders. For example, within-team leaders may be in a better position to contribute to the social well-being (group maintenance) of the group but may face difficulties in emphasizing task performance because of personal relationships with other members.

We think of an elected team leader as being empowered from below. That is, this elected leader acts to organize, motivate, and influence the team, but the power and authority to do so come from the very people the leader is attempting to influence. Note that the team itself may have been empowered from above to carry out this and other self-management responsibilities.

An elected team leader is "empowered from below"; the team itself may have been "empowered from above."

Clearly the leader behaviors of an elected team leader are most consistent with the philosophy of a SuperLeader—that is, a leader who attempts to influence the team to lead itself. Conversely, Strongman behaviors tend to be highly incompatible with the role of elected team leader. An elected leader who behaves as a Strongman is likely to incite a rebellion among team members.

To summarize, at least three types of structures might be possible to express team leadership:

- Foreman or supervisor
- Appointed external facilitator
- Elected internal team leader

These structures provide considerable variance in terms of direct control that is vested in the team itself versus direct control retained by management. In the case of the traditional foreperson or supervisor, virtually all control is retained by management, since most of the power is vested in the supervisor, who represents management. At the other end of the spectrum, a great deal of control is vested in the team itself, which "delegates upward" to the elected team leader.

The appointed external facilitator is a role that is somewhere in between in terms of empowerment, with the philosophy and practice typically moving in the direction of greater team control. A facilitator attempts to move more control into the hands of the team, although in reality, management retains a great deal of control through the power to appoint or remove the facilitator.

In our own experience, we have seen all of these structural forms at one time or another. The traditional supervisor is the usual baseline or beginning point and remains the most common structural form of leadership of work groups in the United States today. Nevertheless, we have seen many successful teams that use the elected team leader concept. We believe, for a team to be fully and truly empowered, team members should have a significant role in deciding who the team leader should be. However, the use of external facilitators and coordinators is probably the most frequent approach to team empowerment and can work very well, especially in a transition mode. Also, we have found the use of external facilitators to be most common when management has lingering doubts, or is not 100 percent convinced about team empowerment.

For a team to be truly empowered, team members should have a significant part in selecting the team leader.

Although the behavior of leaders is correlated with the structure of the leadership position, structure and behavior are not necessarily the same. For example, a supervisor has a wide range of leadership patterns to follow, from Strongman to SuperLeader. Facilitators are more likely to behave as SuperLeaders, although we have seen a few who have difficulty in refraining from giving orders and instructions. Also, we would clearly expect elected team leaders to act more like SuperLeaders or face considerable displeasure from their constituency.

Finally, consider once more the notion of leaderless groups. Again, we don't believe there are any truly leaderless groups in formal organizations. Leadership always exists, and the question is how leadership is structured and how leaders behave. The effectiveness of any work group or team is highly dependent on how the leadership function is designed. We recommend almost any other alternative rather than a "leaderless" group.

BEHAVIORS OF TEAM LEADERS

The role of an external formal leader establishes an apparent paradox or conceptual inconsistency relative to the ideal concept of self-managing teams. The leader is charged with the responsibility of leading teams that are philosophically designed to be self-led. How can they lead when the team is supposed to lead itself? What is the appropriate role and behaviors for these leaders? Why should such a leader be necessary?

In the organizational hierarchy, this external leader—facilitator or coordinator—has replaced roles typically referred to as foreman, general foreman, or supervisor. However, under a self-managing concept, the nature of the authority and responsibility of the leader can become an issue of considerable confusion. To what extent should the leader give direction and evaluate performance yet be a facilitator and communicator? To what degree should he or she directly invoke authority? What are the behaviors that differentiate effective from ineffective facilitators? These questions become particularly challenging when one considers the ideal: that these work teams are supposed to be self-managing. The question, "How does one lead employees who are supposed to lead themselves?" establishes a paradox and exemplifies this dilemma.

The leader is charged with the responsibility of leading teams that are supposed to be self-led— an apparent paradox.

In our own research about self-managing teams, we have found widespread ambiguity and confusion about the role of appointed external leaders. We believe this issue is commonly a very troublesome point of implementation. While executives and workers who have direct experience with self-managing teams are generally pleased with the results, questions about the role of the external leader continue to be particularly bothersome. For managers who must select, train, counsel, and evaluate these external leaders, the questions are not ones of leisurely theory but of immediate pragmatic application.

Consider the case of the coordinators at the Fitzgerald Battery Plant. The coordinator behaviors presented in the following are clearly consistent with our definition of SuperLeadership.

WHAT DO COORDINATORS DO?

In part of our early research on self-managing teams, we investigated team leadership at a manufacturing site with mature self-managing teams. In this section, we describe the results of this elicitation, which was conducted at the Fitzgerald Battery Plant of General Motors Corporation.* The particular role that was the target of this elicitation were the coordinators, or external team leaders. Frequently, these roles are called "facilitators," or "coaches."

What do coordinators do? What are the behaviors and actions of effective coordinators? If employee work teams are supposed to be participative, or self-managed, then why are coordinators necessary? There are no formal guidelines regarding what a coordinator actually does, and coordinator behaviors seem to be loosely defined according to social convention rather than according to any structured set of rules and regulations. There is no job description. At the time of our research, the ambiguities about this position were unresolved.

The inquiry was intended to answer the question: "What important behaviors can coordinators use in their work?" We first asked this question of upper plant management, using a focus group technique. A summary of their answers follows, with the behaviors listed in order of importance."

Coordinator Behaviors Identified by Top Management

Try to get a team to solve a problem on its own.

Facilitate a team's solving conflict within its group.

Tell people—teams and individuals—when they do something well.

Tell the truth even when it may be disagreeable or painful.

---

*See C. C. Manz and Henry P. Sims, Jr., *Business Without Bosses: How Self-Managing Teams Are Building High-Performing Companies* (New York: Wiley, 1993), chap. 2.

Encourage team members to discuss problems openly.

Ask for a solution to a problem rather than proposing (or telling) a solution. People promote what they create.

Encourage teams to set performance goals (e.g., scrap rates, efficiency, QC index, safety).

Provide teams with information they need to run the business.

Anticipate future problems or situations (planning).

Encourage team self-evaluation.

Train teams in the philosophy of the plant.

Be a resource to a team.

The list provides some interesting insights. First, several of the behaviors, including the behavior obtaining the highest importance ratings, reveal an emphasis on getting teams to manage their own efforts: "Try to get a team to solve a problem on its own," "Ask for a solution to a problem rather than proposing (or telling)," and "Encourage teams to set performance goals."

Another major theme is a focus on communication—for example, "Tell people when they do something well," "Tell the truth even when it may be disagreeable," and "Encourage team members to discuss problems openly."

Coordinators would often purposely avoid providing direction to employees even when they knew what should be done.

Finally, several behaviors indicated the role of the coordinator as a facilitator rather than a director. This perspective was indicated in such descriptions of behaviors as, "Facilitate a team's solving conflict within its group," "Be a resource to a team," and "Provide teams with information they need to run the business."

We also asked the same question of internal elected team leaders. A summary of their answers is presented below. Team leaders also seemed to place especially high importance on the facilitation role as opposed to a directive role of coordinators. Two of the top three ranked behaviors support this interpretation: "Ask for solutions to problems" and "Be a resource to a team." Examples of other suggested behaviors indicating the importance placed on the facilitator role of coordinators by team leaders are, "Get tools, supplies, and materials (for a team)" and "Provide information (to teams) to solve its problems."

Coordinator Behaviors Identified by the Team Leaders

Ask for solutions to problems.

Be a resource to a team concerning both technical and personnel problems.

Create an atmosphere of mutual trust and understanding between the coordinator and the team and within the team.

Honestly say the same thing whether you are there or not; provide honest feedback.

Communicate production schedule changes to teams.

Arrange problem solving and present solutions.

Get tooling, supplies, and materials for a team.

Provide backing and communication to the team leader (that is, a within-group team leader who is also a team member).

Learn details about team operations.

Provide information to teams to solve their problems.

Help with team-to-team problem solving concerning quality control.

Try to get the team to set performance goals.

Recheck the production schedule and inventory.

Help in the maintenance of equipment (e.g., getting parts, needed personnel).

Provide support of team leader to the support group (upper management).

Communicate a problem of one team to another team that can help.

Keeps abreast of new machines and processes.

Encourage a team to solve its own problems.

Promote good communication between coordinators to coordinate efforts throughout the plant.

Keep the team leader in the chain of communication.

Encourage a team to evaluate itself.

These results also emphasize the importance of facilitation behavior and the team's apparent dislike of external direction. Views obtained from team members through discussion and observations (including those of team leaders) indicated that they often wished to be left to do their work on their own and solve their own problems. In fact, a general view understood in the plant was that teams resented overly directive coordinator behavior (e.g., a coordinator's giving orders to a team regarding solutions to problems). This view was reinforced by conversations with members of the support group, as well as several coordinators.

At the other end of the spectrum, team leader views and ratings revealed a dislike for some situations in which teams are left totally on their own to solve problems. Some team members expressed frustration and dissatisfaction with difficult situations in which a coordinator provided what they believed was inadequate direction.

It's important for a coordinator to be there, but not with a heavy hand.

We concluded that there is a fine line between overdirection and underdirection on the part of coordinators. While team members placed a high value on independence to manage themselves, they also wanted guidance and assistance when needed. It's important for a coordinator to be there, but not with a heavy hand. Consequently, coordinators must make a decision regarding the appropriate level of involvement based on the nature of each situation.

Overall, these results show a strong similarity with the notion of SuperLeadership: leading others to lead themselves. Most of all, both sources of data emphasize the potential of unleashing the power of team self-leadership.

THE TRANSITION: GETTING TO TEAM LEADERSHIP

Let's say that an organization wishes to implement some form of self-managed or empowered work team—for example, blue-collar manufacturing self-managing teams, white-collar office worker teams, or, cross-functional professional product improvement teams. Whatever the type of team, the transition to teams should always begin with three questions:

1. Where are we now in terms of team capability and team leadership?
2. Where do we want to get to in terms of team capability and team leadership?
3. How long do we want this transition to take?

Typically an organization begins with one of two situations: a new *start-up* (sometimes called a *greenfield*) or a *redesign* of an existing organization (sometimes called a *retrofit* or a *brownfield*). In a start-up, the organization begins with essentially a blank slate, with no existing personnel or organization. Conversely, in a redesign, an organization is in existence, with personnel in place, some of them with considerable seniority and experience. In actual practice, these situations share many issues that must be considered and dealt with as a part of the transition. Let us begin with a start-up situation, and we will later extend these ideas to a redesign situation.

Developing Team Leadership in a Start-up Situation

Typically, a start-up is the creation of a new organization. We will assume that this organization has already developed several important elements, such as a mission, strategy, physical location, logistics, a human resources system (including selection of new personnel), a production or service delivery system and a marketing system. In addition, we will assume that the organization has made a decision to implement an empowered team organization, where the organization structure will largely consist of small groups of employees who are empowered to carryout many of the day-to-day responsibilities associated with their job duties and responsibilities. The issue here is concerned with the design of the leadership of these teams. What kind of leadership do we want? How can we get there?

Actually, we are faced with a rather daunting task. We can select and assemble groups of employees into teams that have logically defined boundaries and at least some initial idea of what their team responsibilities should be. Should we appoint a supervisor or team leader? Should we require the team to elect a team leader?

Also, the question of technical development is important. That is, the employees need to learn the technical or task performance aspects of the particular process or service they perform. Who will teach these task performance skills to new employees? Consider the case of the lead technicians at the Lake Superior Paper Plant, who played a key role in that plant's start-up. When forming the original self-managing teams, Lake Superior decided to "seed" each team with lead technicians who had previous experience with papermaking technology. The main function of these lead technicians was to teach the process to other employees during the plant start-up. According to reports, this start-up was one of the smoothest ever experienced in the papermaking industry.

In the beginning, there is no formal leadership and typically very little informal leadership, so management must do something to create this initial form of leadership. At this stage, we recommend that a team leader be appointed by management to a defined term of service—perhaps six months or a year (but no longer than a year).

At the beginning, teams need informed external leadership. Later, they must be weaned of this dependency on external leaders and look to their own team self-leadership.

At first, this appointed leader frequently needs to behave in ways that are similar to a traditional supervisor. For example, most employees will not be fully trained in the tasks that are necessary to carry out their work, and they are likely to have little or no experience at group self-leadership. They will probably be used to having others tell them what to do. Their lack of technical experience means that they will likely be highly dependent on their appointed leader in this early stage, but soon the team must be weaned of this dependency. Step by step, they must be introduced to team self-leadership. Concurrently, the role and the behavior of the leader must change. At first, the leader provides a significant amount of task instruction, assigned goals, and direct reinforcement for task accomplishment. But then gradually, team members must learn to lead themselves. Now the leader becomes more concerned with stimulating and reinforcing team self leadership instead of dealing with work behavior and team performance. For example, the team leader might encourage a team to define its own goals.

From a process viewpoint, a leader can model the specific self-management strategies, provide encouragement and guidance for teams to use them, and offer reinforcement when they are used. A leader could facilitate the use of team goal setting, for example, by displaying it in his or her own behavior, providing guidance (e.g., suggesting that specific and challenging goals are especially effective), asking for and encouraging the team to begin using self-goal setting, and then praising team members when goal-setting behavior is observed.

Over time, the focus of goal setting and administration of consequences will logically and significantly change. The team leader becomes more concerned with stimulating and reinforcing self-managing behavior than dealing directly with work behavior and performance. For example, eventually the team leader will want to facilitate the team in defining its own goals. There may also be occasions of blatant worker misconduct, which necessitate the use of punishment, but we have observed team self-discipline to be a most effective alternative in our own research—a process we suspect a leader would be wise to encourage at a reasonable level. The point is that the leader's primary task becomes helping the team to manage itself. External modes of influence should mainly be devoted to developing team self-management capabilities, especially in the early team development stages, and also in providing guidance needed when team self-management breaks down.

The team leader becomes more concerned with stimulating self-leadership rather than dealing directly with work performance.

The culture that surrounds team leadership is critical to success, especially in the early stages. The culture must reward leaders for team development rather than short-term performance. A focus on short-term performance is dysfunctional because team implementation is sometimes accompanied by an initial temporary drop in performance. Leaders who are rewarded solely for performance will abandon their patient development of team self-leadership and instead return to older supervisory behaviors of instruction and command. Short-term productivity is always a matter of concern, but it should not overwhelm the objective of developing team self-leadership capabilities for the long term.

Developing Team Leadership in a Redesign Situation

The term *redesign* typically means converting an existing organization from a traditional to a team system. In redesign, a critical question arises in terms of the role of existing supervisors. Can supervisors who have been trained to command and direct change their behavior to team leader behaviors?

According to Kim Fisher, who has extensive experience with conversion to teams at Procter & Gamble, many supervisors become extremely frustrated when asked to convert from a supervisory role to a team leader role. He finds four common reasons for difficulty in the supervisor transition:

1. It is frequently seen as a net loss of power or status.
2. The team leader role has not been well defined for them.
3. Some are concerned that they will lose their jobs as a result of the transition to teams.
4. Many supervisors are asked to manage in a way that is quite different from the way they are managed themselves.[1]

We have encountered similar situations in our own experience. One supervisor in the midst of a transition to a team organization stated, "The atmosphere rewards a high profile [by leaders] and getting personally involved in everything, not in recognizing people who support others."

Some are not very confident about the potential to convert supervisors to facilitators. Fisher quotes John Homan, a previous plant manager of one of the A.E. Staley team plants: "Can all supervisors be successful in the 'new' system, even with extensive training? My assessment right now is no. I have seen too many examples of people who would not or could not change."[2] At the Texas Instruments Malaysia plant, A. Subramaniam (usually called "Subra") recounts how one manager could not make the transition to teams. According to Subra, this manager "completely dominated his team, with his self-centeredness. He never was able to adapt to the give-and-take of the team system and the sharing of authority. He wanted to make all the decisions himself." Eventually he left the organization. "From a technical viewpoint, we regretted his loss," says Subra. "He was excellent at the technical side, but he was never able to accept the team system. I've talked to him recently, and he's much happier in a traditional management setting."

In the end, however, Fisher is upbeat. He concludes that these issues are mainly those of transition, and the problems seem to solve themselves once the supervisors are truly in the new role of team leader.

We do not believe that every supervisor can successfully make this transition (at least not in a reasonable time frame). However, we know of no reliable way of predicting who will make it and who will not. We have seen the most intense bull-of-the-woods foreman become the most passionate advocate of the team system. We believe that every supervisor deserves a chance to change, and most of all, they should be given the training and modeling necessary to make the transition. But in the end, some will not succeed. Even those who do successfully make the transition are aware of the challenge. Consider the following comments from former supervisors at IDS Corporation who undertook the transition to team facilitator:[3]

> In the traditional system it was clear that I had the final word, and right now it is not clear. That's different. Another thing that's different is that we have changed the tasks. It's one thing to be self-managing in your old room and doing the same function, but now we've put together 20 other types of jobs that we didn't know anything about, so instead of having one set of goals and objectives, we've got a variety of them.

> It's frustrating because you feel like you should be knowing it, but you don't, and yet we know it's unrealistic for us to think at this point that we can know everything. We make it a learning experience, and it takes a lot of time to do that.

> The thing I've been struggling with is that there's nothing to call my own. Eventually, if they're truly self-managing, it's going to be the team that gets most of the recognition. Now, I get more satisfaction out of helping someone to do something on their own rather than telling them to do it.

In the traditional structure of supervision, you'd have goals and objectives; it was laid out. I always felt I knew what part of the path I was traveling on. Here as a team facilitator, so far I haven't felt that clarified yet, so I don't quite know where we're going.

The reorganization of the task and the structure of the task are one dimension, and the management style or the division of authority is a different dimension.

SUMMARY

When contrasting a traditional organization with a team organization, leadership roles are the most critical element that changes. The main purpose of the team leader is to create a positive atmosphere for exercising team self-management by stimulating the use of the self-leadership strategies we have presented in earlier chapters. Some of the particularly important elements in this role are that the evaluative and reinforcement functions are gradually shifted from external sources to the work team itself, the progress made in a team's self-leadership behavior is encouraged, and increased emphasis is placed on the goals and expectations of team members themselves rather than external sources (e.g., external leaders).

As the leader shifts to this supportive and facilitating perspective, changes will take place in team member motivation, satisfaction, effort, flexibility of response and, ultimately, performance. Most important, this provides a process by which external leaders can develop and enhance the team self-management. Team leadership can create a foundation for true empowerment. Consider the following quotation from an IDS supervisor who was successful in making the change to facilitator: "Weekly, we just feel more and more comfortable with it. The pilot team is working. They're getting work done. Things are going fine. I'm delighted. I think that it's going to make jobs a lot more interesting for people. There will be a lot more buy-in to decisions if it's a group decision than if it's mine."

BUILDING A SELF-LEADERSHIP CULTURE

Transition to a Culture of Heroes

A journey of a thousand miles begins with a single step, and each of us begins our journey to self-leadership by first focusing on ourself. A company of heroes begins with each person's attending to his or her personal self-leadership. As a next step, we can extend the self-leadership culture by serving as a SuperLeader to other individuals in our organization. The most immediate targets are our own followers.

> **A company of heroes begins with each person's attending to his or her personal self-leadership.**

We then continue the quest to develop self-leadership through the implementation of teams. Now the entire group becomes the target of self-leadership development. Teams and individuals, however, cannot maximize their self-leadership without the support of the larger organizational culture. Self-leadership is optimized only if everyone views self-leadership as the norm for the organization. We call this type of organization a *self-leading organization*. We call the process for getting there *creating a company of heroes*.

Teams and individuals cannot maximize their self-leadership without the support of the larger organizational culture.

In this chapter, we focus on the difficult challenge of leading the transformation of an entire organization to an empowered high-performance system—that is, creating a company of heroes. The fundamental goal that we address is how to create an organization in which empowered self-leaders are the norm, not the exception, and self-leadership becomes the core of a self-sustaining system of empowerment and high performance. The primary goal is to develop an organization at the cutting edge of competitiveness. We see competitiveness as going hand in hand with flat organizations, high-performance norms, and empowered employees—capable self-leaders who are at home working in a team environment.

So how does an organization get from here (a so-called traditional hierarchical organization) to there (a self-leading organization)? Before we tackle this question, it is critical to understand two concepts: culture and deliberate organizational change.

WHAT IS ORGANIZATIONAL CULTURE?

What is culture? Anne Jorden, an organizational anthropologist, defines culture as shared patterns of ideas, behaviors, and artifacts that are characteristic of a society.[1] Culture identifies behaviors and ideas that are unique to a particular human group and distinguish it from other groups. There is individual deviance from cultural norms, and groups within an organization may have subcultures. Nevertheless, members of an organization develop a shared sense of appropriate behaviors and thoughts that are appropriate and characteristic of that organization. These patterns are integrated into the fabric of that organizational society.

The culture of one company can be radically different from the culture of another.

All of us understand intuitively that the culture of one company can be radically different from the culture of another. Certainly the culture of General Motors of the 1960s would be quite different from the culture of Apple Computer in the early 1980s. Differences between organizational cultures can become even more pronounced as we cross national borders. Consider the story of ABB, a European corporation, and the reflections about differences between American perspectives and views overseas gained from an interview with one of its top Swedish executives.

ABB: AN INTERNATIONAL CULTURE OF EMPOWERED HIGH PERFORMANCE

In 1990 ABB (Asea Brown Boveri) of Sweden launched a continuous improvement program dubbed T50. This effort was designed to create flexible work operations that will continue to develop and improve, even when performance is already strong. This continuous improvement strategy combines cycle time reduction (the original objective was 50 percent—hence the label T50), employee competence development, and decentralization, all centered on an overriding customer focus. The central themes of this effort that are emphasized are total cycle time, competence development, and decentralization.

An example of this change is the new work design in the unit that assembles electrical push buttons. This unit had experienced a variety of problems, including unreliable delivery times, high turnover and absenteeism, and employee boredom and burnout. Once the pilot T50 program had been put in place, results improved dramatically. The essence of the program entailed high employee involvement in a team setting. Order cycle time plummeted from 12 days to 1, rejects fell from 15 percent to 1 percent, on-time delivery soared from 10 percent to 98 percent, turnover fell from 39 percent to 0 percent, and absenteeism dropped from 14 percent to 8 percent. Overall productivity increased 15 percent. Moreover, the control unit has experienced continued improvement.

With a concrete success model to draw upon, ABB has continued to roll out the T50 program throughout its Swedish operations and has also begun a change in its international operations.

In a recent visit to Sweden, Charles Manz had an opportunity to visit one of ABB's Swedish operations (ABB Flakt Industri) and to interview division president Anders Wahrolen, who has been extensively involved with the T50 program. During the interview his comments focused primarily on total systems issues. He considered employee empowerment as a fundamental key to the process and thought it was just common sense to involve teams of employees if high performance was desired. At ABB, the supervisor-to-worker ratio had changed from 1 to 7 to 1 to 50.

Every employee is required to develop a personal development plan as part of the company's commitment to individual employee competency. In addition, training is matched to each person's identified developmental areas in his or her plan. Wahrolen also indicated that there was hard negotiating over goals or benchmarks in the company and emphasized that all levels need to have significant input into their own goals.

Employee empowerment is the fundamental key to - cultural transition.

Wahrolen acknowledged the importance of recognizing cultural differences in any work design application. He noted in particular his perception of significant differences between how Americans seem to view the results of new organizational designs versus Swedes. At international conferences he frequently found that American accounts of the success of new organizational designs seemed to be "overly optimistic." He believes Swedes take a "more humble" stance, tending to describe their results as not being as good as they really are. It was apparent from his low-key demeanor that he was no exception to this observation. He described the impressive results of the T50 program in a factual, nonemotional tone and was conservative about what ABB has accomplished through empowered and ever increasingly competent people. The impressive results of this model, however, speak loud and clear. ABB has clearly made a significant transition toward creating a company of heroes.

Although culture can be described in many different ways, one essential defining characteristic of most business cultures is the degree of empowerment of so-called ordinary employees. Are they disenfranchised, or are they integral decision makers? We believe the essence of empowerment is self-leadership. Empowered employees are employees who have a well-developed self-leadership capacity. Furthermore, a self-leadership culture is one in which the normal expectation of all employees is to be effective self-leaders. Again, we call this a self-leading organization. Also, self-leadership behaviors are derived from the overall leadership norms of an organization. Organizational leadership tends to fit a pattern, with new members learning appropriate leadership behaviors from older members of higher status.

Of course, culture fundamentally derives from the basic values of an organization. Consider AES Corporation, whose leaders have carefully defined a set of core values that are closely held throughout the organization. We like to think that some organizations, such as AES Corporation, can be characterized as a strong self-leadership culture. In our opinion, the core values of AES closely resemble our notions of a self-leading organization.

ORGANIZATIONAL STRATEGY THROUGH SHARED CULTURAL VALUES: AES CORPORATION

Kenneth A. Smith and Henry P. Sims, Jr.

This is a story of how shared cultural values are used as a critical element in carrying out an entrepreneurial business strategy. These shared values define the company's culture and contribute to the teamlike atmosphere that permeates AES Corporation. Indeed, these shared values are major drivers of the entrepreneurial spirit of this company and are a critical element in building a self-leading organization.*

AES Corporation: The Company

AES Corporation, formerly called Applied Energy Services, is an independent power producer that develops, owns, and operates electric power plants that sell electricity to utility companies. It was cofounded as a privately held corporation in 1981 by Roger W. Sant (chairman of the board) and Dennis W. Bakke (president and chief executive officer). AES was an early entrant to the independent power generation market and today is one of the largest independent power producers.

AES's stated mission is to help meet the need for electricity by offering a supply of clean, safe, and reliable power. The company has pursued this objective by creating a portfolio of independent power plants. Since 1983, the company has developed, constructed, and is now operating ten plants, with approximately eight other facilities under construction or development. Pursuing a strategy of operating excellence, AES has established high standards of operation and has been a leader in environmental matters associated with independent power production and in plant reliability. In more recent years, AES has also become an important international power producer, with projects in several non-U.S. countries.

By 1994, AES was generating over $500 million in revenues on approximately $2 billion in total assets. In July 1991, it went public by selling

---

*Most of the quotations in this story are from on-site interviews conducted between 1990 and 1992. We are especially thankful to Dennis Bakke, who facilitated the project, and the AES employees for their special cooperation.

approximately 10 percent of the company in an initial public offering. The company has been ranked on *Fortune*'s list of America's 100 fastest-growing companies.[†]

Core Values as a Strategic Driver: Articulating the Culture

An important underlying framework for AES's strategy is its four core or "shared" values:

- To act with integrity
- To be fair
- To have fun
- To be socially responsible

These values emerged over time, mainly from the founders and officers, and have now been articulated to the degree that they were written and published as part of the prospectus for the initial stock offering.[‡] Dennis Bakke describes the corporation as a "learning organization, constantly forcing people to redo things." Strategic flexibility has been characteristic of AES, but the four shared values stay constant. Says Bakke, "The only thing that we hold tightly as to what has to be done are the four values." As a result, the values permeate AES and serve to unify the company as it pursues its objectives. The core values also foster a strong team spirit and philosophy of self-leadership.

Core values are the philosophical driver of the culture of self-leadership at AES.

Bakke describes *integrity* as fitting "together as a whole . . . wholeness, completeness." In practice, this means that the things that AES people say and do in all parts of the company should fit together with truth and consistency. "The main thing we do is ask the question, 'What did we commit?'" At AES, the senior representative at any meeting can commit the company, knowing that the team will back him or her up.

Fairness is the desire of AES to treat fairly its employees, customers, suppliers, stockholders, and the governments of and communities in which it operates. Defining what is fair is often difficult, but the main point is that the company believes it is helpful to question routinely the relative

---

[†]AES Corporation, Prospectus, June 1991; AES, *Annual Report,* 1991, 1994.
[‡]AES Corporation, Prospectus, p. 22.

fairness of alternative courses of action. This may mean that AES does not necessarily get the most out of each negotiation or transaction to the detriment of others. Bakke asks, "Would I feel as good on the other side of the table as I feel on this side of the table on the outcome of this meeting or this decision with my employee or supervisor or customer?"

Bakke also says, "If it isn't fun, we don't want [it] . . . . We either want to quit or change something that we're doing." Sant agrees: "It just isn't worth doing unless you're having a great time." Thus, *fun* is the third value. AES wants the people it employs and those with whom the company interacts to have fun in their work. "By fun we don't mean party fun," Bakke elaborates. "We're talking about creating an environment where people can use their gifts and skills productively, to help meet a need in society, and thereby enjoy the time spent at AES."

The fourth value is *social responsibility*. "We see ourselves as a citizen of the world," says Bakke. This value presumes that AES has a responsibility to be involved in projects that provide social benefits, such as lower costs to customers, a high degree of safety and reliability, increased employment, and a cleaner environment. "We try to do things that you'd like your neighbor to do."

"By fun, we mean crating an environment where people can use their gifts and skills in a productive way."

One might question whether a commitment to these shared values might be detrimental to profits or to the value to the shareholders. This is how Bakke responds: "We have specifically said that [maximized profit] is not our objective." In fact, the company stated in its prospectus, "Earning a fair profit is an important result of providing a quality product to [our] customers. However, when a perceived conflict has arisen between these values and profits, the company has tried to adhere to its values— even though doing so might result in diminished profits or foregone opportunities. The company seeks to adhere to these values, not as a means to achieve economic success, but because adherence is a worthwhile goal in and of itself."

AES's shared values contribute to the spirit of self-leadership that pervades the company. First, the content of the values encourages its personnel to think of themselves not as individuals but rather as members of the AES team. Integrity stresses the need for individuals to fulfill commitments: their own and those made by the company. Fairness generates sensitivity to the positions and perspectives of others, both inside and outside the company. Fun, as defined at AES, results from using one's abilities to contribute to the effort of the whole. Social responsibility stresses being aware of and serving the needs of others. Together, these values build an outward-looking orientation in the minds of AES personnel and foster a desire to work with others.

Second, the processes by which the values are implemented and evaluated contribute to AES's team orientation. For example, each manager gets rated every year on "values performance"—that is, how the manager performs in relation to the four shared values. According to Bakke, "We rate each other, fifty–fifty, on the basis of technical performance and values performance." More broadly, all AES employees are encouraged to challenge any and all others on how strategic and operating decisions reflect the core values. This fosters an air of mutual accountability and serves as a constant reminder that everyone is a member of the same team. Thus, the shared values contribute to a company-wide culture that is characterized by an unusually high degree of self-leadership.

Teams at the Plants: Operation Honeycomb

One of the more interesting ways that AES attempts to evoke employee psychological ownership is through the use of teams at the generating plants. As outsiders, we would call these structures self-managing teams or employee involvement teams, but AES uses the term *honeycomb*. Dennis Bakke described the evolution of Operation Honeycomb in this way:

> *Our plants were running wonderfully when we said, "This isn't really consistent with our values and the way we want people to operate and relate to each other." We need to make huge changes in the way we do operations if we're going to be consistent with our values. We did this massive change that came to be known as Operation Honeycomb. It's based on the premise that people will take responsibility and can be trusted. We didn't want arbitrary rules, detailed procedures manuals and handbooks, punch clocks, etc. We wanted a "learning organization," where people close to the action were constantly creating and recreating.*

After getting a green light, developing self-leadership at the plant became a bottom-up transition.

> *For example, I went down and asked, "What if you didn't have shift supervisors? What if you didn't have this manual that tells you everything to do?" Two months later, they totally revolutionized the place. We discovered these people are no different from the managers. They have the same motivations, the same concerns, and*

they like to care about people and about the company. Why were we treating them differently?

Then one of the plant people came up with, "Why don't we just divide up into teams?" The next thing I knew, the plant manager called me and said, "We got this all done. We've implemented it." They said, "We're going to call this stuff 'Honeycomb,'" and they had worked out all this symbolism regarding beehives and how all the bees were working together.

Now the plants do their own capital allocations. The plant managers decided to change the order of criteria for hiring. First, how well does this person fit with our shared values? Then, technical skill [is next]. They make almost every decision. They have the responsibility and authority to make every single decision in that plant. There are no exceptions that I know of.

Today, all of the AES generating plants are organized according to some form of self-managing teams. Since the process of change essentially is implemented bottom-up (although mandated top-down), the specific forms, labels, and language vary considerably from plant to plant. Further, the path leading to self-management has been quite different among the plants: some were changeovers of existing nonunion plants; one was a changeover of a union plant; and others have been implemented from the beginning at greenfield plant sites.

Most of all, the conversion to honeycomb-like teams has always been inspired and guided by the core values of the organization and always features a bottom-up process that displays great confidence in the employees to work out the details of implementation.

Self-Leadership Through Natural Teams

The term *team* is not widely used in everyday vocabulary at AES. Nevertheless, a sense of "teamness" pervades the company, embedded in the culture. Roger Naill articulated it best: "I don't think *team* is an AES word, in the sense that we don't go around calling ourselves teams." But the concept is clear. In addition to Project Honeycomb, AES obviously exhibits team characteristics in numerous ways and at many levels. We have identified a number of clearly distinguishable team structures within AES.

First is the core vision team. This group of three top executives serves together in a type of "office of the CEO" concept, sometimes exchanging roles and responsibilities. Next, each energy-generating plant acts as a team, especially when they undertake their annual formal strategic planning event. As a derivation, most plants also have "teams within the team," with subgroups of employees clustered into "cells" of a "honeycomb," who also act as a team on more of a day-to-day basis.

The new venture groups also act as teams, with different individuals serving different roles depending on the stage of development of a particular project. We call these "virtual" teams because of their unusual flexible structure and process. (See Chapter 18 for further details on AES's new venture teams.)

A strategic planning group also behaves like a team. In a supportive role, the group helps the corporation obtain the information necessary to behave as "informed opportunists." The members of the planning group give and take responsibility for gathering, analyzing, and reporting information. Finally, the operating committee acts as a team, especially as it goes about the annual strategic planning cycle and through the monthly meetings as it deals with strategic implementation.

The Advantages of AES Culture

This emergent team concept has contributed to the well-being of the company in a number of ways. First, self-leadership provides a unique stimulus to enhance the motivation, initiative, and self-responsibility of employees throughout the company. Indeed, the word *ownership* is most appropriate to describe how teams influence the psychological perspective of employees. We use the word *ownership* here in the psychological sense rather than the financial or legal sense, though the company has used stock options as a means of building ownership. That is, employees feel ownership in the company and especially in their own jobs. Roger Sant says that from the very beginning, they wanted "something that really makes people feel that they own us. Our instincts were that everybody likes to feel important." Ownership leads to strong motivation and sometimes exceptional effort to perform well. Thus, individual ownership contributes to organizational competitiveness. (We note with interest that many employees are also financial owners through a stock participation plan.)

Psychological ownership leads to strong motivation and exceptional effort to perform well.

In addition, a culture of self-leadership leads to a highly adaptive, nonrigid organizational structure. Job assignments and roles are not engraved in granite, and they sometimes change significantly as the situation demands. Assignments are not characterized by rigid boxes. The phrase "that's not my job" would be highly incompatible with the self-leadership philosophy at AES. In fact, contrary to most other companies, AES deliberately avoids drawing and publishing a formal organization chart. The use of teams provides an adaptive structure that can change quickly to meet the demands of an emerging situation or a shift in strategic implementation. In fact, the annual strategic planning cycle is seen mainly as a starting place; often, significant strategic changes will be undertaken with short notice.

Finally, teams contribute to high productivity and competitiveness. Bottom-line results speak for themselves. AES's energy-generating plants significantly exceed industry standards of availability—that is, the proportion of time that energy generation is on line. AES's plants typically operate at less than 50 percent of allowable emissions; safety statistics are consistently below industry averages; and the real cost per kilowatt hour of electricity produced has decreased over three years. Finally, the company as a whole has maintained a high degree of profitability consistently.

"We think it's too early to draw long-term conclusions concerning our 'experiment' with regard to these traditional measures of excellence," Bakke is quick to point out. "We are fairly bullish, however, regarding adherence to the values, especially the fun environment that has been created by the decentralized teams and other aspects of the corporate approach."

We suspect some would call AES a "high-involvement" organization, and we would certainly classify AES as a self-leadership and a SuperLeadership type of culture. AES emphasizes the importance of individual self-leadership and teamwork throughout the entire organization. The executives of this company do not see themselves as bosses, and they clearly attempt to design a total organization that represents the essence of business without bosses. Whatever the label, AES has found a way to make self-leadership an essential ingredient of entrepreneurial strategy that creates a company of heroes.

ORGANIZATIONAL CHANGE

Organizational cultures are dynamic, and they change through various means. Sometimes the change is wanted and welcomed; sometimes it is deliberate, perhaps even planned; and at other times, the change is involuntary, unwelcome, and painful.

Executives who wish to change an existing culture deliberately need to identify desired new cultural patterns and to replace existing ideologies, symbols, and practices with new and different forms. From an organizational viewpoint, a transition to a SuperLeader culture inevitably requires that an old culture must die. Here, we focus on this transition from an organizational view and explore what is required to change a traditional organization to an empowered SuperLeader form of organization. To explore this question, we define three types of organizational change: incremental, greenfield, and retrofit.

Executives who wish to change need to find new cultural patterns.

Incremental (sometimes called "linear") change indicates an evolution over a period of time. For the most part, such change takes place in times of stability. Perhaps it would be nice if every organization could change through incremental means because it is less frustrating and stressful to all parties. Deliberate change to a self-leading culture through incremental methods is rare, although it can be done, and sometimes done effectively. Consider the story of Texas Instruments Malaysia, where change took place in a planned, relatively orderly manner over a decade.

TEXAS INSTRUMENTS MALAYSIA: CHANGE OVER THE LONG RUN

Alan B. Cheney

In today's breakneck global business environment, companies that survive accept change as a means of seeking new and better ways of doing business. *Kaizen*—continuous improvement—has become much more than the phrase du jour; today, it is the imperative for success.* An excellent example of the planned evolution of total quality management (TQM) into a system of team self-management is Texas Instruments Malaysia.

Texas Instruments Malaysia Sdn. Bhd. (TIM) is a wholly owned subsidiary of TI Incorporated, located near the capital city of Kuala Lumpur. It produces about 3 million high-volume semiconductor integrated circuits *per day,* many of which are shipped to companies in Japan, a mark of their high quality. Most of TIM's 2,600 employees are Malaysian nationals, drawn from the three major ethnic groups: Malay, Chinese, and Indian. Malaysia is one of the world's fastest-growing economies and is now the world's third largest producer of computer chips.

Over the years, managers at TI Malaysia have attempted to build a

---

*We thank the staff at Texas Instruments Malaysia, especially Jerry Lee, Mohd Asmid Abdulla, A. Subramaniam, and Gene Carlone. An earlier version of this story was published in Charles Manz and Henry C. Sims, Jr., *Business Without Bosses* (New York: Wiley, 1993).

flexible organization that is flatter and pushes decision making to lower levels in the organization. When the plant opened in 1972, the baseline, or originating structure of the plant, was the traditional functional-vertical hierarchy, characterized by separate and specialized planning, manufacturing, control, and facilities maintenance departments. As Malaysia's economy began to boom and industrialization grew, however, it became clear that TIM would one day face a labor shortage of educated and experienced professionals. At the same time, Malaysia and the rest of the world was being swept up in the total quality movement, with its emphasis on customer focus, continuous improvement, and employee involvement. By the early 1980s, TIM managers, including Jerry Lee, Mohd Azmi Abdulla, and A. Subramaniam, were searching for ways to blend the changing economy and demographics of Malaysia with an emphasis on the elements of total quality. They developed an evolutionary long-term plan that would meet their changing business needs.

The objective was to build a flexible organization that was flatter and pushed decision making to lower levels.

The plan called for the gradual and evolutionary phasing in of increasing levels of worker self-management through structural realignment, task redesign, and commensurate training and education. An early step was to create quality circles and quality improvement teams (QITS) in the managerial and engineering offices. These cross-functional teams were charged with finding ways to cut costs and improve quality. Later, following the example of management, workers were encouraged to form QITs and attack selected work-related problems.

Beginning in 1985, TIM managers began to put operator self-control into practice. Operators were given extensive training in the knowledge and skills needed to monitor their own work, look for and recognize variances in quality, and know how to respond to problems. To implement operator self-control, three requirements are necessary. The first, a *knowledge of what one is supposed to do,* was accomplished by expanding the job of each operator to include monitoring the quality of their work, known as "quality at the source." Now workers actively look for defects in their own work and in the work passed to them by others. They receive quality awareness training, and their job descriptions were changed to promote quality at the source.

The second point, the *ability to monitor one's own performance,* was accomplished through training that provided knowledge and skills in quality inspection and control. Line operators were taught statistical process control (SPC) techniques and other quality tools.

Workers would actively look for defects in their own work.

The third requirement, the *ability to regulate one's own activities through a decision-making process,* was taught through the use of Deming's PDCA (Plan-Do-Check-Act) cycle, the "Q.C. Story," and other frameworks for problem solving and decision making. Former quality control (QC) inspectors, now out of a job, became trainers for this task as the QC function was integrated into each operator's job.

After operators were taught the principles and tools of quality at the source, they were empowered with the authority to act on decisions. At TIM, operators may shut down the line when they find a defect; previously, only QC inspectors could do this.

In 1988, TIM moved into the pilot stages of self-managed teams. By mid-1992 about 85 percent of the manufacturing workforce were members of self-managed teams. Teams gradually began taking on routine activities formerly performed by supervisors, such as time cost allocation, setup, control of material usage, quality control, monitoring cycle time, safety, and line audits. TIM benchmarked several American and Japanese companies for ideas and methods and then adapted these to its own needs.

As self-management abilities grew, workers began to manage higher-level functions such as incorporating quality, cost, delivery, and service and monitoring customer satisfaction, all according to the original plan. Teams began to detect abnormalities and take corrective action, as well as make improvements in their work area using problem-solving techniques and QC tools. To accomplish this, each team member received about 50 hours of training in QC tools for problem solving, team building, daily management, analysis, capacity, communication, and other areas.

Workers began to manage higher-level functions such as incorporating quality, cost, delivery, and service and monitoring customer satisfaction.

As for the numbers, they are most impressive:

- TIM attributes a savings of U.S. $50 million in ten years to quality improvements alone.
- There is a significant positive change in attitude among employees, shown by annual attitude survey results that increase each year and are often the highest within TI worldwide.

- Thirty-five percent of TIM's production goes to Japanese customers, as opposed to none prior to 1985. Every major Japanese electronics company buys products from TIM, and several have exclaimed that quality at TIM rivals Deming Prize winners in Japan.
- As a result of putting operator self-control into practice, sustainable increases in yield and quality have been recorded.
- In 1989, TIM received Malaysia's Award for Manufacturing Excellence and International Standards Organization (ISO) 9002 certification.
- From 1980 to 1991, units shipped increased from 400 million to almost 1 billion per year, while the number of employees decreased from 2,500 to 2,000, showing a dramatic increase in output per person.
- The operator-to-supervisor ratio increased from 60 to 1 to 200 to 1, while the number of supervisor positions decreased from 79 to 18. The plan is to reduce supervisory positions even further.
- There have been demonstrable increases in cleanliness and machine up-time: the equipment mean time between failures has increased four times and downtime is only 25 percent of what it was in the past.
- Product cycle time has been cut in half.

The transition has been marked by patient but steady progress over a relatively lengthy period of 12 years. At no time was an overnight transformation from a vertical hierarchy to a flat, delayered, largely self-managed organization expected. The defining characteristic of the transition to an empowered organization was the unusual evolutionary nature of the change. The transition was *not* crisis driven. Most of all, the transition shows that self-leadership can be achieved by an orderly implementation of self-managing teams.

Changing to a SuperLeadership culture, however, is typically not linear. Transition involves a deliberate disturbance of the equilibrium and status quo and is a major event in the life of an organization. Most of the time, these events are drastic and intense, and, indeed, such change can be revolutionary and traumatic. Cultural change involves a disruptive break with the past and substantial changes in the way leaders lead others and the way employees lead themselves. We believe that the majority of today's organizations can be classified as Transactor types of leadership cultures, with the prevailing assumption about employee motivation based on the exchange principle: "We expect you to do a good job because you are paid to do that job." Rewards are the motivating driver of this organization. And, of course, a Transactor pattern of leadership is typically accomplished by a vertical hierarchical pyramid. One hears comments like this one; "If you pay your dues, you make your way up the corporate ladder."

TQM is an example of incremental change; moving to a team organization is definitely not incremental.

Many times, organizational leaders believe that they can change the organization in a meaningful way through evolution. We believe that the total quality management (TQM) movement in the United States is an example of attempts at incremental change. The tools and techniques of TQM are useful to a certain degree, but they do not constitute a cultural change. TQM involves incremental change, whereas moving to a team organization is definitely not incremental. Consider the following discussion of the difference between TQM and self-managing teams.

ARE SELF-MANAGING TEAMS AND TQM THE SAME THING?

Gregory Stewart

The airplane began its descent. Bill was excited to visit his best friend, Darin. They had been roommates in college and had not seen each other since graduation a year ago. Darin had taken a job with a West Coast manufacturer, while Bill stayed in the Northeast to work as an engineer. It had been a challenging year for Bill, but it was vacation time now, and he had decided to visit Darin.

As they left the airport, Bill and Darin began to reminisce about their college days. Their conversation turned to a discussion of Professor Wada's class. Bill said, "Yeah, I thought that class on TQM was really neat. But I'm not so sure now."

"What do you mean," asked Darin.

"Well, we have a TQM program where I work, and it just seems like a way for management to intrude more in what we do," replied Bill. Their conversation continued, and Bill was surprised to hear himself talking so negatively about his job. He decided to ask Darin if his company had a TQM program.

"Oh sure," said Darin. "We do focus on quality as a part of our

self-directing teams. In fact, my team just received an award for quality improvement. But we also consider other issues besides quality."

"But don't you feel constrained by all the technical requirements?" queried Bill.

"No, not really. Our team is empowered to make improvements, and TQM provides us with concrete tools to put them into practice," responded Darin.

Bill wondered if they were even talking about the same thing. He had been excited about TQM when he left college. It sounded like a great way to manage a business. Yet when he started his job, he often heard people complain about statistical process control, Pareto charts, and fishbone analyses. His boss even claimed that TQM held their department back and made it impossible to enact large-scale changes. Now Darin was sitting here telling him that TQM provided freedom. How could this be?

Bill listened attentively as Darin described how his team had won the award for quality improvement. This confirmed Bill's suspicion that they were talking about two different things. His organization had teams too, but they didn't seem to have nearly as much authority and responsibility as the teams in Darin's organization. Rather, his company used fairly traditional management practices to manage its employees, who were clustered into groups they called teams but in reality had little decision-making discretion. In fact, these so-called teams had very little real authority. Their TQM program ensured that the work was carefully monitored and done according to rigid, detailed specifications to avoid and correct work errors. As he talked with Darin, he concluded that Darin's teams seemed to be truly empowered.

Self-managing teams and total quality management (TQM) are two popular approaches to work design. TQM principles include the recommendation to use teams. Self-managing teams are often credited with improving quality. Both self-managing teams and TQM require line employees to do tasks traditionally performed by managers. However, these two approaches are potentially very different.

In its original form, TQM focused on eliminating variation in work processes. Managers using it clearly described the proper way to make goods and provide services. Conformance to rigid quality specifications was essential. Statistical analyses aided the identification and solution of problems. Inputs into the production process (e.g., labor and raw materials) were standardized. Employees monitored quality but did not have the authority to change how work was done. In sum, the beginnings of TQM were based on the idea that change is undesirable.

Recent advances in TQM focus more on the need to satisfy custom- ers. These updated practices acknowledge the importance of change; however, top-level managers normally retain control over work pro- cesses. Line employees provide information about quality improvement but are rarely given the power to make adjustments.

TQM encourages a standard way of doing things, while self-managing teams encourage change.

In contrast, organizations using self-managing teams encourage change because a "best" method of production does not exist. Teams have the discretion to alter work processes, and indeed, top-level man- agers encourage line employees to explore new ways of accomplishing work. Variations in how work is done are positive because they represent effort to adjust to changing conditions and increase flexible response capabilities.

TQM thus favors stability; self-managing teams encourage flexibility. Effective organizations need to balance these two forces. By combining elements of TQM with applications of self-managing teams, organiza- tions can develop dynamic quality improvement. This is achieved as teams (rather than the organization as a whole) use principles of TQM.

Self-managing teams encourage flexibility.

Teams within the organization are coordinated by a shared vision of quality improvement. Quality control techniques, such as statistical pro- cess control, help define areas where the output of one team can be improved to serve the needs of another team better. Autonomy of the team helps employees develop feelings of ownership for the work they do, while tracking of quality improvement helps them see ways they can better accomplish their work.

Many organizations use a mixture of self-managing teams and TQM concepts. Moreover, many authors and speakers fail to distinguish be- tween the two approaches. The fundamental assumptions underlying TQM and self-managing teams are, however, quite different.

We believe the real goal of a cultural transition to a company of heroes should be an organization in which SuperLeadership is the dominant form of leadership, and followers define themselves through effective self-leadership. The main objective of leaders is the creation of self-leaders throughout the organization. Establishing a company of heroic self-leaders is the overriding target.

This transition is arduous, complicated, and challenging and may not succeed. Further, this change sometimes happens in mysterious and spontaneous ways. A successful transition to SuperLeadership is typically instigated, deliberately and consciously, by the top executives of the firm. Indeed, usually at least one person is obsessed with creating a culture where self-leadership is the defining pattern of behavior. Sometimes, in an apparent contradiction, this person even uses authoritarian means to instigate the change to a self-leading organization.

The most straightforward transition to a self-leading organization is to begin from the bottom up with a brand-new organization—the so-called greenfield approach (taken from the notion of creating a new manufacturing plant entirely from the ground up at a site that is currently only a "green field"). Indeed, most of the early pioneer efforts of creating team-based manufacturing organizations were done at greenfield sites. The earlier story of the Fitzgerald plant is an example of self-managing teams that were initiated at a greenfield plant.

The main objective of change should be a transition in which SuperLeaders create self-leading followers.

These greenfield operations were extremely useful in the pioneering days of cultivating empowered organizations. They provided a venue for learning—learning how to do teams right and also learning from the mistakes that were made. One example is the New United Motors operation located in Fremont, California. This joint venture between General Motors and Toyota used a version of the team concept from the very beginning. In many ways this operation has been a stunning success, with high performance in quality and productivity. Indeed, the Fremont venture was a substantial learning opportunity for General Motors that led to the more famous Saturn operation, another greenfield operation.

But not every organization can afford the luxury of starting over. How many companies can fund a new startup? Usually the main challenge in the United States is converting existing organizations with so-called traditional designs into self-leading cultures—the retrofit type of organizational change. Indeed, most of the major organizational changes in the United States are retrofit transitions. In the next chapter, we relate the story of IDS Corporation and its interesting transition of office workers to a self-leading organization.

Some may think that a major organizational transition can be carried out in a relatively short period of time, but old ideas die hard. Our experience is that major cultural change can be initiated relatively quickly, but it takes years for these changes to permeate and transform the organizational culture.

RESISTANCE TO CHANGE

We have good news and bad news about the spread of self-leading organizations. The good news is that many organizations have begun the journey to self-leading organizations. The bad news is that only a small minority of employees have actually been touched by this new organizational form.

If the gains can be so substantial, why isn't it spreading faster? Why is there resistance to a change to a more empowering pattern of leadership? There are several philosophical and practical barriers to the ready acceptance of new leadership concepts. Many stem from discomfort with the unknown and general resistance to change.

The good news is that many organizations have begun the journey to empowered self-leading organizations.

While we are clearly advocates of empowerment as an effective means for creating self-leadership, it's important to understand that the road to teams is indeed challenging. Some of the more notable reasons for resistance follow.[2]

Emphasis on Individuality. Today the main structural form through which self-leadership and empowerment is diffusing throughout the United States is teams. Thus, in practical terms, becoming a SuperLeader means the implementation of teams. In the United States, we have a strong political and personal tradition of individualism that can run counter to the collective nature of teamwork. For both managerial and nonmanagerial employees, an emphasis on team values threatens both their traditional views of work and their fundamental philosophical approach to life.

A History of Dependence. Many employees find it difficult to adjust to the idea of working as a self-leader without a traditional boss or supervisor after so many years of dependence. We recently learned of a case where a large, burly production worker, after hearing about his company's move to self-managing teams, banged his fist on a table and demanded his right to have a boss to tell him what to do.

Distrust. Some companies, especially those with a history of management-induced fads and poor management of industrial relations, have scant credibility with first-line employees, especially unionized employees, to earn the trust needed to implement self-leadership. If management sees employee development as an expense rather than an investment, and employees see empowerment as another effort to co-opt employees to management's views, an attempted shift to participative values and work may fail. It is not surprising that many stories of successful change efforts have come from threatened companies or industries, whose employees and management were forced to confront and discard traditional distrust in favor of teams in order to survive. We do encounter organizations that end up moving one step forward and two steps backward.

Loss of Perceived Personal Power and Employment Opportunities for Middle Management. A shift to self-leadership and corresponding flatter organizations reduces managers' opportunities for advancement in the traditional organizational hierarchy, if only because there is no longer much of a hierarchy. Advancing up the ladder gets to be problematic when several of the critical rungs have been removed. But the restructuring of organizations is mainly driven by economic factors, not just a movement to self-leadership. Downsizing and delayering will continue in order to enhance competitiveness, whether teams and self-leadership are used or not. In fact, self-leadership frequently provides the competitiveness boost that is needed to save jobs over the long run.

Managers who have been trained to manage in a forceful, even threatening way may not readily accept the concept of empowering leadership. Changing to a self-leading organization is perceived as resulting in a variety of disincentives to the traditional, hard-charging manager. Most of all, many managers sincerely experience a sense of loss of power, whether the loss is real or not. This sense of loss can be a severe short-term impediment that can be overcome only by a positive experience with an empowered organization.

Unrealistic Expectations. In the transition to a self-leading organization, things sometimes get worse before they get better. Remember there is a social learning curve as well as a technical learning curve. That is, it takes some time for self-leadership to become fully vested, and some confusion and readjustment in the early stages is inevitable. Sometimes this means a temporary decrease in performance. An inexperienced executive will be tempted to abandon the transition, because of the apparent threat to performance. At this point, one commonly hears comments like this one: "I knew this team stuff wouldn't work!" A bit of patience to get through this initial learning period is essential.

Frequently, outside facilitation of the transition process can be helpful. The "outside" facilitator need not necessarily come from outside the organization; temporary help from the human resources staff will sometimes do. Whatever the source, an experienced outside view can be genuinely useful in helping to guide the transition.

Also, we sometimes see sink-or-swim transitions, where a work group is supposedly turned into a "team" overnight by removing the supervisor, with no real training or development effort provided for the team. While this can sometimes work, we generally think this approach is a sure recipe for failure. The so-called team is in danger of sinking.

A Sense of Loss.   In some situations, particular positions in a hierarchy have gained a certain amount of status, and perhaps a pay advantage. We recall the senior clerks at IDS who had difficulty accepting the change to teams, and the lead technicians at the Lake Superior Paper Company eventually became an impediment to full teamwork. Stakeholders who think they have something to lose can be a critical obstacle to a successful transition. Their concerns must be addressed.

Difficulty in Diffusing Throughout the Organization.   For large organizations, successful implementation of self-leadership at one site does not necessarily mean successful transition at another one. When it comes to implementing self-leadership, a severe "not invented here" syndrome seems to be active. Each site must somehow find its own way.

Requirement for Sophisticated Information Systems.   Many organizations fail to consider the burden on the existing information systems that a transition to a self-leadership culture will require. Teams, for example, tend to see themselves as a minibusiness and demand all kinds of indicators to measure how they're doing and to control their own efforts. Our experience is that a complete information system cannot be designed ahead of time; rather, it more naturally follows a transition as new information requirements become known.

THE KEY TO CULTURAL TRANSITION: A NEW PERSPECTIVE ON LEADERSHIP

The management of empowered followers requires the ability to listen, change views, empathize, and change basic leadership patterns. Without an adequate investment in the training and development of new, social-oriented work skills, development of enlightened leadership will be retarded or even thwarted. This issue is the most critical element in ensuring a smooth transition.

In the end, organizational culture is the garden that enables self-leadership to flourish or causes it to die. The wise leader will pay significant attention to SuperLeadership as the foundation of empowerment. If a true self-leadership culture is established, ordinary leaders can grow to become SuperLeaders, ordinary employees can grow into empowered self-leaders, ordinary groups can transcend to self-leading teams, and an ordinary organization can blossom into a company of heroes.

Part IV

Creating a Company of Heroes

DEVELOPING SELF-LEADERSHIP IN OTHERS

How Do I *Really* Do It?

The main focus of the SuperLeader is to reduce dependency of followers on leaders—to instead help and teach them to influence themselves to achieve top performance. Followers can become heroes when they learn the art and practice of self-leadership. In this chapter, we focus on the question of how SuperLeadership might be implemented or executed. What might be included in a plan of action to unleash the power of self-leadership in others? Here's the real question:

OK, I've got the idea, but how do I *really* do it?

The development of a SuperLeader typically takes a specific sequence:

1. Understand the *philosophy* of SuperLeadership.
2. Learn the *concepts* of SuperLeadership.
3. Execute the *actions* and *behaviors* of SuperLeadership.

The philosophy and concepts of SuperLeadership have been introduced in the previous chapters of this book. Throughout, we have provided suggestions and tips about how SuperLeadership might be carried out. Here, we summarize and emphasize the actions and behaviors that managers and executives can take to execute SuperLeadership, truly empowering others to lead themselves.

STRATEGIES FOR DEVELOPING SELF-LEADERSHIP IN OTHERS

Generally the idea of developing follower self-leadership can be divided into three categories: structural strategies, process strategies, and interpersonal strategies. *Structural strategies* refer to the way that organizational structures may be changed to facilitate SuperLeadership. For example, tall organization structures make it difficult to empower employees through the layers of hierarchy. Highly specialized departments work counter to self-leadership. Most of all, strong central staff organizations retard self-leadership.

SuperLeadership can also be executed by changing organizational processes—*process strategies*. That is, some patterns of material flow, information flow, or formal communication channels can deter empowerment, while other flow designs may enhance empowerment. For example, a company policy that requires all operational decisions to be reported and approved through a lengthy chain of command will inhibit self-leadership. A SuperLeader might arrange for work to be redesigned so that each employee does more of a whole job rather than a specialized part.

Perhaps the most important means of executing SuperLeadership is through *interpersonal strategies*: changing the way we talk and behave in everyday interactions with others, especially followers. Certain patterns of verbal behavior are critical if we wish to empower followers. An example is to focus on asking good questions rather than providing all the answers.

Tall organizations make it difficult to empower employees through layers of hierarchy.

In the following sections, we elaborate each of these strategies in some detail. Note that none of these strategies is a stand-alone approach; rather, some combination of structural, process, and interpersonal is typically required to execute SuperLeadership. To undertake a major organizational change, such as creating a company of heroes—that is, self-leaders—all three strategies are critical.

Structural Strategies

In organization terms, *structure* refers to the way that functions, roles, responsibilities, and duties are apportioned in an organization. The structure is the skeleton of the organization. Structures are typically divided into vertical hierarchy, which refers to the layers of responsibility and authority in an organization, and horizontal differentiation, which refers to the way roles and responsibilities are clustered and differentiated from each other—in effect, role specialization.

Specialization is the enemy of SuperLeadership.

In a more traditional organization, specialization is emphasized. For example, authority is divided along some vertical hierarchical dimension, with those at the top of the hierarchy specializing in making decisions and those at the bottom specializing in carrying out decisions. The lines dividing decision making from implementation are sharply drawn.

Specialization can also be emphasized with horizontal structure, where roles, functions, and job specifications are drawn more narrowly. One is more likely to hear the dreaded phrase, "That's not my job!" in a highly differentiated structure. In general, specialization is the enemy of SuperLeadership. SuperLeaders want organization structures that are less specialized and less differentiated. How can this be carried out?

Following is a list of some specific actions for redesigning organization structure in order to reduce specialization, facilitate empowerment, and generally create a SuperLeader type of organization. For the most part, these strategies are consistent with a horizontal organization:

- Create self-managing teams.
- Create concurrent engineering teams.
- Create product or quality improvement teams.
- Create task force or ad hoc teams.
- Remove one or more layers from the organization structure.
- Organize according to geographical or customer lines rather than by specialized functions.
- Reduce or remove staff functions, and incorporate these activities into line functions.
- Appoint "facilitators" or "coordinators" rather than "supervisors."
- Reduce the number of job classes or categories, thus expanding the range of job responsibilities within each classification.
- Reduce the number of pay classifications, and expand the range of each one.
- Eliminate organization charts or design one so that employees are assigned to teams with multiple tasks.

DOWNSIZING AND TEAMS: A MISMATCH MADE IN HELL?

"Have you heard the news?" whispered Julia. "The whole contracts division is going to be downsized."

"Yeah," replied Jim. "I've heard they're going to reduce the headcount by 35 percent and cut down to three levels in the division. Did you also hear they're going to initiate teams in the division to replace the supervision level?"

"Well, I don't know about you," said Julia, "but I wouldn't want to be part of a team after all that pressure and stress. How can you be an enthusiastic team member when bodies are flying around like that?"

Julia has a point. In our opinion, it's difficult to implement self-managed teams in the midst of a substantial downsizing or delayering. Yet it is logical to presume that teams might be an appropriate organizational form once delayering has occurred.

After downsizing has taken place, self-leadership is a logical follow-up.

In our experience, the simultaneous execution of delayering (or, downsizing) and initiation of self-managing teams is not a wise policy. Clearly delayering is a structural change usually accompanied by a good deal of pain and stress. Typically morale plummets. The survivors feel guilty and demotivated and do not have much enthusiasm or excitement for organizational change. Through association with the downsizing, the word *team* itself takes on a negative connotation. The prospects of a successful team implementation are severely threatened.

But once delayering has taken place, teams are a logical organizational form. Flatter organizational structures are more consistent with the idea of SuperLeadership and empowered, self-led employees. Teams can become the vehicle to take the organization to new heights of effectiveness.

We are not proponents of radical downsizing or delayering, especially accompanied by significant reductions in force. Nevertheless, some organizations find themselves in a position to make this necessary change. In this case, we recommend that restructuring precede team implementation by at least three to six months. This interval allows some time for psychological healing and provides a more stable foundation to build effective teams.

Process Strategies

Process strategies for executing SuperLeadership typically entail redesigning the way material, information, or communication flows in the organization. As one example, the prominent book by Michael Hammer and James Champy, *Reengineering the Corporation*, for the most part describes efforts to redesign the flows of material and information in order to improve productivity, service, and/or quality. Generally these efforts are intended to streamline the way business is done and in many cases entail the empowering of lower-level units in the organization.

We suggest caution with reengineering. Management may see this organizational change as a means to boost productivity, but employees frequently see this approach as a slash-and-burn attack on the existing workforce. Even James Champy, one of the originators of reengineering, has recently decried the means by which this process has been implemented. Consider the following look at the record of reengineering.

TRANSITION THROUGH REENGINEERING: WHAT'S THE RECORD?

Reengineering is a word that exploded into the American business vocabulary a few years back.* *Reengineering the Corporation* (1993), by Michael Hammer and James Champy, became the best-selling business book since Peters and Waterman's *In Search of Excellence* (1982) Most of all, the notion of reengineering has inspired organizations to redesign many business processes according to the objective of improving customer service.

But what kind of revolution has this book spawned? Clearly reengineering is a major organizational transition, and sufficient time has passed for an assessment.

Perhaps the best and most concise evaluation is captured by a quotation from Champy's new book. *Reengineering Management: The Mandate for New Leadership.* The book opens with his candid admission that although reengineering has worked for some organizations, the technique has fallen far short of its potential. "Reengineering is in trouble," he

---

*The original reengineering bible was the book by Michael Hammer and James Champy, *Reengineering the Corporation* (New York: Harper Business, 1993). The following quotations are from James Champy, *Reengineering Management: The Mandate for New Leadership* (New York: Harper Business, 1995).

says. "If I've learned anything in the last 18 months, it is that the revolution we started has gone, at best, only half way." He goes on to say, "I have also learned that half a revolution is not better than none. It may, in fact, be worse."

Some have equated reengineering with an excuse to conduct a slash-and-burn downsizing. Champy quotes one manager as saying, "What we do is downsize the company and leave it to the three people who are left to figure out how to do their work differently." Some have called reengineering a heartless exercise in downsizing.

Reengineering is in trouble.

Champy faults management as the main culprit. He suggests they either don't understand how to manage the process or are unwilling to surrender the power that reengineering requires. Speaking of power, he states that "the paradox of power [is] that the best way to get it is to let go." Indeed, Champy's follow-up book is more about leadership, teamwork, and organizational change than reengineering itself.

In our own experience, we have found that "natural reengineering" is often an outcome of moving an organization to self-managed or empowered teams. In essence, reengineering is an extremely important element of what teams actually do. Natural reengineering is one of the reasons that empowered teams work as well as they do. In contrast to classic reengineering, however, the process is carried out by the *real* experts—the people who know the job. In classic reengineering, this redesign is assigned to so-called outside experts. (One of the first steps of these outside experts is to conduct intensive interviews of the people who are actually doing the work.)

Natural reengineering is often an outcome of self-managed teams.

In the future, we would expect to see a blending of reengineering concepts with empowered teams and more reliance on the inside experts, who do the work day in and day out. Experience is showing that the real issue when it comes to reengineering is implementation. Employees who are seen as "enemies" by the reengineering experts can ravage the best-designed reengineering effort. Instead, empowered, self-led employees, the real reengineering experts, need to become the owners of the reengineering process.

Here are some specific process redesign actions that might be taken to execute SuperLeadership:

- Conduct process flow analysis with a view to combining or unifying departments that have responsibilities for sequential operations and services.
- Use authority empowerment. Require decisions to be made at the lowest level possible.
- Have weekly meetings where a member of the group is the leader, rather than having the meeting led by the manager.
- Send reports directly to the person who has the responsibility for action rather than routing reports up and down the organization chain of command.
- Establish direct liaison relationships between employees and clients, suppliers, and others outside the department.
- Appoint temporary leaders of projects where others on the team may be senior in grade, status or pay.
- Elect from within rather than appoint a team leader.
- Assign responsibility to employees or units to conduct their own quality control (subject to audit).
- Challenge individuals or teams to specify their own goals.
- Challenge individuals or teams to solve specific problems that have traditionally been outside their own narrow responsibilities.
- Conduct celebrations for achievements.
- Provide generous training for developing personal skills and capabilities, especially self-leadership training.
- Reengineer the task so that employees have responsibility for whole jobs rather than parts of them.

Interpers onal Strategies

On a day-to-day basis, the execution of SuperLeadership is mainly vested in the interpersonal verbal and nonverbal behavior that occurs between a leader and a follower. Whatever structural or process changes have been made, empowerment can be destroyed by relatively few authoritarian remarks from a leader to a follower. Indeed, SuperLeaders speak to followers in very different ways from the Strongman, Transactor, and even Visionary Hero leaders. The purpose of everyday conversation for a SuperLeader is to give a follower the confidence and capability to stand on his or her own.

Here are some of the specific interpersonal actions that might be used to develop follower self-leadership:

- Listen more.
- Reduce verbal behaviors such as direction, instruction, and command. Ask followers to provide their own direction: "What's next?" or "Where are you headed?"
- Reduce the proportion of assigned goals. Ask a subordinate what his or her own goal is.
- In response to a failure or mistake, ask what can be learned. Use direct punitive language only as a last resort.
- Ask followers to orally work through their logic and analysis of how they have come to a decision.
- Ask followers to relate what other alternatives have been explored when they come to a decision.
- Ask about feelings: "How do you feel about that?"
- Overturn a follower's decision only as a last resort.
- Express confidence in a follower's potential and capacity to achieve a specific goal or accomplish a specific task.
- Decline to solve directly a follower's problem unless it's a crisis or a last resort. Ask followers to solve problem on their own.
- Decline to answer directly when asked by a follower to make a decision that should be made by the follower. Reflect the decision back onto the follower.
- Ask followers if there are ways this job can be done more effectively.
- Verbally reinforce when a follower shows initiative. Look for opportunities to accept and implement follower initiative.

MOVING TOWARD FOLLOWER SELF-LEADERSHIP: EXECUTION IS NOT DONE OVERNIGHT

Executing self-leadership is not an event that occurs over the weekend—suddenly you awake on Monday morning and your followers are skilled and empowered self-leaders. Becoming a SuperLeader takes time and requires substantial development of both the leader and the follower. The leader must learn new behaviors that facilitate and encourage follower self-leadership. The follower must develop new skills, along with the confidence and capacity to express self-leadership.

A SuperLeader learns new behaviors that facilitate and encourage follower self-leadership.

Empowerment—that is, transforming followers into effective self-leaders—is a process with four stages:

1. Leader modeling of self-leadership behavior.
2. Guided participation of the follower.
3. Ensuring follower resources, training, and capability.
4. Follower self-leadership and performance—in essence, an empowered follower.

It's clear that these stages cannot be implemented simultaneously. Most of all, a complete transition will entail changes in structure, process, and interpersonal behavior.

Moving from a traditional to a SuperLeader organization requires time, patience, and resources. Each of the strategies that we have described is useful as a stand-alone approach, but a truly successful transition to a SuperLeadership system will require concurrent changes in structure, process, and interpersonal behavior that are attuned to both individual followers and teams of followers. For example, changing structure is an important precursor to a SuperLeadership system, but it must be accompanied by concurrent changes in processes and interpersonal behavior. It's the consistency and synergy that stems from changes in all parts of the system that, in the end, will really make it work.

A real transition will entail concurrent changes in all three elements: structure, process, and interpersonal behavior.

Consider the story of IDS Corporation in Minneapolis, whose mutual funds operations were transformed into a self-leading team-based organization in the late 1980s. The IDS experience, a classic retrofit, provides some interesting lessons on how this transition can be undertaken by changing elements of structure, process, and interpersonal behavior. The IDS experience also points out that the transition is accompanied by many stressful moments. In our opinion, IDS's management was particularly venturesome, because its changeover was one of the earliest experiences with service and knowledge workers. Nevertheless, it was able to draw fruitfully from and adapt earlier experience from transitions in manufacturing organizations. Note in particular the time frame in which the change took place.

GETTING TEAMS STARTED AT THE OFFICE: THE STORY OF IDS MUTUAL FUNDS OPERATIONS

Henry P. Sims, Jr., Barry Bateman, and Charles C. Manz

In 1988, after extensive self-analysis, executives of IDS Financial Services in Minneapolis decided to undertake a transition to self-managing teams in their mutual funds operations division. Prior to the change, the employees were organized into specialized roles and departments and overseen by supervisors who worked in a traditional vertical hierarchy.

IDS offers a wide range of financial services and products, including personal financial planning, insurance and annuities, mutual funds, certificates, limited partnerships, consumer banking, lending, and brokerage services. The Mutual Funds Operations division can be viewed as a service organization that processes information and financial transactions. A typical transaction is the investment of a certain amount of money in an IDS mutual fund for a client or a withdrawal or redemption from an account. The transactions are carried out by core workers, who undertake the back-room operations for the division. Accuracy and absence of errors are critical for maintaining both efficiency and customer goodwill.

Several temporary organizational structures were formed to implement the change to self-managing teams. The effort was launched by a

---

*This story is abridged from Charles C. Manz and Henry P. Sims, Jr., *Business Without Bosses: How Self-Managing Teams Are Producing High-Performing Companies* (New York: Wiley, 1993). Barry Bateman was a coauthor of the chapter, which provides a much more detailed account of the teams at IDS.

steering committee, which consisted of the vice president of operations and his staff of managers, the vice president of information systems, the vice president of human resources, and an external consultant. The steering committee was charged with initiating the change, getting the people in place to implement the change, and establishing the overall guidelines for the change.

After considerable discussion, the committee empowered a design team, a group of 11 employees selected from 57 volunteers. This team consisted of 8 core workers, 2 supervisors, and 1 assistant supervisor and was supported by the same consultants who supported the steering committee. Each team member was relieved of his or her regular job and assigned to the design team full time.

The steering committee empowered a design team to develop a plan, conduct a task analysis, and conduct a social analysis.

The design team's work consisted of three major steps: developing a plan, conducting a technical (task) analysis, and doing a social interaction analysis. Over eight and one-half months, the team conducted its analysis and prepared the new organizational design. Despite difficulties along the way, it finally proposed a design that consisted of the following elements:

- Teams would be organized according to geographical or regional lines.
- Each team would have 25 to 40 members.
- Each team member would be trained to perform multiple skills and tasks.
- Each team would be multifunctional. It would include all the different functions and processes within the team.
- Each team would be empowered to make the decisions needed to process the work in a timely and accurate fashion.
- Supervisors would be eliminated and replaced by two facilitators for each team.
- Information systems would be developed that would provide each team with the information it needs to operate effectively as a small business.

After substantial discussion, the plan was approved by both management and the workforce, and a transition plan was implemented. The transition consisted of a pilot team of about 25 employees who were assigned to the first geographical area and were empowered to begin operations as an experimental team for several months. Then the entire organization was converted to teams over a weekend—a change called the "big bang." Both the pilot team and the subsequent big bang included the conversion of supervisors to facilitators. Not surprisingly, this transition did not always proceed without difficulties. Not every supervisor was well suited to assume the radically different role of facilitator; employees who had previously been classified as senior clerks (a position providing special expert status) felt disenfranchised because of a perceived loss of status; and some managers, who now assumed the role of strategic directors, perceived a loss of control. Nevertheless, the overall results of the transition to teams were quite positive. Team members developed a more personal relationship with their primary customer, the financial planner in the field; accuracy and quality improved; and the organization became much more flexible.

The transition did not always proceed without difficulties, yet overall the results were quite positive.

Perhaps one of the most interesting indicators of the benefits of moving to the team system was the improvement in flexibility that came when the system encountered a traumatic surge of workload. In 1987, during the mini-crash of the stock market, an extremely large swell of customer telephone calls—mainly requests for redemptions—was thrust upon the division without advance warning. Call volume to the organization quadrupled within a single day, placing a tremendous load on the system. The result was chaos. The average speed of answer— that is, how long it takes to begin to service a call—was 7½ minutes. The system was gridlocked.

Subsequent to the transition to teams, a similar mini-crash occurred in 1989. With no new technology and the same-size workforce, the teams handled a larger volume than the 1987 crash, and the average speed of answer was 13 seconds!

This comparison deserves a second look:

1987, before teams	7½ minutes
1989, after teams	13 seconds

Detailed analysis showed that the improvement in response came from the actions that the teams themselves took to deal with the crisis. As one manager said, "This team concept really works!"

The change at IDS included revisions to structure, process, and in-terpersonal behavior. Structural changes included delayering and the formation of geographical teams. Changes in process included less spe-cialization and broader responsibilities within each team so that a team member could handle well over 90 percent of the transactions without transfer to another employee. Finally, the change included substantial shifts in interpersonal behavior as supervisors met the new role of team facilitator. Team members undertook the self-leadership behaviors that are necessary for the team to be self-managed.

Today the team system at IDS is alive and well. Their experience is one of the early examples that teams can work with knowledge and infor-mation workers as well as those in manufacturing environments. Most of all, this system is a classic example of how changes in structure, process, and behavior can be an instrument for creating a company of heroes.

EXECUTING SUPERLEADERSHIP: LEADING OTHERS TO LEAD THEMSELVES

When an organization seeks to spearhead a change from traditional leadership to a self-leading system, perhaps the most important change is in interpersonal behav-ior. The way a leader talks to a follower lies at the heart of SuperLeadership. The SuperLeader empowers followers through the daily verbal and nonverbal commu nication with them.

The mature SuperLeader is insistent that followers become true self-leaders.

The main overarching objective of all these strategies is follower empower-ment—indeed, challenging followers to lead themselves. It's also important to realize that the SuperLeader is not a laissez-faire leader who abdicates responsibil-ity. Frequently, in our executive development programs, we hear the expression "*allowing* subordinates to make decisions." In our view, a SuperLeader is not one who allows but instead is one who expects—perhaps even requires—followers to carry out the responsibilities necessary to their own job.

In our view, follower self-leadership is not a permission or a privilege but a requirement of doing one's job effectively. SuperLeaders want empowered followers who are fully capable of self-leadership, of carrying out the full range of duties associated with their work. The mature SuperLeader, in fact, is rather insistent—perhaps even demanding—that followers become true self-leaders. *It's not an option on the part of the follower!* SuperLeaders are not the heroic leader of myth but leaders who create a company where heroism is expressed by the many self-leaders.

THE
DESTINATION
Creating a Company of Heroic Self-Leaders

As Thomas Jefferson said, "That government is the strongest of which every man feels himself a part."[1] To extrapolate this idea to modern organizations, "That organization is strongest of which every person feels a part."

This brings us back to where we began. Organizations founded on self-leadership will have many pillars of strength to reinforce and sustain. These strong companies cannot be significantly damaged by the loss of single leaders. SuperLeaders create companies of heroes—companies in which members take pride in themselves and experience commitment to work they own. It's a natural human tendency to take greater care when we have a stake, when we are committed to a piece of ourselves.

> "The new consensus is that the greatest competitive advantage for the American company lies in a skilled empowered and adaptable work force."
> —Robert B. Reich, U.S. Secretary of Labor[2]

What greater gift or more sound investment can a leader deliver than to provide an opportunity for followers to discover their achieving self and to experience the pride of being their own heroes? Employees can experience a taste of heroism through their sense of self-respect, confidence, and their skill to face major challenges independently. Add to this a sense of cooperation with other capable self-leaders in a team–oriented organization, and the recipe for creating a company of heroes is truly established.

Consider the new venture teams at AES Corporation. Are these teams the prototype of the organization of the future?

THE VIRTUAL TEAM: AN ORGANIZATION OF THE TWENTY-FIRST CENTURY

Amy L. Kristof, Kenneth G. Brown, Henry P. Sims, Jr., and Kenneth A. Smith

A virtual team is a new form of work organization to meet the challenges of turbulent world competition.* It is a self-managed knowledge work team, with distributed expertise, that forms and disbands to address specific organizational goals. A virtual team is characterized by fluid human resources in terms of membership, leadership, and boundaries. Most of all, virtual teams represent a sophisticated alternative that emphasizes flexibility to use the most competent individuals at the most appropriate time.

Our model is based on an analysis of new venture teams at AES Corporation, a company we described in Chapter 16. One of the major efforts of the company is the development of new generating plants— new ventures. Typically, a new venture team organizes and develops each new plant. AES has committed itself to maintaining a flat organizational structure with a minimum of supervisory levels. No formal organization chart or job descriptions exist, and high levels of empowerment are found throughout the company.

AES employs approximately 70 people internationally who work on project development issues. A project development team has multiple responsibilities: finding a specific site for the plant, handling public relations with the local residents, obtaining necessary permits or permitting, financing plant construction, and bringing the plant on-line. The budgets for these projects vary anywhere from $2 million to $20 million, depend-

---

*We thank the officers and employees of AES who willingly contributed their time to develop the information on project teams. We especially thank Dennis Bakke, Tom Triborne, Roger Hemphill, and members of the Warrior Run team. All quotations are from interviews with AES employees or from written documentation and comments.

ing on the size of the plant, the location, and the amount of time spent in development. Here, we present the story of the Warrior Run Team, one of these teams.

The Warrior Run Team

The Warrior Run project development team has been in existence since 1988, when a power sales agreement was signed with utility officials at Warrior Run, Maryland. At the time of this study, the team had purchased land for a power generation site, was working to obtain the necessary permits, and was arranging for financial closing of the project. The structure of the Warrior Run team and its place in the organizational structure of AES is shown in Figure 18-1.

The upper-right-hand portion of the figure depicts the total human resources allocation in the project development area at AES. As the lines and ellipses on this smaller picture demonstrate, project teams generally follow a pattern of forming around a few individuals, gradually growing to some maximum capacity, shrinking, and finally disbanding. This pattern reflects the needs of each project as it progresses from a tentative business deal to a completed business transaction. As the construction phase of a power plant is completed, a plant management team assumes operational responsibility, and the project development team disbands.

The larger portion of the diagram illustrates what occurred within the Warrior Run team. The lines and labels (e.g., team member 3 or consultant 2) indicate employees who have been or are working with the team. Notice how members enter and exit the project while the team has maintained a pattern of growth. As Warrior Run moves nearer the end of its plant construction phase, many of the employees noted here will move on to other project development teams.

The characteristics of the Warrior Run team, such as fluid membership, fluid leadership, and flexible boundaries, are represented by the lines and labels that appear within the half-ellipse. In order to describe and characterize the team, we organized our observations into themes that emerged from our observation of teams at AES. In all, ten themes were identified:

- Person-organization fit.
- Project-dependent existence.
- Fluid team composition.
- Multiple team memberships.
- Fluid team leadership.
- Individual specialty areas and general responsibilities.

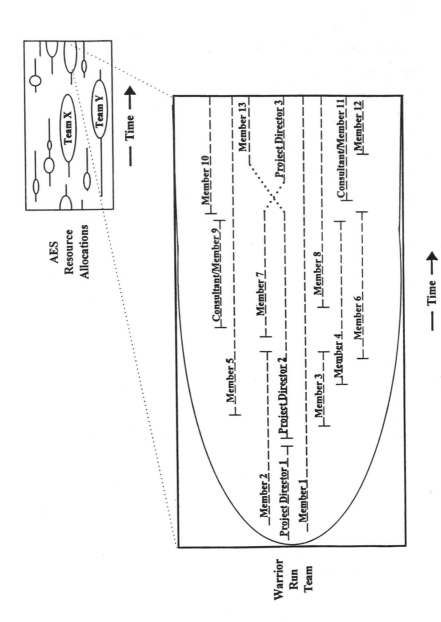

Figure 18-1. The team environment in the AES corporation.

- Informal communication channels.
- Open information culture.
- Trust in company and fellow employees.
- Team identity with permeable boundaries.

Person-Organization Fit

This theme relates to the individuals within the team. All Warrior Run members shared at least four individual characteristics: appreciation for challenge, desire for individual growth, tolerance for ambiguity, and solid academic background. Given the nature of the fluid organizational structure at AES, individuals must fit with the company in terms of these attitudes in order to be successful.

The nondirective atmosphere at AES requires that each individual cope with large degrees of uncertainty. Dennis Bakke, president and CEO, says, "They don't want to be told to follow certain directions and say, 'here's the rule book,' because there isn't any rule book. . . . We want a learning organization." One team member said he did not know for sure what he would be working on tomorrow, but knew there would always be something to do. Another Warrior Run team member said the uncertainty provided in the AES team structure bothered him slightly at first, but he soon came to enjoy it. All Warrior Run employees have a tolerance for the lack of structure in their individual assignments and development. Moreover, this lack of structure appears to be effective because each individual values challenge, enjoys learning, and seeks growth opportunities.

Project-dependent Existence

Project development teams are formed only after a solid idea has emerged from the business development phase. Once an agreement has been signed, a project director and one or two others form an initial team to develop the facility. The team evolves, with team members joining and departing as the project progresses toward the final goal; a completed, on-line cogeneration power plant.

Every person clearly understands that his or her work is defined by the project, not by a position in a hierarchy.

If at some stage the project is canceled, for whatever reason, team members turn to other projects and look for new opportunities within the company. Interestingly, the team dissolves if the project is successful and transferred to a plant manager. Whatever the final outcome, all team members know that team membership is temporary and that they will eventually move on.

Fluid Team Composition

The Warrior Run team at the time of this study consisted of nine members. Only one of these employees was on the team when it began. Individuals have joined, exited, and changed roles within the team depending on the varying project demands. Three team members were added in the past year to address specific project needs. Bob Hemphill, executive vice president, says that the teams "tend to add or subtract people from the project depending on what has been completed and what's . . . still left to be done."

The composition of the team varies with project requirements. One of the team members captured the essence of fluid team composition when he compared AES project development teams to football teams. During a football game, the team puts in different players depending on field position. Similarly, a project development team utilizes different team members based on stages of the project. According to Bob Hemphill, at the early stage, the project is "totally at risk, high value added. . . . Then you need to raise the money. That's generally a pretty intense activity. . . . Then you build it. . . . It takes two and a half years. . . . There's some risk to that, but it is a very different kind of risk, and it takes a very different kind of skill. . . . Then you operate it. . . . again, that's a different set of skills."

Multiple Team Memberships

Another theme that characterizes the culture of AES is the simultaneous involvement of employees on more than one team or project. Because individuals enter teams as their skills are needed, they may begin involvement with a project by spending approximately 20 percent of their time with a team. As their role in the project becomes more critical, they begin to sever ties with other projects and focus more and more time on that one particular team. When their skills become less required due to the changing nature of the team's task at hand, they begin to look to other projects where their skills can be utilized. Warrior Run members maintain involvement in several projects and shift their time and energy toward the projects requiring their skills at any given time.

Fluid Team Leadership

As with general composition, the project director or coordinator of the team varies according to the broader needs of the team. Typically, technical knowledge and expertise determine who becomes the director at various stages in the development project. The first coordinator of the Warrior Run team was a person described as having an entrepreneurial spirit and excelling at investigating available options. His skills were well suited for the start-up phase of a fledgling project. As the project progressed, new skills were required. Thus, the first coordinator left the team and a new person, skilled in financial closing, assumed the role of project director.

The idea is to get the most qualified person as project leader.

A recent change in the project precipitated a second transfer of leadership. The main reason was a change in the projected completion of the project from the near term to a more extended timetable, reducing the need for a quick financial close. Given the more extended nature of the project, revisions of previously issued environmental permits became the critical element. The concept of fluid leadership ensures that the team is represented by a leader with the skills most suited to current project demands.

Individual Specialty Areas, But Also General Responsibilities

All members of the Warrior Run team possess a sense of ownership for a specific job on the team. Each contributes a unique set of skills and is encouraged to use and develop those skills for the betterment of the entire company. One team member said, "We tend to have specialized roles once we get to this point in project development." However, a dynamic tension exists between individual specialization and general responsibilities. Team members also participate in topics outside their specialty area. Each team member is counted on to donate time to other specialty areas in order to keep the project underway. Thus, team members try to avoid becoming overcompartmentalized in a specific area. "We do not try to be specialists, [or] make people do the same thing over and over again." As Bob Hemphill puts it, "We believe in a lot of decentralization, a lot of individual responsibility, a lot of attempts to get people to understand that they have to work across a broad range of skills and not just what they are specially trained for."

Informal Communication Channels

Another theme that emerged from the interviews was a reliance on informal communication. Each Warrior Run member felt that the majority of important communication takes place in the hallways of AES and through unplanned telephone conversations. "You walk out of your office and yell down the hall to the other person," commented one team member. If a team member learns of a piece of information that may be valuable to other team members, he or she has an unspoken responsibility to call them and let them know. Information rarely flows entirely through the team director.

The informal communication network is supplemented by occasional team meetings, attended by all available team members. The agenda includes a discussion of significant developments in the project. Although team meetings are beneficial, Warrior Run team members emphasized that the most important information was communicated on a one-to-one basis. Informal communication is also apparent in the minimal amounts of written information. This is partially due to the flatness of the organization. The lack of bureaucracy limits the need for routine paperwork, and the informal communication networks facilitate the necessary information sharing. However, formal channels do exist at the organizational level in AES. Bob Hemphill says, "Every month we meet for generally two days, and go through each project case by case. . . . We look at every project at every plant every month."

Open Information Culture

All types of information, positive and negative, are shared openly within AES and with interested outsiders. AES has been open about sharing information not only concerning its triumphs but also reflections on some of its most challenging moments. This open information system contributes to the atmosphere of trust that permeates AES and its teams.

Trust in Company and Fellow Employees

The element of trust was frequently identified by members of the Warrior Team. First is the trust that AES places in its employees. Dennis Bakke says, "Although we are strong on accountability, we don't have a lot of regulations. It comes down to the premise that people are going to take responsibility and you trust them." AES spends a significant amount of time recruiting and selecting highly capable people. Once an individual joins AES, a high level of trust is placed in his or her abilities. Employees do make mistakes, and sometimes these mistakes may be costly; however, because the culture relies on trust as the basis for empowering employees to make decisions, words such as *blame* or *fault* were not spoken during our contact with AES and very little finger pointing was observed.

Trust in employees . . . trust in company.

The second element of trust mirrors the first. Not only does AES have trust in its employees, employees have trust in AES. Ambiguity is the norm, and structured careers are almost nonexistent, so employees must trust that challenging and interesting work will be made available. If a project fails, team members must trust that they will have a job the next day. "Where I go from here is pretty much where they need me," commented one team member. When talking with the Warrior Run project director soon after the postponement of the financial closing date, this point was well illustrated. He stated that he did not worry about his next day's work, because he trusted AES would provide him with interesting opportunities.

Team Identity with Blurred Boundaries

The themes of the open information system and fluid team membership combine to create a related theme concerning the permeable boundaries between AES project teams and outside help. The only way for a team of eight to ten people to develop a cogeneration power plant is to maintain contacts with multiple outside agents. In the Warrior Run team this is exemplified by the inclusion of an outside public relations consultant as a team member. When critical competencies cannot be located within AES, the company looks elsewhere.

Blurred boundaries also exist geographically and functionally. There are no functional homes for project development personnel, and team members do not necessarily work in the same location. Thus, the boundaries of the team become blurred as people in various locales, organizations, and functions become critical elements for the project's success.

The Virtual Team: A Model for the Twenty-first Century

In some ways the Warrior Run team is an empowered, self-managed team of highly educated knowledge workers. Members have a wide range of cross-functional skills, have improved access to information, have been extensively trained in the skills required to maintain a self-managed team, and have increased authority to make decisions regarding their work. The teams often differ from traditional work teams by having fewer and broader job categories within a team, control over daily team activities, and a reward system tied to both team performance and individual breadth of skills.

The key to successful operation of a virtual team is the fluid nature of assignments to and from, as well as within, the team. For example, official leaders, whether they are called project directors or team coordinators, change over time depending on the needs of the team. Individual personality characteristics, skills, knowledge, and professional expertise determine who undertakes the responsibility of coordinating the group's activity. According to Bob Hemphill, "Basically, we've got a pool of people here and we try to match the right person to the right project . . . especially with regard to who is leading the project." The person whose skills are most aligned with the proximal goals of the team is generally chosen to lead. Of course, individuals selected for leadership roles must also have demonstrated the ability and the knowledge to coordinate a team effectively. Management experience is not required, although coordinator potential as identified by peers and higher management is crucial.

Virtual teams provide the flexibility to combine the most competent individuals at appropriate times to meet organizational goals. Flexibility is accomplished through ever-changing leadership roles, functional roles, and team membership. By functioning in an atmosphere of trust, individuals, teams, and the entire organization benefit from the constant opportunity for growth presented by this flexibility. Through a network of virtual teams, an organization can make effective use of its human resources by creating synergistic groups directed at achieving company goals.

Virtual teams depend on employee self-leadership as a critical element of success.

Does all of this work perfectly? No. As Hemphill says, "We've certainly never been able to manage so adroitly that the number of people is always perfectly matched to the workload. It's not that predictable, but it's not infinitely variable either. . . . If we had a preference, we'd prefer to be short-handed. . . . Now this causes us, every so often, to have internal heart failure when we think of how much stuff has to be done and how few people we have to do it. . . . But that's the best way as opposed to having a bunch of really good people sitting around bored and angry because you don't have enough for them to do." In their letter to shareholders in the 1993 *Annual Report,* Dennis Bakke and Roger Sant explained, "When there are too many people jobs are divided too precisely and too narrowly to be fun. We believe that increasingly expanded ownership and responsibility are what most people want."

There are other examples of virtual teams in existence today. Many consulting firms use this type of structure to accommodate multiple projects simultaneously, with consultants rotating between projects as their skills are required. Similarly, concurrent engineering teams and integrated project development teams, which are being established in manufacturing companies, are virtual in the sense that they represent cross-functional teams in which members contribute core competencies. When the product they were assembled to produce is completed, the team disbands.

Undoubtedly in our enthusiasm, we have painted too flattering a picture of both the team and the company. Therefore, we close with a dose of reality. Dennis Bakke's words reflect a knowledge of the difficulties that all teams face daily and an appreciation for the people who contribute to make teams an effective way of conducting business:

> Your . . . description and analysis . . . is probably more complimentary than we deserve, since the team characteristics you describe do not always exist or work the way we'd like them to.

> The road map to teamwork is not through technical analysis and structure, but through an understanding and affirmation of how we have been created as people and through the development of "character" in each individual and team.

In this final chapter we address what we see as the past, the present, and the future of leadership. In doing so we will revisit many of the primary themes presented throughout this book and our belief that as we move into the twenty-first century, successful organizations will be the ones that can create a company of heroes.

THE PAST: STRONGMEN— THE BOSS-REX

Over the centuries, Boss Rex has been the dominant form of leadership. These tough and overpowering bosses made the decisions; their view was the only one that counted. Followers were simply expected to do what they were told. If followers were not willing to comply or screwed up in trying to do so, the leader's job was to come down on them, and come down hard.

"In a hierarchical organization, bosses don't do much. . . . They just . . . take all the credit. . . . A lot of good . . . people are buried down there, and their bosses are happy to keep them buried."
—Michael Walsh, former CEO, Tenneco[3]

The leader was like a tough cop who both made and enforced the laws. For Boss-Rex, bending others to the will of the leader was the path to power. The selection of those with leadership potential was centered on finding self-focused, self-important individuals. And frequently the leaders were self-chosen through the exercise of power. They craved power, influence, and importance. Satisfaction of these cravings came at the expense of the self-respect, dignity, and freedom of others. Boss-Rex, or the Strongman, was a king who ruled with an iron fist.

The result of Boss-Rex type of leadership is well-known. They create yes-men followers who are not only dependent but cowed by the leader. There is no creativity or initiative on the part of the follower. Politics replaces performance.

FROM PAST TO PRESENT: TRANSACTORS

A more recent arrival on the leadership scene is the Transactor, a leadership approach that centers on goals and incentives. Fundamentally, the leader wishes to make an exchange. When followers comply in reaching leader-specified targets, the leader loosens the purse strings, offers recognition, perhaps even praise, and provides a variety of other desired rewards.

On the surface, the Transactor appears to operate in ways that come across as much more humane than the Strongman. After all, all of us want to be rewarded when we perform well. Nevertheless, both types share a fundamental focus on the leader and a quest for follower compliance and sometimes exploitation. The leader is still expected to have the answers and to drive problem solving and goal setting. Good followers are obedient and serve the leader. Serving others—customers, society, or even themselves—is secondary.

Some might believe the Strongman and the Transactor have already passed on to the leader graveyard, but the reality is that they are still alive and well, even if their subordinates seem to be asleep. Indeed, these archetypes represent dated views of leadership. At least the rhetoric about leadership seems to be calling for more than Strongmen or Transactors. Follower compliance to the thinking and direction of one person, who happens to be called a leader, is not generally regarded as an effective strategy for competitiveness and survival.

The Strongman and the Transactor are still alive and well, even if their subordinates seem to be asleep.

The sad fact is that the behavior of many practicing leaders is not current with the latest thinking about leadership. For these leaders, new thinking challenges what they have come to believe over their time as a leader. Thus, this forms the intersection between the past and the present. Many Strongman leaders still exist, and Transactor leaders probably remain the majority of today's practicing leaders.

THE PRESENT: VISIONARY HEROES AND TALK OF EMPOWERMENT

Keep in mind that actual practice does not usually keep up with the current thinking about leadership. Nevertheless, much current leadership thinking points to the need for leaders to create visions that inspire followers. According to current popular reasoning, an effective leader is expected to articulate the future through a meaningful vision of a better tomorrow. The dominant current rhetoric calls for visionary leadership. The advantage is that the Visionary Hero seems to have a capacity to generate follower emotional involvement.

The Visionary Hero leader is at the center, with others pushed to the background. This kind of leader creates a company of dependent followers.

There are, however, two primary limitations of Visionary Hero leadership. First, many individuals do not possess a natural talent for creating a vision and communicating it in an inspiring way. Second, even if they do manage to learn these behaviors, the leadership process inevitably comes full circle to focus on themselves. The leader becomes the center, and followers are pushed to the background, where they are dependent on the leader. Most of all, the capability of the organization becomes restricted to the limitations of one mortal human being. This Visionary Hero leader creates a company of dependent followers. Only one hero, the leader, is allowed.

Another side to recent thinking about leadership reflects a movement toward employee empowerment, but as history continually reminds us, it is much easier to talk the talk than walk the talk. Thinking about leadership has progressed, but practice lags. A major shift toward various forms of participative management and employee teams is sweeping across the United States and much of the rest of the world. Most reasonably intelligent organizational leaders will not argue with the logic of this shift, and most people occupying positions of leadership will pledge their own commitment to this leadership philosophy. They can mouth the right words: "participation," "teamwork," "empowerment," "cooperation," "win-win." They can even share an example or two of how they have used this kind of leadership with their own employees. But the reality of common leadership practice is more like a statement made in a recent *Fortune* magazine article. "Ninety-five percent of American managers today *say* the right thing. Five percent actually *do* it. That's got to change."[4] Leadership that truly empowers and develops followers is more difficult to uncover.

237

THE FUTURE: UNLEASHING THE POWER OF SELF-LEADERSHIP

The future of successful leadership is represented by those who have the capacity to bring out the inner self-leadership potential of followers. SuperLeaders enable and expect followers to serve as leaders for themselves. The power of self-leadership is released. This means leaders who can walk the talk, not just talk it. High value is placed on developing the capabilities of followers. The leader's own essence as a leader is largely based on the effectiveness of followers. This leader is called the SuperLeader: one who leads others to lead themselves. A SuperLeader takes pride in the accomplishments and achievements that followers have initiated and carried out on their own. By empowering others to lead themselves, the leader's own leadership influence and capability is greatly enhanced. Indeed, a leader becomes a SuperLeader by bringing out the self-leadership capabilities of others.

SuperLeaders begin by becoming expert self-leaders themselves. Then they concentrate on leading others to be self-leaders.

Self-Leadership begins at home. To lead others, first lead ourself.

Effective self-leaders serve as pillars of strength throughout the organization. They manage their own behavior through strategies such as self-set goals, self-observation, and evaluation. They create positive thought patterns by managing their self-talk, mental imagery, and overall beliefs. And they learn to build natural motivation into their work. Through the power of self-leadership, they become the heroes in a company of heroes.

TRANSITIONS TO SUCCESS: CREATING A COMPANY OF HEROES

A successful transition will be guided by a relatively simple underlying philosophy: the presumption that people are capable. When leaders act according to this philosophy, employees respond with enthusiasm and commitment, as employees recently did at Southwest Airlines.

Herb Kelleher, Southwest's CEO, has made a practice of openly expressing his appreciation for Southwest employees. In countless ways, he has demonstrated his high regard for employees as his heroic self-leading peers. Not only has he made it a point to learn their names, he hasn't been too shy to roll up his sleeves and chip in to get the work done. He is widely recognized throughout the company for symbolic acts such as lugging baggage and greeting holiday passengers in an Easter Bunny costume. He has served as a living model of SuperLeadership that treats individual employees as the real heroes of the company. Not too long ago, Southwest employees reciprocated with their own expression of appreciation. They pooled their own money and paid for a $60,000 ad in *USA Today* to thank Kelleher on Boss's Day. The ad concludes by thanking him "for being a friend, not just a boss."

Eventually the practice of SuperLeadership becomes a consistent pattern. The main focus of leadership is the development of self-leadership in others. Instead of always having the answer, the SuperLeader asks good questions. Expecting others to find their own way to get the job done rather than forcing compliance to the leader's wishes becomes a habit. Encouraging teamwork replaces an obsession with individual performance. Initiative and creative problem solving are emphasized, while mindless adherence to a multitude of rules and procedures is discouraged. Learning from honest mistakes takes precedence over vindictive punishment.

If we believe in others and give them the opportunity, they will respond with positive self-leadership.

All the while, the SuperLeader becomes a model of self-leadership. By mastering one's own self-direction, self-motivation, and committing to allowing others to become strong and self-reliant, SuperLeaders set the tone for a truly empowered work system. The system is characterized by effective empowerment-based action, not just talk.

If given the confidence, training, resources, and empowerment, most people will respond in a positive, responsible way. Each person can become an effective self-leader—in effect, his or her own boss. Most of all, the culture of the entire organization can reinforce and support self-leadership through a normal expectation that people can and will perform on their own, through either individual self-leadership or team self-leadership. By changing the culture, especially the leadership culture, any organization has the potential to become a company of heroes.

Many contemporary leaders have made this transition. One of the more interesting is Jack Welch, CEO of GE, who has made an interesting journey in seeking to discover his own true pattern of leadership. This consistent practice of Super-Leadership represents the future. Companies that are led in this way will possess the strong self-leading employees that enable survival and success.

WILL THE REAL
JACK WELCH PLEASE
STAND UP?

Pamela J. Derfus

Jack Welch has led General Electric through a revolution and today is hailed as one of America's most successful CEOs. In the last few years, two books on GE's transformation, several Harvard cases, and countless articles have presented Jack Welch in a positive light. But earlier, at the height of his negative image, it's estimated that over 200,000 GE employees were against him, and public sentiment toward Welch was generally negative.* How did he get GE, and the media, on his side? Did he change, or did he just finally get his communications clear, his message across?

Let's review Welch's history to assemble clues and answer this question. Welch is a particularly good candidate for study, since we have seen seemingly contradictory leadership patterns over the course of his career. At different times and in different ways, he has been Strongman, Transactor, Visionary Hero and SuperLeader. In this piece, I draw mainly from two books on Welch, to highlight his evolution as a leader.†

Welch as Strongman

Although GE didn't seem unhealthy when Welch became CEO in 1981, he believed it was in serious trouble—too bloated and wasteful for international competition. Little more than a year after Welch was named CEO, the April 6, 1982, issue of *Newsweek* labeled him "Neutron Jack." The reference referred to his seemingly diligent efforts to "vaporize" employees while leaving buildings standing. He was feared, both inside and outside GE.

GE had nearly 420,000 employees when Welch became CEO in 1981. In 1992, the number was under 285,000, yet revenues had roughly doubled. Over 170,000 positions were eliminated, and 135,000 GEers worked for businesses Welch sold—Neutron Jack indeed.

Welch's style as a leader was forged in his earlier days, when he engaged in constructive conflict to make decisions. He stimulated "fierce, no-holds-barred debates" to gather information. Additionally, he "lacked the patience to wait for formal reports. Instead, he just dropped in on people

---

*Noel M. Tichy and Stratford P. Sherman, *Control Your Destiny or Someone Else Will* (Garden City, N.Y.: Doubleday, 1993), p. 8.
†Slater, Robert. *The New GE: How Jack Welch Revived an American Institution* (Homewood, Ill.: Irwin, 1993), and Tichy and Sherman, *Control Your Destiny*.

and grilled them. Anyone who couldn't answer a basic question wouldn't last long." Welch could be demanding and intimidating. One story described him in this way: "He was white hot in anger. . . . We were going around the table making business presentations, and the next guy walked up, and Jack just started ripping the business presentation to shreds."‡

Welch was shocked when *Fortune* named him one of America's toughest managers.

In 1984, *Fortune* ranked Welch "the undisputed premier" among America's toughest bosses. According to former employees, "Welch conducts meetings so aggressively that people tremble. He attacks almost physically with his intellect—criticizing, demeaning, ridiculing, humiliating."§

Interestingly, the *Fortune* story was a blow to the earnest CEO, and in a recent interview, he recalled that "it marked one of the worst moments" in his career.* Was the story a milestone leading to change? Some saw Welch's most important characteristic as his ability to change.

Welch as Transactor

Day in and day out, "Welch relied very heavily on goal setting, not direct commands, to trim GE down. [Welch] insists that he has never told a business leader to cut headcount by a certain percentage." Those who performed remained and advanced in Welch's organization; those who didn't perform endangered their business. In other words, those who performed were rewarded; those who did not suffered the consequences. This was clearly Transactor behavior, although we normally don't think of Welch as a Transactor.

The Visionary Hero

In 1981, when he first became CEO, Welch had a massive change project in mind, but he had a difficult time communicating his vision early in his tenure. His now-famous "Number One, Number Two" speech (referring to first or second in market share), delivered late in 1981 to Wall Street financial analysts at the Hotel Pierre, laid out a blueprint of a corporate mission. Unfortunately, the speech wasn't understood, although it was truly a remarkable visionary statement. Despite the content of the

---

‡Slater, *The New GE,* pp. 47–51.
§Steven Flax, "The Toughest Bosses in America," *Fortune,* August 6, 1984.
*Tichy and Sherman. *Control Your Destiny,* p. 120. The balance of the quotations in this story are from this book.

message, Welch recalls, "I knew I wasn't hitting a chord with them. My agenda and theirs were passing in the night."

Inside GE, things weren't any better. As Welch noted recently, "I was intellectualizing the issues with a couple of hundred people at the top of the company, but clearly I wasn't reaching hundreds of thousands of other people." GEers outside corporate headquarters didn't know or understand what Welch was doing and didn't agree with what they saw and experienced. Welch clearly had difficulty communicating the vision he was conceptualizing.

Welch has clearly excelled at articulating a strategic vision for GE.

Welch marshaled the forces of GE's internal media and management development programs to communicate his values message. He especially relied on Crotonville, GE's executive development school, to communicate the GE values of ownership, facing reality, integrity, and constructive conflict. Welch himself observed that it's one thing to work with several hundred people every day, but something else entirely to communicate with several hundred thousand people you never even see, let alone debate with.

But Welch was still frustrated. In 1986, five years after he became CEO, he realized people still hadn't gotten his message. He said, "I'm getting the same questions I've gotten for five years! Doesn't anyone understand anything? I'm just not getting through to them." He understood then that it wasn't just simplicity but also repetition. He had to keep communicating the vision over and over again.

The SuperLeader

Nevertheless, by 1988, the GE transformation was a success by almost all accounts. Revenues and profits were up, and even annual productivity growth had increased somewhat. Yet Welch still wasn't happy. He knew productivity was a critical factor with regard to worldwide competitiveness, but he needed some way to communicate this to all of GE, not just the elite at headquarters. Welch knew improved productivity had to come from the floor, not from buying and selling or negotiated goals with top managers. Welch realized he needed the commitment of all of GE's workforce.

There were still holdouts—bureaucratic managers from the old days who hadn't gotten the message and were still trying to manage their employees in the old way. Welch didn't want to control employees; he wanted to liberate them. To be the best, the most agile, a healthy, grow-ing company, GEers had to manage differently, work differently, think about their businesses differently. Welch explains it this way: "The old organization was built on control, but the world has changed. The world is moving at such a pace that control has become a limitation. It slows you down. You've got to balance freedom with some control, but you've got to have more freedom than you ever dreamed of."

Because of restructuring, the number of people or businesses re-porting directly to each manager had increased from about 6 to as many as 12, and sometimes more. It was done to encourage employees to delegate more, look over each other's shoulders less, and eliminate un-necessary work. But people weren't free or weren't liberated; they were just working twice as hard. GE had slashed and burned about as much as it could.

Welch needed to push these ideas to the lowest levels. "One of the things we can't do as top management is solve local problems"; that's why he had been "preaching liberation and empowerment and responsi-bility." To explain the basis for his next big step, Welch tells this story: "This engineer says to me, 'The plant is nothing like it used to be. It's nowhere near as much fun as it was ten years ago. What the hell are you going to do about it?'"

"I looked at him and said, 'Let me tell you what I'm going to do. I'm leaving for Paris in about thirty minutes and I won't be back within a year, maybe two years. So, personally, I'm going to do very little about it. . . . Why don't you get fifty people together . . . and why don't you, for the next two and half days, go and write down, in the left-hand column, why it was fun before? And in the right-hand column, put down why it isn't fun now. And then, why don't you fifty people change it and move everything back to the left side, so you're having fun again. Because you're the only people who can do it."

More recently, Welch has been very proactive in his attempts to unleash the power of self-leadership.

Welch had finally realized that only the people themselves could re-ally change GE. His vision, no matter how well communicated, would not produce real productivity gains unless middle managers shared the val-ues and took action to implement them. Thus, Welch instituted Work-Out in 1989—the implementation designed to change the culture of GE.

Modeled after town meetings, Work-Out sessions gathered employ-ees in groups from 30 to 100 for three days at off-site conference cen-ters. A casual but serious atmosphere prevailed. The first job was to break down barriers between employees and managers. Bosses were locked out, and employees met in small groups to define problems and develop concrete solutions. On the last day, bosses were brought in to hear the proposals. They were required to make instant decisions about each proposal and commit right in front of everyone.

This simple process worked. Employees aired grievances in a constructive fashion; ideas were frequently adopted. The results were very positive. Finding success with Work-Out, GE went after it with gusto. By mid-1992, over 200,000 GEers had attended Work-Out sessions. Today, Welch, and the rest of GE, are committed to pursuing Work-Out for at least ten years.

"Welch believes in teamwork, not out of idealism, but because he grew up playing hockey: He know that teamwork wins games. When his teammates score goals, he feels good. As a manager, he knows that the most valuable innovations often come from the shop floor."

Will the Real Leader Please Stand Up?

Can Jack Welch's behavior be explained in terms of the leadership archetypes presented in Chapters 2 through 6? Certainly his early behavior as CEO seemed to be Transactor in orientation, laced with occasional Strongman outbursts. Lately, he's been hailed as a Transformational or Visionary Hero leader. Further, Work-Out, as well as Welch's more recent rhetoric on freedom, ownership, and teamwork, implies an affinity for certain SuperLeader behaviors. In essence, at one time or another, Welch seems to have emphasized behaviors from all four leadership archetypes while transforming General Electric. Yet an interesting question remains. Did Welch evolve from one leadership style to another?

Tichy and Sherman maintain, "During his years as CEO, Welch has evolved from a demanding boss to a helpful coach, from a man who seems hard to one who allows his softness to show. That is part of what enabled him, long after he had gotten GE's businesses into shape, to win over GE's alienated employees." And, according to one GE manager, "I've watched the rebirth of Welch, or the renaissance of Welch, or whatever has happened to him. I don't know all the elements that went into his being born again, and I don't even care what they are. But I'm sure glad it's happened. He's a different man than he was in 1981." Welch disagrees with this assessment:

I haven't changed a thing! I try to adapt to the environment I'm in. In the seventies, when I was helping grow new businesses—at Plastics, at Medical—I was a wild-eyed growth guy. And then I got into the bureaucracy and I had to clean it out, so I was different in 1981.

And now I'm in another environment. But that's not being "born again".

The ideas were always the same. . . . We just got it simpler and more carefully articulated over time: Work-Out, eight years later, is a more meaningful way of communicating the idea of ownership— but it's the same idea . . . you keep refining and improving them; the more simply your idea is defined, the better it is.

Given the vividness of the early labels pinned on Welch—"Neutron Jack" and "America's Toughest Boss"—and, the eloquence with which people rhapsodize about the General Electric and Jack Welch of today, it is tempting to think of Jack Welch as the evolved leader. But although Welch has grown as a public leader over the years, perhaps his core leadership style has remained the same.

Welch clearly espouses empowerment and self-leadership for GE as a whole.

In some ways, he remains the hybrid Strongman and Transactor: "[He] gives me all the resources and independence I need. If I perform well, I can make more money here than anyplace else. If I don't, I'm out. That's the way it works at GE, and I knew it when I came. We all know it." But clearly Welch's behavior In recent years has focused much more on motivation via inspiration. As Larry Bossidy, one of Welch's direct reports for many years, commented: "I do think there was a change, vividly, from yelling and screaming for performance, to a much more motivational kind of approach. He became a lot more understanding, much more tolerant: *Hey if you get the job done even though your style is different from mine, that's fine.* He wasn't that way in the beginning. The nice thing about Jack is that he keeps growing. The Jack Welch who took over GE is not the Jack Welch you see today."

As for SuperLeader behaviors, Welch is clearly espousing this approach for the company as a whole. But at this point, we don't have enough detailed information about his one-to-one relationships to make conclusions about his day-to-day leader behavior. We do know that Welch has recently adopted Work-Out on a grand scale. As we have seen, this program encourages group problem identification, problem solving, and implementation efforts. Welch professes to want these groups to redefine the way work is done at General Electric, which seems consistent with developing a self-management culture.

Clearly Welch desires to leave an empowered SuperLeader culture as a legacy at GE. Whether he personally behaves as a SuperLeader in one-on-one interaction is open to question. Most of all, Welch has shown he is not subject to quick and easy labeling but is indeed an exceedingly complex leader.

FROM THE PAST TO THE FUTURE

When contrasting a traditional organization with a self-leading organization, the role of the leader is the most critical element that changes. Following is a general summary of some of the major differences between a traditional leadership culture and a self-leading organization—a company of heroes. This list is not intended to be exhaustive but provides a good sample that illustrates the pattern of differences.

Traditional Leadership Culture	*Company of Heroes*
Leader Structure and Roles	
Appointed by management	Input or elected by team
Always external to group	Sometimes a member of the team
A "boss"	Not a "boss"
Characteristics of a Leader	
Limited leadership training	Extensive leadership training
High need for power	Low need for power
Low need for affiliation	Moderate need for affiliation
Moderate need for achievement	High need for achievement
Verbal Behaviors of Leaders	
Talkers	Listeners
High level of instruction and command	Low level of instruction and command
Asks few questions	Asks many, many questions
Assigns goals	Asks for goals
Low positive compliments	High positive compliments
High intimidation	Low intimidation
High reprimand	Low reprimand
Low encouragement	High encouragement

Traditional Leadership Culture	Company of Heroes
Characteristics of Organizational Setting and Culture	
Workers are controlled	Workers control themselves
Workers seen as expense	Workers seen as investment
Training seen as cost	Training seen as investment
Short-term perspective	Long-term perspective
Employees seen as individuals	Employees seen as teams
Individual goals	Team goals
Low delegation	High delegation
Individual rewards	Team rewards
Extrinsic rewards as motivational driver	Intrinsic rewards as motivational driver
Centralized	Decentralized
Inward quality focus	Customer quality focus
Top-down information flow, "need to know"	Top-down, bottom-up, lateral, and open information flow
Autocratic past leadership models	Empowering leadership models
Tall, differentiated, specialized hierarchy	Flat, unspecialized structure
Functional organization structures	Project or process structures
Episodic organizational change	Ongoing organizational change
Structured job descriptions	General or no job descriptions

CREATING A COMPANY OF HEROES

To create a company of heroes, we begin with ourselves—we become master self-leaders. Then we work to stimulate and enhance the self-leadership capability of individual followers. Next we focus on teams of self-leaders. Finally, when we create a community of self-leaders, we create the culture that nourishes a total self-leadership culture: a company of heroes.

We are captivated by the words of Dennis Bakke, CEO of AES Corporation, whom we have come to regard as an executive-philosopher on the subject of leadership. He thinks deeply about organizations and the challenge of empowering others.

Your analysis . . . suggests that [empowering others] is a technique—that it can be engineered. In reality, it's more about character than technique, and more about relationships than engineered structure. It is about creative, thinking, trustworthy, capable, accountable, and fallible *people*—not machines—working in community.[5]

We admire Bakke's unbounded optimism about people. We also wish him, and all the other SuperLeaders and would-be SuperLeaders, success in their quest to create a company of heroes.

In the end, it's all about the follower. True leadership comes from within. In truth, this fact has been known for centuries. Consider the following poem from Lao-Tzu, sixth-century Chinese philosopher:

> A leader is best
> When People barely know he exists,
> Not so good when people obey and acclaim him,
> Worse when they despise him,
> But of a good leader, who talks little,
> When his work is done, his aim fulfilled,
> They will say,
> We did it ourselves.

We are optimistic about the organizations of the future. We have considerable hope that employees can and will develop the independent self-leadership that leads to high achievement. But self-leaders do not emerge from thin air. SuperLeaders make it happen. SuperLeaders create heroes by unleashing the power of self-leadership, and together they create a company of heroes.

Notes

Chapter 1

1. John Huey, "The New Post-Heroic Leadership," *Fortune*, February 21, 1994, pp. 42–50.
2. Ibid., p. 42.
3. John A. Byrne, "The Horizontal Corporation," *Business Week*, December 20, 1993, pp. 76–81.

Chapter 4

1. This is a literary interpretation of a true story told by Pekka Padatsu, CEO of an entrepreneurial company located in Finland. While this annual ritual is clearly a Transactor event, as a leader, Pekka himself is mainly a Visionary, who is seeking to move his company into an empowered SuperLeadership culture.

Chapter 5

1. Speech before the Hamilton Club, Chicago, April 10, 1899.
2. Speech accepting renomination, June 27, 1936.
3. Interview by Marshall Loeb, "Jack Welch Lets Fly on Budgets, Bonuses, and Buddy Boards," *Fortune*, May 29, 1995, p. 146.

Chapter 6

1. Dwight D. Eisenhower, *At Ease: Stories I Tell to Friends* (Garden City, N.Y.: Doubleday, 1967), p. 119.

Chapter 7

1. For earlier work, see C. C. Manz, "Self-Leadership: Toward an Expanded Theory of Self-Influence Processes in Organizations," *Academy of Management Review* 11(1986): 585–600; *The Art of Self-Leadership* (Englewood Cliffs, N.J.: Prentice Hall, 1983); *Mastering Self-Leadership: Empowering Yourself for Personal Excellence* (Englewood Cliffs, N.J.: Prentice Hall, 1992). See also C. C. Manz and H. P. Sims, Jr., "Self-Leadership as a Substitute for Leadership," *Academy of Management Review* 5(1980): 361–367; and *SuperLeadership* (New York: Berkley, 1990).
2. We acknowledge the inspiration of Fletcher and his interesting work on how to discover the unique pattern of high performance in each individual. See Jerry L. Fletcher, *Patterns of High Performance: Discovering the Ways People Work Best* (San Francisco: Berett-Koehler Publishers, 1993).
3. Ibid., p. 2.

Chapter 8

1. The roots of this self-leadership philosophy lie in the self-regulation literature of psychology. Notable early references include E. E. Thoreson and M. J. Mahoney, *Behavioral Self-Control* (New York: Holt, Rinehart & Winston, 1974); and M. J. Mahoney and D. B. Arnkoff, "Self-Management: Theory, Research, and Application," in J. P. Brady and D. Pomerleau, eds., *Behavioral Medicine: Theory and Practice* (Baltimore: Williams & Wilkins, 1979), pp. 75–96.
2. *Analog* (July 1994): 253.

Chapter 9

1. These quotations are taken from interviews conducted at AES by Kenneth A. Smith and Henry P. Sims, Jr., and originally appeared in Charles C. Manz and Henry P. Sims, Jr., *Business Without Bosses: How Self-Managing Teams Are Building High-Performing Companies* (New York: Wiley, 1993), p. 175.

2. See Charles C. Manz, *Mastering Self-Leadership* (Englewood Cliffs, N.J.: Prentice Hall, 1992).
3. Norman Vincent Peale, *A Guide to Confident Living* (Greenwich, Conn.: Fawcett Crest Books, 1948), p. 59.

Chapter 10

1. See, for example, the writings of Albert Bandura, most notably his book *Social Foundations of Thought and Action: A Social Cognitive Theory* (Englewood Cliffs, N.J.: Prentice Hall, 1986).
2. Some of our early work on cognitive self-leadership can be found in *The Art of Self-Leadership* (Englewood Cliffs, N.J.: Prentice Hall, 1983).
3. An example is the book by D. Michenbaum, *Cognitive Behavior Modification: An Integrative Approach* (New York: Plenum Press, 1977).
4. Mike Tyson, while in jail, interviewed by Larry King, CNN.
5. For comprehensive discussions on dysfunctional thinking, see Albert Ellis, *A New Guide to Rational Living* (Englewood Cliffs, N.J.: Prentice Hall, 1975), and Aaron Beck, *Cognitive Therapy and the Emotional Disorders* (New York: International Universities, 1976).
6. See David Burns, *Feeling Good: The New Mood Therapy* (New York: William Morrow, 1980).

Chapter 13

1. Quoted from John Huey, "The New Post-Heroic Leadership," *Fortune*, February 21, 1994, p. 42.
2. *Our Story So Far: Notes from the First 75 Years of the 3M Company* (St. Paul, Minn.: Minnesota Mining & Manufacturing Co., 1977), p. 12.
3. C. C. Manz, D. Keating, and A. Donnellon, "On the Road to Teams Overcoming the Middle Management Brick Wall," in Charles C. Manz and Henry P. Sims, Jr., *Business Without Bosses: How Self-Managing Teams Are Building High-Performing Companies* (New York: Wiley, 1993), pp. 23–40.
4. For a more detailed description of this case, see C. C. Manz and H. L. Angle, "The Illusion of Self-Management: Using Teams to Disempower," in Charles C. Manz and Henry P. Sims, Jr., *Business Without Bosses: How Self-Managing Teams Are Building High-Performing Companies* (New York: Wiley, 1993), pp. 115–129.

Chapter 14

1. This story is inspired by one told by Kelvin Throop III in *Analog* (May 1994): 81.
2. From Brian Dumaine, "The Trouble with Teams," *Fortune*, September 5, 1994, pp. 86–89.

Chapter 15

1. For further development of these ideas, see Kimball Fisher, *Leading Self-Directed Work Teams: A Guide to Developing New Team Leadership Skills* (New York: McGraw-Hill, 1993), p. 48.
2. ibid., p. 223.
3. Charles C. Manz and Henry P. Sims, Jr., *Business Without Bosses: How Self-Managing Teams Are Building High-Performing Companies* (New York: Wiley, 1993), pp. 85–114.

Chapter 16

1. Ann Jorden is currently at the University of North Texas. This definition was adapted from her working paper, "Managing Diversity: Translating Anthropological Insights for Organizational Studies."
2. These ideas are adapted from Charles C. Manz and Henry P. Sims, Jr., *Business Without Bosses: How Self-Managing Teams Are Building High-Performing Companies* (New York: Wiley, 1993).

Chapter 18

1. Thomas Jefferson to Governor H. D. Tiffin, February 2, 1807.
2. Letter to the editor, *Fortune*, May 29, 1995, p. 15.
3. Quoted in Michael Walsh, *New York Times*, January 18, 1993, p. D4.
4. John Huey, "The New Post-Heroic Leadership," *Fortune*, February 21, 1994, pp. 42–50.
5. Personal communication from Dennis Bakke, CEO of AES Corporation.

Index